RADICAL PROJECT MANAGEMENT

ISBN 0-13-009486-2

9 780130 094865

90000

Selected Titles from the
YOURDON PRESS COMPUTING SERIES
Ed Yourdon, *Advisor*

JUST ENOUGH SERIES / YOURDON PRESS
DUÉ, Mentoring Object Technology Projects
MOSLEY/POSEY, Software Test Automation
THOMSETT Radical Project Management
YOURDON, Managing High-Intensity Internet Projects

YOURDON PRESS COMPUTING SERIES
ANDREWS AND STALICK Business Reengineering: The Survival Guide
BOULDIN Agents of Change: Managing the Introduction of Automated Tools
COAD AND MAYFIELD with Kern Java Design: Building Better Apps and Applets, Second Edition
COAD AND NICOLA Object-Oriented Programming
COAD AND YOURDON Object-Oriented Analysis, Second Edition
COAD AND YOURDON Object-Oriented Design
COAD WITH NORTH AND MAYFIELD Object Models, Strategies, Patterns, and Applications, Second Edition
CONNELL AND SHAFER Object-Oriented Rapid Prototyping
CONSTANTINE The Peopleware Papers: Notes on the Human Side of Software
CONSTANTINE AND YOURDON Structure Design
DEGRACE AND STAHL Wicked Problems, Righteous Solutions
DEMARCO Controlling Software Projects
DEMARCO Structured Analysis and System Specification
FOURNIER A Methodology for Client/Server and Web Application Development
GARMUS AND HERRON Measuring the Software Process: A Practical Guide to Functional Measurements
HAYES AND ULRICH The Year 2000 Software Crisis: The Continuing Challenge
JONES Assessment and Control of Software Risks
KING Project Management Made Simple
PAGE-JONES Practical Guide to Structured Systems Design, Second Edition
PUTNAM AND MEYERS Measures for Excellence: Reliable Software on Time within Budget
RUBLE Practical Analysis and Design for Client/Server and GUI Systems
SHLAER AND MELLOR Object Lifecycles: Modeling the World in States
SHLAER AND MELLOR Object-Oriented Systems Analysis: Modeling the World in Data
STARR How to Build Shlaer-Mellor Object Models
THOMSETT Third Wave Project Management
ULRICH AND HAYES The Year 2000 Software Crisis: Challenge of the Century
YOURDON Byte Wars: The Impact of September 11 on Information Technology
YOURDON Death March: The Complete Software Developer's Guide to Surviving "Mission Impossible" Projects
YOURDON Decline and Fall of the American Programmer
YOURDON Modern Structured Analysis
YOURDON Object-Oriented Systems Design
YOURDON Rise and Resurrection of the American Programmer
YOURDON AND ARGILA Case Studies in Object-Oriented Analysis and Design

RADICAL
PROJECT
MANAGEMENT

Rob Thomsett

Prentice Hall PTR
Upper Saddle River, NJ 07458
www.phptr.com

Library of Congress Cataloging-in-Publication Date

Thomsett, Rob,
   Radical project management/Rob Thomsett.
      p. cm. -- (Just enough series)
   Includes bibliographical references and index.
   ISBN 0-13-009486-2
      1. Project management. I. Title. II. Series.

HD69.P75 T485 2002   2002020039
658.4'04--dc21

Editorial/Production Supervision: *Laura Burgess*
Acquisitions Editor: *Paul Petralia*
Marketing Manager: *Debby vanDijk*
Manufacturing Manager: *Alexis Heydt-Long*
Cover Design: *Nina Scuderi*

©2002 Prentice Hall PTR
A division of Pearson Education, Inc.
Upper Saddle River, NJ 07458

Prentice Hall books are widely used by corporations and government agencies for training, marketing, and resale.

For information regarding corporate and government bulk discounts please contact:

   Corporate and Government Sales
   Phone: 800-382-3419 or
   corpsales@pearsontechgroup.com

All product names mentioned herein are the trademarks or registered trademarks of their respective owners.

Printed in the United States of America

10 9 8 7 6 5 4 3 2 1

ISBN 0-13-009486-2

Pearson Education LTD.
Pearson Education Australia PTY, Limited
Pearson Education Singapore, Pte. Ltd.
Pearson Education North Asia Ltd.
Pearson Education Canada, Ltd.
Pearson Educación de Mexico, S.A. de C.V.
Pearson Education—Japan
Pearson Education Malaysia, Pte. Ltd.

Contents

Preface *xvii*

Part 1

Chapter 1
The New Project Environment
3

Forces Driving Change *4*
Driving Force 1—A Power Shift *4*
Driving Force 2—The Free Agent Army *10*
Driving Force 3—The Global E-Economy *12*

Chapter 2
Project Management Evolution
15

The Four Waves of Project Management *18*

Chapter 3
eXtreme Concepts
23

Project Management Versus Technical Management *24*
Context and Content *25*
Whole-of-Life Project Management *27*
Project Manager as Facilitator *29*
Sponsors as Executive Project Managers *31*
Scenario Planning *33*
The L.A. Law Model *34*

Rapid Planning   *34*

Virtual Teams   *36*

It's the Context, Stupid   *37*

Part 2

Chapter 4
eXtreme Project Management Context

41

Two Very Different Types of Work   *41*

Process Work   *42*

The Two Cultures in Conflict   *42*

The Categories of Project Work   *43*

Project Size   *45*

Chapter 5
The eXtreme Project Management Model

49

Project Management Processes   *49*

Project Justification, Approval, and Review   *50*

The Critical Information for Project Approval   *52*

Project Planning   *52*

Project Tracking   *54*

Project Reporting and Change Control   *54*

Postimplementation Reviews   *55*

A Note on the Project Initiation and Feasibility Study   *55*

The Project Charter or Business Case   *57*

The Only Stable Thing Is Change   *58*

Chapter 6
The RAP Process

61

Why Should We Run RAP Sessions?   *62*

Different Stakeholders, Different Agendas   *63*

Great Idea...But I Don't Have a Team Yet   *65*

The RAP Structure   65
   RAP Technology   67
   How Long Should a RAP Take?   67

Chapter 7

Analyze Project Success

69

What Are Expectations?   71

The Seven Success Criteria   72
   Degree or Level of Stakeholder Satisfaction   72
   Meeting of Objectives and Requirements   72
   Meeting Budget   73
   Meeting Deadlines   73
   Added-Value Requirements   73
   Quality Requirements   74
   Team Satisfaction   74

eXtreme Tool 1: Success Sliders   74
   Don't Panic! It Is Meant to Be Subjective   76

Chapter 8

Define Scope, Objectives, and Stakeholders

79

What Is the Difference between Scope and Objectives?   79
   Conflict Is Inevitable   83
   Levels of Objectives   84
   Refining Your Objectives   84
   Let's Not Get Physical   85
   Don't Fence Me in   85

Stakeholders and Related Projects   86
   What Is a Stakeholder?   86

Related Projects—A Special Case of Stakeholder   87
   Focus and Communicate   88
   Formalizing Stakeholder Relationships   89
   Sponsor Agreement—The Most Important of All   91
   Who Is Your Team?   91

Chapter 9
Analyze Added Value 95

The State of the Art   95
Problems with Traditional Cost–Benefit Approaches   97
The Ultimate Fiddle   100
Added-Value Analysis   101
The Added-Value Chain   101
The IRACIS Model   103
Actual Versus Notional Costs   104
Shadow Pricing: Hedonic Costing and Contingent Valuation   105
Benefits Realization   107
Cost-Effectiveness Model   108
Another Form of Double-Counted Benefits   110
Additional Added-Value Drivers   110
A Final Note on Added-Value Analysis   111

Chapter 10
Define Quality 115

Project Quality Deployment   115
Linking Product and Process Quality: QFD   117
What Is a Quality?   119
Toward an Effective Quality Plan: PQD in Action   121
Step 1: Define the Product Requirements   123
Step 2: Negotiate Product Quality Attributes   123
Step 3: Review Quality Attributes with Your Sponsor   123
Repeat Until...   124
Quality Index   124
Quality in Action   125
Quality Assurance Drivers   127
Quality Assurance Principles   128
Quality, Estimates, Costs, and Risks   128
The Impact of Quality   128
The Hot Buttons   129
A Final Note on Quality for Now   129

Chapter 11

Select a Development Strategy 133

Strategy Ain't Methodology 135

The Four Development Strategies 136

Monolithic or Waterfall 136

Release, Version, or Incremental 139

Fast Track, Evolutionary, or Production Prototyping 142

Hybrid 145

Rapid Application Development (RAD), Agile, and Other Variations 145

RAD or Time-Boxing 146

Radical Fast Track 146

Microsoft's Daily Build 146

Agile, Lite, or Extreme Methods 147

Mixing and Matching 147

Partitioning Guidelines 147

By Function or Data 147

By Stakeholder 148

By Benefits 148

Strategy Selection 148

Strategy as a Change Control 149

Strategy and Risk Assessment 149

Chapter 12

Analyze Risk 155

Project Risk Assessment Overview 157

Many Classes of Risk 159

Project Risk Management 160

Project Risk Assessment 161

Subjective Versus Objective Risk Assessment 164

The Risk Assessment Process 165

Overall Project Risk Assessment 167

Risk Containment or Reduction 167

Risk Management Plans 169

Risk Tracking and Reporting *170*
Shooting the Messenger *170*

Chapter 13
Develop Task Lists *175*

Develop Project Task Lists *175*

Methodologies: A Brief Introduction *177*
1. Tailor Methodology *177*
2. Brainstorm Project Tasks *178*
3. Fine-Tune Your Methodology *179*
4. Review with Other Experts *179*
5. Repeat the Process *179*
The Amazing 5/10 Day Rule *180*
The Risk of the Project or Task *181*
The Nature of the Task *182*
The Experience of the Team Members *182*
The Degree of Trust *182*

A Moral Dilemma *183*

Where Is the Moral Dilemma? *184*
Scenario and Real-Time Planning *185*

Chapter 14
Estimate Tasks *189*

Causes of Estimation Error *189*

Misestimating the Scope *191*
Misestimating the Stakeholders' Effort *191*
Misunderstanding the Quality *192*
Miscalculating the Project Risk *192*
Forgetting Tasks *193*
Misunderstanding Your People *193*
Estimation Overview and Principles *194*
Getting Our Language Right *194*
Project Estimation Points *195*
Estimation Principles *195*

Avoid Single-Person Estimation   *195*
Always Complete a Risk Assessment Prior to Estimation   *195*
Where Possible, Use Relevant Experts   *196*
Always Carefully Document Estimating Assumptions   *196*
Review the Work Breakdown Structures   *197*
Always Undertake Sensitivity Analysis   *197*

The Detailed Estimation Process   *197*
Saying No Revisited   *198*
A Review of Risk Assessment   *199*
Develop a Work Breakdown Structure   *200*
Complete a Function Point Estimate   *201*
Complete Team-Based Estimates   *202*
Not Another Note on Sensitivity Analysis!   *204*
Adjust for Quality Agreement   *206*

Chapter 15
Develop Schedule   *211*

Develop Project Execution Plan   *213*
Step 1: Develop a First-Cut Network   *214*
Step 2: Adjust Estimates to Elapsed Days   *215*
Step 3: Develop First-Cut Schedule   *215*
Step 4: Schedule Actual Resources   *217*
Step 5: Adjust the Schedule as Required   *219*

Scenario Planning Revisited   *219*

Develop Project Staffing Agreements   *221*
Oops! Wrong Planet, Wrong Person   *221*
A Typical Skill Model   *222*
Virtual Team Twist   *224*

Chapter 16
Develop Return on Investment   *227*

Develop Cost and ROI Scenarios   *229*
ROI Fundamentals   *229*
Analyzing Project Costs   *234*

Future and Present Values   *234*

Developing Your ROI   *235*

Cost-Effectiveness   *236*

Chapter 17
Project Tracking and Reporting   *239*

Project Tracking   *239*

The Tracking Mechanism   *240*

The Use of Automated Project Management Tools   *242*

Various Tracking Concepts   *242*

We Aren't Painting Walls: We Are Building Dreams   *244*

Tracking Mechanism   *245*

Tracking Summaries   *245*

Building a Project Metric Database   *246*

Project Reporting   *246*

Project Management and Technical Deliverable Reviews   *247*

The Project Reporting and Review Process   *248*

Really Radical Reports   *250*

Assistance to Projects   *251*

Reporting to Stakeholders   *253*

The Project Change Control Process   *253*

Maintaining the Project Management File   *255*

The Business Case Is the Focus of Everything   *255*

Chapter 18
Postimplementation Reviews   *259*

The Postimplementation Review   *259*

The Postimplementation Review Focus   *260*

Don't Forget Your Sliders   *262*

The Timing of Postimplementation Reviews   *263*

The Learning Loop Concept   *265*

Client Satisfaction Surveys   *267*

The Postimplementation Review Team   *267*

The System Support Review   *268*

Benefits Realization Planning   *268*

  The Benefits Realization Plan   *271*
  The Project Sponsor's Role   *273*
  Benefits Reviews   *273*

Chapter 19

Support

275

The Support Problem   *276*

  The Production Portfolio Concept   *276*
  Portfolio Investment Effort   *277*

The Production Support Portfolio   *278*

  The System Efficiency Review   *278*
  Production System Activities and Support Costs   *280*

Passages: The Life Cycle of Production Systems   *280*

  1. New Product or System: Childhood   *281*
  2. Mature Product or System: Adulthood   *281*
  3. Old Product or System: Geriatric   *281*

Conclusion   *282*

Part 3

Chapter 20

Getting the Sponsor You Deserve

287

Rule 1: The Bag of Money and the Baseball Bat   *288*

Rule 2: The Passive Conduit   *290*

Rule 3: You Generally Get the Sponsor You Deserve   *292*

Rule 4: In the Absence of Information, Executives
Still Make Decisions   *293*

Rule 5: Educate as Well as Inform   *295*

Rule 6: The Level of Help You Get Is Inversely
Proportional to Your Delay in Asking   *296*

Rule 7: Show Them the Money   *298*
Rule 8: "Beam Us Up, Scotty"   *299*
Rule 9: No Sponsor, No Start   *300*

Chapter 21
Getting the Stakeholders You Deserve   *303*

Rob's Corporate Mathematics   *303*
Why You Need Your Stakeholders   *304*
How to Win Stakeholders Over   *305*
   Remember They Have Other Jobs as Well   *307*
How to Get the Project You All Want   *308*

Chapter 22
A Question of Ethics   *311*

Situation 1   *311*
Situation 2   *312*
Situation 3   *312*
Situation 4   *312*
Situation 5   *313*
Best Practice and Best Behavior   *313*
Organizational and Individual Impact   *315*
Drawing the Line—An Extreme Project Management
Responsibility   *316*
A Draft Code of Ethical Behavior for eXtreme Project
People   *317*

Chapter 23
The Success Sliders Redux   *319*

Requirements Are Not the Same as Expectations   *320*

So, What Are Expectations?   *320*

The Swiss Army Knife   *321*

Other Tips for Understanding Expectations   *323*

    Become a Culture Vulture   *324*

    Check out the Scenery   *324*

    Learn Their Language   *324*

    Say It Once, Hear It Many Times   *325*

Chapter 24
In Case of Emergencies

327

The Dark Side   *328*

    Dark Side 1: Don't Tell Anyone   *328*

    Dark Side 2: Hope It Will Get Better   *328*

    Dark Side 3: Covertly Degrade Quality   *329*

    Dark Side 4: Covertly Degrade Functionality   *329*

    Dark Side 5: Work Harder—Long-Term   *329*

    Dark Side 6: Hire Consultants or Contractors and Blame Them   *329*

    Dark Side 7: Blame Your "Users"   *330*

    Dark Side 8: Blame Everyone—A Witch Hunt   *330*

    Dark Side 9: Leave the Project   *330*

    Dark Side 10: Add Lots of People—The Horde Model   *330*

    Dark Side 11: Stop the Project   *331*

The Good Side   *331*

    Good Side 1: Shift the Deadline   *331*

    Good Side 2: Shift the Requirement   *331*

    Good Side 3: Partition and Add People   *331*

    Good Side 4: Overtly Degrade Quality   *332*

    Good Side 5: Change the Technology   *332*

    Good Side 6: Change the People   *332*

    Good Side 7: Work Harder—Short-Term   *332*

    Good Side 8: Leave the Project   *333*

    Good Side 9: Mix and Match   *333*

    Good Side 10: Stop the Project   *333*

Come to the Dark Side, Luke   *333*

Chapter 25
The Secret of Great Project Managers   *335*

References   *337*

Index   *341*

Preface

This book confronts many of the myths, beliefs, and practices of project management. It presents a new and radical approach to managing projects that has been proven more effective in the turbulent business environment of the 21st century.

Acknowledgments

I wish to thank the following people:

Ed Yourdon, Gerry Weinberg, Larry Constantine, and Peter Lonsdale, who opened new doors and started me on my journey.

Trevor Boucher, Michael Carmody, and Graeme Harrison, current and previous change leaders of the Australian Taxation Office, who had faith and gave me the chance to experiment, innovate, and work without a safety net.

Peter Mullins, Tom Fraser, Gavin Pearce, Rodney Cook, Chris Macdonald, Cathy Pekar, and all the brilliant people in AMP who share our dream of a creative, flexible, innovative, and profitable work life.

Jack McElwee, who has always believed.

The brave people who have attended our workshops and went back into darkness to light a candle.

Miles Davis, Joni Mitchell, Bob Dylan, Robert Johnson, Frank Zappa, The Byrds, David Sylvian, and Bill Connors, whose innovation in music should inspire all business people as they inspired me.

Charles Rex, Graham Hawkins, and Ann Smith, who are true believers.

Most of all, my partner, wife, colleague, and best friend, Camille. None of this could have happened without her support, creative comment, input, and love.

Introduction

On a recent trip to London, I was amazed as my cabbie, Steve, nudged forward into the face of three lanes of oncoming traffic to cross a busy intersection that we had been waiting at for over five minutes. "Only a cabbie could pull that off," I commented, as we avoided potential accidents. Steve laughed and replied, "I have been driving cabs for 23 years. We cabbies have a term. We use the road. Other people drive but we use the road."

By bending rules, taking calculated risks, and using his experience of the many roads, lanes, and alleys of London, Steve made the journey faster, more efficiently, and safer by using rather than driving on the road.

Later I thought about the difference between "using the road" and "driving on the road" and the difference between eXtreme project management and traditional project management.

For people faced with too many projects, projects that seem to change every day, not enough good people, and not enough time and money, eXtreme project management is about using the road.

Why Should *You* Read This Book?

The simple answer to this question is for you to answer a couple of other questions:

	Yes	No
I have a completely stable and realistic project plan.	☐	☐
My organization has a stable strategic plan.	☐	☐
My stakeholders are fully committed to my project.	☐	☐
My sponsor is fully effective and available to me quickly.	☐	☐
I have a completely clear statement of scope and objectives.	☐	☐

My team is loyal and devoted to the project. ☐ ☐

We have effective risk and quality management plans. ☐ ☐

My organization understands project management. ☐ ☐

I have access to a group of expert project managers. ☐ ☐

I have all the tools, technology, and techniques I need. ☐ ☐

My project and organization are not changing rapidly. ☐ ☐

If you answered "Yes" to all these questions, this book should be used to raise your Project Manager of the Century award higher for all to see and envy. If you answered "No" to any of these questions, this book will help you get a perfect score.

This book is about a new and radical approach to managing projects and teams—project management (XPM). It represents a quantum leap in project management.

Our group has been developing, implementing, and refining this approach over the past 25 years. This new project management approach is not based on academic theories or esoteric models. Rather, it has been forged through the experience of thousands of hours of practical experience in hundreds of real projects. The projects have been in virtually all sectors of business—most government areas, insurance, banking, health, computing software, information technology (IT) hardware and IT services, research and development, retail services, policy development, and manufacturing.

What Makes This Book Different?

eXtreme project management is fundamentally different from mainstream and traditional project management approaches.

eXtreme Project Management Test

To show the radical difference between eXtreme project management and traditional project management, let's explore the answers to this question: How do you determine the progress of a project?

The traditional project management answers to this question include:

- Is the project meeting agreed deadlines?
- Is the project in budget?
- Have there been changes to the scope and objectives?

Indeed, most project management systems are based on reports only on budget and deadline compliance.

eXtreme project management adopts a completely different approach to measuring project success and progress:

- Are stakeholders being informed and consulted about project status?
- Have there been unapproved changes to scope and objectives?
- Are the cost and benefits assumptions still valid?
- Has the agreed product quality been compromised?
- Are project risks unchanged?
- Is the sponsor completely aware of the project status?
- Are the team members satisfied with the project?

In effect, traditional project management looks inward and downward whereas, eXtreme project management looks outward and upward.

Over the past 25 years, we have studied and researched project management and related topics from as many perspectives as possible. We have read every book (currently more than 100) and article (many hundreds) on project management we can find. We have searched the Internet and have attended meetings of professional project management groups such as the Project Management Institute and the Australian Institute of Project Management. In addition, we have discussed our views and models with more than 20,000 project managers in our workshop series.

The longer we look, the more we are convinced that most published project management material has *missed* the mark. Either the models are too basic and simplistic or too theoretical and complex. In many cases, they are just unrealistic. For example, many project management texts suggest that you have to acquire and implement complex system or project development methodologies (at the cost of hundreds of thousands of dollars). Critical management issues such as quality, benefits realization, and risk were either completely ignored or plugged in as afterthoughts.

Sometimes we wonder whether the author or expert even lives on the same planet that we do! Their world seems so organized, so rational, so structured, and so devoid of the complex interpersonal politics we see every day in our clients that we wonder whether we have a distorted view of reality.

However, 20,000 people cannot be wrong. Our workshop participants do live on the same planet as we do and in the same world of complex organization dynamics.

Traditional project management approaches reflect the engineering and construction models of project management. They are based on a set of assumptions that are increasingly irrelevant in the chaotic and ambiguous world of organizations facing the new millennium. Concepts such as fixed requirements, long development time frames, stable teams and technology, and passive involvement of project stakeholders who trust their expert project managers have become historical myths.

Our new project management approach has been continuously refined and expanded to reflect the realities of the new business paradigm. It is based on a different set of assumptions that include dynamic requirements, compressed development schedules, virtual teams, unstable technology, and total involvement of project stakeholders. Our project management approach is totally focused on the analysis, measurement, and realization of financial benefits from the project, managing the *total* whole-of-life project cycle, complete integration of quality issues, and proactive project risk management.

We have evolved our project management approach to be as simple as it can be and as complex as it needs to be.

In his terrific book, *Management of the Absurd,* Richard Frason (1996) described how James Watt saw something that millions of other people had also seen but "not seen." It was Watt's observation of how steam coming from his tea kettle could be used to power steam engines that sparked the Industrial Revolution. Watt also saw the "invisible obvious" that so many others could not.

So much of this book is about the invisible obvious. Time and time again throughout this book, you'll find yourself saying "Of course! Why didn't I think of that? It's so obvious. It is so simple."

However, as Richard Riodan said when he was mayor of Los Angeles, "Simple and easy aren't the same words."[1]

Most important, as we first stated in 1981 in *People and Project Management* (1981) and in *Third Wave Project Management* (Thomsett, 1992), our project management approach is totally focused on people and the relationships among the many people involved in projects.

People, not resources or users, work on projects.

What This Book Is Not About

This book is not about how to develop work breakdown structures and project schedules. It is not about developing simplistic and mechanical models such as project plans (which are never followed anyway). Most important, it is not *boring*. Many

---

1. We caught Riodan making this wonderful distinction between the simple statement "We should eliminate all gangs" with the not-so-easy task of implementing it on a TV news broadcast in 1992.

of the project management books that we have read present project management as some dry, cold, and quasi-scientific "pursuit."

We totally reject this view of project management. Our experience is that project management is one of the most challenging, creative, and exciting activities you can undertake. We hope that this is reflected in this book.

The Structure of the Book

To assist our readers who are under eXtreme project deadlines and working conditions, we have structured the book into three parts for quick access.

Part 1—eXtreme Concepts

This covers the background to XPM. We look at the evolution of project management, the emerging project environment, and the forces driving the need for XPM.

Part 2—eXtreme Tools

This introduces the XPM tools such as RAP sessions, learning loops, success sliders, and the detailed techniques used in XPM planning and tracking.

Part 3—Additional Resources

This includes readings that provide further tips; advanced tools; and related issues such as project sponsorship, negotiation, communication, ethics, and other critical project management concerns. There are additional readings available on our Web site *www.thomsett.com.au*

Each part is related but they can be read independently if you are in a hurry; though we hope you get to read the entire book eventually. Great project managers will read all of this book.

During our journey as consultants to major organizations, we have seen many strange and wonderful things. In many cases, what we observed put the bizarre events in the series *The X Files* to shame. At the end of the chapters in Part 2, we have included a section called *The P Files* (where *P* represents people or politics). *The P Files* entries support the points raised in the associated chapter.

A Note on Terminology

Throughout this book we refer to *business projects*. This term includes all the typical elements of business process redesign and development, new policy development, IT development, and change management. Readers who have either a business or IT background will find the concepts and techniques relevant. After all, there is no such thing as an IT project. eXtreme projects embrace and include all aspects of business, IT, policy, administration, human resources, change, and research effort that all projects should include. We also do not use the term *user,* which we dislike intensely, to refer to non-technical people. As we explain in the next chapter, this term has been used to marginalize and diminish the critical role that business experts and clients play in contemporary projects.

PART

1

eXtreme Concepts

The New Project Environment

"A good plan today is better than a perfect plan tomorrow." ∎

Conrad Brean (Robert De Niro)[1]

A series of advertisements for a well-known project scheduling tool provide a fascinating insight into the state-of-the-art of project management.

One of the ads shows a person, alone, in a high-tech, darkened room with a wall of 20 terminals displaying various outputs from the project management software. The project manager is saying "Excellent." Clearly, the project is going fine, thanks, in part, to the scheduling tool.

 Never confuse the map with the journey.

To our group, this ad could not be further from the truth of contemporary project management.

---

[1]. *Wag The Dog*, Barry Levinson, Director; Larry Beinhart (book); Hilary Henkin, Writer, 1997.

There are three major forces driving the need for a new paradigm of project management.

eXtreme project management has been developed to deal with the nature of contemporary or "e-projects" and Internet time. E-projects are projects that:

- Must be delivered rapidly,
- Are both research-like and mission-critical, and
- Have to be managed in a turbulent business and technology environment.

These types of projects have become the most common as a series of forces continue to accelerate the rate of change.

Forces Driving Change

Although new technologies such as the Web, Wireless Access Protocol (WAP), and Java play a part in the need for new project management models, the major forces are not technological. They are:

- Driving Force 1—A power shift;
- Driving Force 2—The free agent army; and
- Driving Force 3—The global e-economy.

Driving Force 1—A Power Shift

Our group first documented this phenomenon more than 10 years ago (see our Web site). The use and abuse of expert power by computer people[2] have resulted in a major shift in the control of Information Technology (IT) and other expert project groups back into the business areas.

There are four broad stages in the evolution of expert and business professional relations that are discernible in most organizations. Each stage has its own written and unwritten codes of practice and behavior—in essence, its own culture. The prevailing culture is evidenced in every interaction between business and computing professionals. It *totally* dominates the processes of project management, systems analysis, and system and product support.

The key cultural difference between the stages is the direction and nature of the control and power relations, as shown in Figure 1.1. Simply, the power relationship revolves around who controls the IT and system development activities.

---

2. Although we focus on computer and IT people here, the same patterns exist for other expert areas such as architecture, engineering, medicine, and so on.

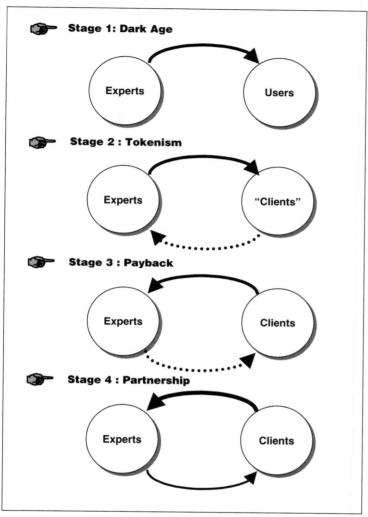

Figure 1.1
Four stages of power relationships

There are four stages of professional behavior that are currently evidenced in organizations:

- Stage 1—Dark Age
- Stage 2—Tokenism
- Stage 3—Payback
- Stage 4—Partnership

Each stage seems to be a prerequisite for the next. However, this is not inevitable, as there are a few organizations that have bypassed Stage 2 and some that have the potential to bypass Stage 3.

We'll use computing people as our example, however. As shown by Alan Patching (1994), a similar model has emerged for construction and engineering project management as well. Indeed, the shift in power from experts to clients in project management is mirrored more broadly in the shift to consumer power being experienced in many organizations.

We also accept that there is a possible fifth stage in which the distinction between expert and client ceases to exist.

Stage 1—Dark Age

For most organizations, the Dark Age stage was associated with the first introduction of computing into the organization. In general, this stage lasted through the 1960s into the late 1970s. The prevailing ethic was that of expert diagnosis and expert power. There was little standardization of the system development and project management process, and each senior programmer or project manager had his or her way of doing things.

A typical scenario in this stage was that a perceived business problem was quickly outlined by the client with the computer person asking specific questions about the nature of the problem. The business person would be told how long the system development process would take and then, unless he or she was required to provide more information, the business client would not be disturbed until system testing and implementation.

The key to this was that the business user was completely dependent on the computer professional. Should the project take longer than originally estimated, there was little that the business client could do, with the exception of complaining (which, in many cases, further *reduced* the likelihood of satisfaction, because the computer professional had been upset).

In summary, this stage was marked by a directive, often aggressive attitude toward the clients (i.e., Trust us. We know what's best for you in computing solutions), little or no client involvement in the system development process, and the issues of quality and project management left to the computing group to define and manage.

In essence, computing people were left alone to practice their dark art. The key word here is *dominance*.

This stage inevitably led to a serious organizational conflict and a maintenance nightmare. With the arrival of database technology coupled with the structured revolution (data flow diagrams, data modeling, structured design, and programming) in the mid-1970s, organizations began to move to the second stage.

Stage 2—Tokenism   The second stage, which emerged in the mid- to late 1970s, is marked by the redevelopment of many of the systems developed in the first stage to take advantage of the benefits offered by database technology and the emerging communications and network technology. In addition, this stage marked the first attempt to automate new types of information systems such as management information and decision support.

However, the key element of the second stage was the development of more disciplined approaches to system development, project management, and quality assurance. Implicit in these techniques was the need for more active client involvement in the specification and testing of computer systems. However, it is revealing that *none* of the classic texts in these techniques really addressed the social and political issues associated with client involvement in system development, product quality, or project management impact.

In addition, as we discuss later, the disciplined approaches to project management introduced by people such as Phillip Metzger (1979) were based on engineering models that also excluded any meaningful client participation in estimation, scheduling selection of strategy, and so on.

As a result, although the intrinsic quality of the system development and management process was considerably higher in Stage 2, client involvement was restricted to initial systems analysis, system testing, and documentation. In many organizations, a token business analyst or client representative was recruited to the computer project team or, in some cases, specific business analysis or special project groups were formed using business people that were designed to represent the business areas. Typically, members of these groups were corrupted by computing people and these groups eventually entered a "Twilight Zone" existence, representing neither the interests of business groups nor of computing groups.

The Tokenism stage was typified by computing groups still firmly in control of project management issues such as cost, effort, quality, and priorities. There was some participation by business clients in the development process, but this involvement was on the terms of computing people. It is not surprising that in this stage, business people get to undertake testing and documentation, the two stages of the development process least liked by IT professionals. Many organizations are still in Stage 2 but moving rapidly to Stage 3. Others have moved on to Stage 3. The key word here is *bureaucracy.*

Stage 3—Payback or Get Even   This stage reflects both the years of frustration of business people with their lack of control of the computing effort and a series of major technological and environmental factors influencing organizations throughout the 1980s. Simply, in Stage 3, the pendulum swings dramatically from computing control to business control.

The major factors behind Stage 3 are business factors that have been well documented in landmark books by people such as Tom Peters (1988), Peter Drucker (1989), Charles Handy (1989), and many others. Competitive, financial, and social pressures forced all organizations (private and public) to evaluate their methods of working, managing, and planning. As a result, senior management began, for the first time, to critically examine its organization's investment in computing. In particular, senior management became focused on issues such as how computing technology and systems were aligned to business fundamentals such as strategic planning, return on investment, client service, and added value.[3] As a result of Stages 1 and 2, most internal computing professionals were left wanting.

Features of Stage 3 are concepts such as "a business within a business," computing as an internal service bureau or cost center, best practice, benchmarking and, in extreme cases, outsourcing computing as an independent business area. In practical terms, this means that clients are charged fully for their use of computing people and equipment. It means that return on investment and the associated techniques of risk assessment and risk management are taken more seriously and that projects that cannot be objectively measured and justified from a business (not computing technology) perspective are not supported. In extreme cases, it means that internal computing groups are forced to submit project estimates or quotations in competition with quotations from outside organizations (in many cases, they are threatened with outsourcing). Stage 3 also involves penalties for nondelivery and for poor estimation. In other words, business clients are demanding from internal computing people the same level of service that they would expect from commercial consulting and system integration organizations.

Stage 3 might give the business professionals a legitimate power and perhaps a less legitimate feeling of "getting even" with computing professionals, but it does little to address the fundamental issues of lack of meaningful participation and organizational impact that typified Stages 1 and 2 and led to Stage 3 with its shift of power to the business groups.

OUTSOURCING AS PAYBACK

Among the unspoken factors underlying the rapid growth (>30% per annum) in outsourcing are the factors covered in this chapter. Despite evidence that outsourcing results in higher costs, many business groups have indicated that they will continue to outsource their IT and other expert effort. The answer lies mainly in the higher degree of professional service and attitude exhibited by better outsourcing groups.

---

3. In addition, the increased level of computing and IT studies in schools has created a class of business people who are more knowledgeable about IT issues.

In many ways, Stage 3 has made matters worse as it has led to an antagonistic attitude between IT and business professionals. Although they are now "in control," business people can do little to really ensure that they obtain quality systems because they have simply removed themselves further from the development process by adopting a contract-at-arms'-length attitude. In essence, they have become victims of their own control and this continues the lack of understanding between the two groups. The key word for this stage is *antagonism*.

Stage 4—Partnership Stage 4 is marked by a shared recognition from both computing and business people of the need for a collaborative partnership based on professional behaviors. This partnership includes all the return on investment, cost recovery, and other project management and quality concerns of Stage 3, in addition to open negotiation of these issues and full client participation in planning, managing, and developing the computer system.

WE'RE ALL MIXED UP

In larger organizations, all stages can be evident at the same time. Because the behaviors covered in this chapter are cultural, they exist in the "heads" of the various project managers. It is possible for one project manager to be exhibiting Dark Age behavior and, in the very next room, another project manager to be in Partnership with his or her clients. Unfortunately, as in many human interactions, the worst behavior tends to be taken as representative of the whole group.

Rather than the "closed bidding" of project costs, effort, and delivery schedules typical of Stage 3 (and to some extent Stages 1 and 2), projects in Stage 4 are planned in joint planning sessions that include the formation of essential "contracts" for project delivery and quality requirements. These contracts are not the one-way contracts associated with Stage 3 but rather, joint contracts that also require commitment from business clients.

Another key feature of Stage 4 is complex, interdisciplinary project teams that shift throughout all system development and support phases (see "Driving Force 3—The Global E-Economy").

Inherent in Stage 4 is the expansion of both business and computing professionals' awareness of each other's concerns and the project dynamic. Computer professionals become more aware of the strategic business issues associated with the use of information systems and are fully trained in cost–benefit and risk management processes. Business professionals are educated in project and quality management processes as well as in systems analysis, cost–benefit analysis, and associated system development techniques.

This is not to suggest that business professionals will become computer professionals and vice versa, but rather that education and communication are necessary to ensure a deeper appreciation of each group's concerns and to facilitate more meaningful participation. Each group must act professionally and respect the other group's professionalism. The key word for this stage is *cooperation*.

This force, more than any other, is driving the new project management paradigm.

Driving Force 2—The Free Agent Army

In the 1960s and 1970s, belief in concepts such as jobs for life and corporate loyalty was accepted as the norm. In addition, many organizations provided a "corporate family" for their employees and, as documented by many management experts, the rules were simple: Look after your organization and it will look after you.

As a result, there was a generally stable organization structure and culture, which meant that long-term investment was made in building the skills and knowledge of people and teams. In addition, the relative stability and security of employment meant that personnel turnover was low and when it did occur, it was well planned.

During the 1990s, an organizational environment emerged that was more complex, more turbulent, and more chaotic. Again, as well documented by experts such as Peter Drucker (1989), Charles Handy (1989), and many others, one of the side effects of the new organization environment is that corporate loyalty and careers for life are no longer accepted dogma.

An excellent example of the new corporate reality can be seen in one of our favorite magazines, *Fast Company*. In the August/September 1997 and December/January 1998 issues, *Fast Company* headlined two "state of the art" pieces. The first, from Tom Peters, was called "A Brand Called You." In a wonderful revision of the famous statement, "There is no I in team," Peters argued that "There is a You in team" and that the focus of people must be on their own career interests rather than that of others or of the organization. In the December/January issue, Daniel Pink described the concept of free agents or, in more conventional terms, corporate mercenaries.[4] In *Fast Company*'s terms, free agents are people who understand:

> The old social contract didn't have a clause for introspection. It was much simpler than that. You gave loyalty (to the company). You got security. But now

---

4. The term that *Fast Company* offers as an alternative for free agents is *condottiere,* which is the Italian term for soldiers who traveled Europe fighting for any sovereign who would pay them.

that the old contract has been repealed, people are examining both its basic terms and its implicit conditions.

Nina Munk (1998), in an article entitled "The New Organization Man" in *Fortune,* parallels the conclusions reached in the *Fast Company* articles, quoting from a senior in a U.S. university:

> My dad worked for Sears for 19 years as a security guard, and he was laid off. I have to position myself so that I can constantly look out for myself. I have to be self-serving.

These views are typical of those of the members of the virtual teams[5] with which we are familiar.

These concepts are not new and, in fact, were first proposed in 1989 by Charles Handy in his seminal *The Age of Unreason.* In that book, Handy argued for people to adopt the concept of work not as an upward and hierarchical career in one organization, but rather as a horizontal portfolio of different jobs for different organizations.

The new team environment also includes the additional factors of continuous restructuring, outsourcing, and dynamic planning driven by increasing competition and technological innovation.

The other major driving force for new team structures is the increasing subspecialization of business and information skills. Traditional project teams were based on a group of people who possessed the requisite skills to undertake the project work. Only a decade ago, the typical IT team would need access to a project manager, a systems analyst, a data modeler, a couple of COBOL programmers, a documentation expert, and perhaps a tester. Now, the range and complexity of technical issues, development platform concerns, higher business group participation, graphical user interface (GUI) and prototyping requirements, business process redesign considerations, change management, complex network and database design, implementation factors, and so on, have vastly increased the range and sophistication of skills required for successful product and system development. As a result, few teams can permanently accommodate all required skills, so the flexibility of the virtual team has given it an edge.

---

5. A *virtual team* is a shifting group of part-time and "borrowed" people who have reporting lines to other people as well as the project manager. We discuss this in greater detail later.

The project management models required to effectively manage a virtual team working under extreme pressure are fundamentally different from those required for stable, traditional teams.

Driving Force 3—The Global E-Economy

A quick visit to the management section of Barnes & Noble or Borders shows the overwhelming pressure being bought to bear on contemporary business executives. Hundreds of books with titles including *Blown To Bits, Faster, Innovate or Die, Business at the Speed of E,* and *The Networked World* exhort executives to rapidly adopt e-technologies and strategies.[6] In one week, in both the leading daily business papers of Australia and the United Kingdom, over 50% of the advertisements were for e-commerce or e-technology companies. For most senior executives, the message is clear: innovate or liquidate.

Discounting the massive vendor hype and the dot-com failures of 2000, there is a fundamental shift occurring in the global business economy. In his wonderful book, *The Lexus and the Olive Tree,* Thomas Friedman (1999) detailed the broader impacts of globalization. He argued that the Cold War created an international system that is now being replaced by another system—the globalization system:

To begin with, the globalization system, unlike the Cold War system, is not static, but a dynamic on-going process: Globalization involves the inexorable integration of markets, nation-states and technologies to a degree never witnessed before—in a way enabling individuals, corporations and nation-states to reach around the world, farther, faster, deeper and cheaper. (p. 00)

Globalization and the e-economy have resulted in a business and regulatory environment of:

- Increased growth;
- Increased levels of takeovers, mergers, and alliances;
- Higher levels of competition;
- More aware consumers;
- More choice for consumers;
- More complex product requirements; and
- Rapid product development cycles.

---

6. In September 2001, while browsing in a bookshop at Changi Airport in Singapore, I counted more than 100 books on e-business management practice. In fact, there were more e-business management books than traditional management books.

In particular, increasing consumer awareness, availability of Internet-driven alternatives, shifting of labor to low-cost countries, the push for reduction of trading barriers and free trade, and many other factors are forcing organizations to reexamine their product, project, and service-delivery processes.

In our group's client base, which is mainly major financial organizations, the widely held belief in business groups is that traditional IT and other project development approaches are too bureaucratic and slow. This belief, coupled with the other driving forces, has enabled us to design and implement more radical project development and management approaches—eXtreme project management.

eXtreme project management is not just a new set of tools; it is a new project culture.

Project Management Evolution

2

"The past is a foreign country. They do things differently there." ■

Michael Redgrave (Narrator)[1]

The engineering and, more significantly, the IT professions have heavily influenced the evolution of business project management.

As a new profession, information systems looked to other professions for guidance and for models to assist in formalizing and establishing best practices. Given the dominance of hardware engineering and research in the early days of computing, it is not surprising that many of the initial models for development and management were drawn from engineering and construction.

The classic product and system development lifecycles and methodologies were drawn directly from the product development cycles of construction and engineering. The evolution of formal methodologies first discussed in the North Atlantic Treaty Organization (NATO) conferences[2] during the late 1960s was based on the concept of phase-by-phase progress through the processes of analysis, design, construction, test, and implementation.

---

1. *The Go-Between*, Joseph Losey, Director; Harold Pinter, Writer, 1970.
2. NATO Software Engineering, Naur & Randell, 1968.

Most important, the first formal models of project management in information systems also reflected those developed in the defense and construction industries.

As discussed by James Adams (1991), the development of technology as we know it can be traced from around 10,000 years ago. Although there is evidence of crafted implements such as fire-hardened spears as far back as 400,000 years, the Neolithic period marked the move from hunting and gathering to domestication of animals and farming. With this shift, the development of human-designed implements (engineering) began to accelerate and, by 3000 B.C., the Egyptians had developed sophisticated technologies such as boats, wheels, plows, and sewage systems. The construction of major buildings such as the pyramids and large canal works was common.

The management of these major engineering works was undertaken by people such as Khufu-onekh, who designed and built the Great Pyramid, and Imhotep, who designed and built the Pharaoh tombs. Similar large projects were being undertaken during the same period in Mesopotamia, China, and Greece.

By the end of the Roman Empire, technology and engineering had a "base of ingenuity, craft, art, empirical relations and, some quantitative reason" (Adams, 1991). However, it wasn't until some 4,000 to 5,000 years later during the Industrial Revolution that the move from guilds of craftspeople to professional societies such as the British Institute of Civil Engineering (1818) began to occur.

The formalization of teaching, knowledge, techniques, measures, and behaviors associated with professional societies was complete in all areas of engineering by the early 1890s, but the formalization of the management of complex engineering projects did not emerge until some 60 years later in the 1950s.

Project management in other industries had also faced the difference between technical management and project management briefly discussed in our Introduction and explored further in later chapters.

Until the 1950s, the management issues in engineering such as cost estimation, change control, scheduling, management and direction of resources, contract negotiation, and so on were undertaken by the project's architect. However, the management of both the technical aspects and the overall project by the same person often led to a conflict of interest.

A dramatic example of this conflict of interest can be found in the Sydney Opera House project. Joern Utzon was awarded the contract to design and build the Opera House in 1959. Some nine years later, Utzon had not produced any architectural construction drawings and he resigned after a series of heated discussions with the new Minister of Public Works, Sir Davis Hughes, who stated to the New South Wales Parliament in 1966 that "If the complete control of the Opera House was left in the hands of Mr Utzon, the building would never be completed" (Hughes, 1993).

After Utzon's resignation, an engineering management team completed the project in 1973. Hughes maintains that Utzon was overwhelmed by the technical difficulties associated with the construction of the large shells and cost control, schedules, and other project management concerns were basically ignored.

During the late 1950s and early 1960s, the integration and development of a body of project management were driven by difficulties faced by the U.S. Department of Defense. Most of the concepts came from major projects such as the Manhattan Project (the building of the atomic bomb), the Polaris, and the 688 submarine projects under Defense Secretary Robert McNamara and implemented by Admirals Raborn and Rickover. The predominant approach to project management mirrored the construction industry, in that the management of defense projects was undertaken by the technical experts. However, the underlying issue of conflict of interest existed in these projects as well.

As documented brilliantly by Richard Rhodes (1995), until the Manhattan Project clearly separated the overall management of the project's budget, schedule, and mission under General Groves and the technical management of the project under Robert Oppenheimer, the project to build the atomic bomb was facing failure.

The concept of project management as a separate discipline is now well established in engineering. In contrast to the Sydney Opera House, the construction of the new Federal Parliament House in Sydney was managed by a specialist project management group with clear separation of management and technical roles. We return to this concept in the next chapter.

However, this brief examination of the history of project management enables us to identify the fundamental myth that is the foundation of traditional project management: Business and engineering projects are the same type of projects.

This is one of the most enduring of the traditional project management beliefs. The analogy between engineers constructing a building, a bridge, or a ship and a business or IT professional building a new product is often used by advocates of software engineering and traditional project management. The well-known waterfall model of system development in which design does not commence until formal specifications are signed off on by the client is a direct "copy" of the traditional engineering models.

As shown in Figure 2.1, there are few, if any, parallels between building business processes, products, or software and building skyscrapers.[3] The dynamic nature of business project construction is in complete contrast to the "stable" process of building. In addition, as documented by Chris Meyers (1993) and many others, the building, automotive, chemical, and many other engineering groups are moving to

---

3. In fact, the closest project to business projects is making films, which is why we use film and TV quotes in this book.

Engineering Projects	Business Projects
Small number of professionally certified service providers with formal legal contracts	Large number of disparate often political service providers with informal verbal contracts
Specifications generally fixed and formally specified	Specifications flexible and informally specified
Well-established code of practice and ethical standards	Poorly established code of practice and ethical standards
Well-established methodologies founded on physical and mathematical principles	Conflicting methodologies founded on theoretical and marketing principles
Physical deliverables and modular components	Abstract deliverables and unique components
Clear performance indicators and accurate metrics	Poor performance indicators and inaccurate metrics
Variation reduced through consistent and standard process	Variation amplified through individualism

Figure 2.1
Engineering versus business projects

iterative and concurrent development models, abandoning the waterfall model to be first to market.

The Four Waves of Project Management_____

Project management has evolved through a number of stages or waves. Table 2.1 highlights the major differences between the waves of project management.

Table 2.1
The Four Waves of Project Management

First Wave—Initial	1950–1970
Project Justification	Projects were justified by experimentation and proof of technology.
Senior Management Role	Generally unaware of major project issues—IT were trusted as "scientists/experts."
Business Expert Role	Little or no involvement in development process.
Management Focus	Focus on development effort only.
Team Structure	Single teams with dominant technical leader.
Planning Approach	Informal and verbal planning.
Project Dynamic	Generally unlimited time and budget.
Second Wave—Engineered	**1970–current**
Project Justification	Projects were justified by token cost–benefit analysis—no effective benefits realization.
Senior Management Role	Involved in token steering committees—IT were still trusted as "scientists" or "experts."
Business Expert Role	Token involvement as business analysts and in testing and documentation—Some business project managers with little support or training.
Management Focus	Continuing focus on development effort only—Formal metrics recorded on development productivity.
Team Structure	Single teams with dominant technical leader and related technical experts such as database experts.
Planning Approach	Macro planning based on engineering concepts such as one-off planning at front, fixed, formal specifications.
Project Dynamic	Expert-driven where the IT and other specialists set budgets and technology.
Third Wave—Dynamic	**1980–current**
Project Justification	Cost–benefit taken more seriously and greater awareness of benefits realization.
Senior Management Role	Committed sponsor and steering committee roles with greater awareness of project management issues.

Table 2.1
The Four Waves of Project Management (*cont.*)

Third Wave—Dynamic	1980–current
Business Expert Role	Business experts involved more actively in development and project management process.
Management Focus	Whole-of-life focus is adopted with development and support cycles measured.
Team Structure	Virtual teams emerge with small project team supported by contractors, specialists, and business people as stakeholders.
Planning Approach	Micro planning based on flexible plans with deliverables or time-boxes of 3 to 6 months.
Project Dynamic	Constraint-driven by fixed deadlines, limited budgets, and resources.
Fourth Wave—eXtreme	**1990–**
Project Justification	Projects are totally focused on added value and benefits realization.
Senior Management Role	Project sponsors as executive project managers for total life of product or system.
Business Expert Role	Business and technology teams completely integrated.
Management Focus	Focus on total whole-of-life product life cycle with integrated process and product management and metrics.
Team Structure	Virtual teams within virtual organizations based on partnerships and networks.
Planning Approach	Organic planning using micro plans and very short development cycles (daily builds).
Project Dynamic	Increasingly constraint-driven but balanced by return on investment considerations.

Clearly, this book is based on fourth-wave principles. However, in the assessment of our group, based on direct contact with more than 500 companies over the past 25 years, the majority of companies are still using second-wave project management practices.

NEWTONIAN VERSUS QUANTUM

Doug DeCarlo (*Cutter Consortium, www.cutter.com/consortium/consultants*) used a wonderful model that is identical to our distinction between second- and fourth-wave project management. He described project managers with Newtonian neurosis, which is a pathological need to bring structure to projects. He argued that extreme projects require project managers with a quantum view of the world that embraces and accepts change, chaos, uncertainty, and relaxation of control to gain control.

In addition, the majority of published material on project management is clearly second-wave with some notable exceptions such as Steve McConnell's *Rapid Development* (1996) and Jim McCarthy's *Dynamics of Software Development* (1995). We provide a guide to the other people who have joined us in developing this new mind-set at the end of this book.

The good news is that the group is finally growing.[4]

Managing projects is the management of creativity.

JAZZ AS EXTREME PROJECT MANAGEMENT

John Kao in *Jamming: The Art and Discipline of Business Creativity* (1997), and others use jazz as a metaphor for creative work. Anyone who has heard Miles Davis letting his awesome colleagues improvise within a highly organized but shifting structure knows the power of jazz. He was the first extreme project manager.[5] The key here, of course, is that you have to be a brilliant player to jam effectively. The same goes for creative teams: You need the best for eXtreme models to work.

---

4. Greg Howell and Lauri Koskela (www.leanconstruction.org) join Alan Patching (op cit) and others in addressing the need for a similar shift in project management approaches in the construction industry. You should also access the views of leading IT consultants such as Jim Highsmith, Doug DeCarlo, and Scott Ambler at www.cutter.com/consortium/consultants.
5. Rock bands such as The Grateful Dead, Phish, and King Crimson also get into creative jamming.

eXtreme Concepts

3

"I don't care about what anything was designed to do,
I care about what it *can* do." ■

Gene Kranz (Ed Harris)[1]

There are a number of values that underpin eXtreme project management. These values result in project management behaviors that are:

- Participative: The management of projects is based on meaningful participation of stakeholders.

- Proactive: Project management is a creative and proactive problem-solving process.

- Open: Everything about the project is shared openly with all stakeholders.

- Outward-oriented: The focus of the project manager is outwards toward the stakeholders.

- Trusting: The project team is treated as professionals who are to be trusted.

[1.] *Apollo 13*, Ron Howard, Director; Jim Lovell, Jeffrey Kluger, Writers, 1995.

In addition, eXtreme project management incorporates radical concepts such as these:

- Project management is completely different from technical management.
- Context is more important than content.
- Whole-of-life project management.
- The project manager is a facilitator and integrator rather than a manager.
- Senior management are executive project managers.
- Scenario planning rather than macroplanning.
- Participative rapid planning.
- Virtual teams rather than traditional teams.

This chapter explores these concepts in more detail and provides the framework for the eXtreme project management tools and techniques.

Project Management Versus Technical Management

The distinction between technical and managerial information in a project is critical in understanding eXtreme project management. To understand a project and manage a project, you must make a distinction between the information dealing with the business aspects of a project and the information that represents the technical issues such as the development technologies and deliverables that are being developed in the project.

A TEST FOR TECHNICAL OR PROJECT MANAGEMENT PREFERENCE

Let's assume that your team comes to you with the following problem. They have been evaluating the Aardvarker database versus the Blahdanger database technology and they can't decide which to adopt. How would you assist them? A technical manager would use his or her technical expertise to arrange various volume benchmarking, referential integrity, efficiency, and other technical evaluations, undertaking some of the more difficult technical tests themselves. A project manager would ask the team what skills and assistance the members need to make the decision and arrange for the team members to get the help they need. In addition, the project manager would evaluate the risks, costs, schedule, and impact on project objectives of each option.

In the broadest sense of the term, all professions deal with technical information. The structure, components, and behavior of the human body form a highly technical set of information studied by doctors. The complexity of legal processes, precedents, and law is another set of technical information required by lawyers. The rules, procedures, and legal issues in business accounting provide another example of technical information understood by accountants. The complex policy, analysis, and assessment issues associated with implementing competency-based assessment are as technical as any information system design. In computing, the techniques of systems modeling, systems design, data design, programming, testing, and integration are examples of technical information. To develop and normalize an entity-relation model, to program in C++, and to design a DB2 database are highly technical skills that are required to develop information systems.

As shown in Figure 3.1, the project management of a project has a different but related focus and is driven by a different set of information that is not technical in the pure sense, but rather represents the business and managerial context of the project. The technical and managerial aspects of a project are integrated through the scope, objectives, strategy, and quality requirements of the client. We call this set of information a *business case* (see later).

The effective management of a project requires a balance between and integration of the *content* (technical deliverables, tasks, internal dynamic) and the *context* (managerial, political, social environment) of the project.

As discussed in Chapter 2, "Project Management Evolution," the emergence of specialist project managers who are not involved in the technical detail of the project is a recent innovation in other areas such as construction and engineering. The project manager's focus must be the context, not content.

Context and Content

Whereas the traditional project manager could personally review the detailed project technical deliverables, this was often achieved by ignoring the business aspects of the project. Further, as the rate of technological change increases and the various system development techniques become increasingly complex, it has become difficult, if not impossible, for a project manager to have all the requisite skills to enable him or her to undertake such technical reviews. As a result, the role of a project manager has gradually shifted to ensuring that processes are in place to assure the technical quality of the project's deliverables, rather than personally reviewing the quality. This shift reflects the distinction between technical management and project management that emerged in other professions, such as civil engineering, discussed earlier in this book.

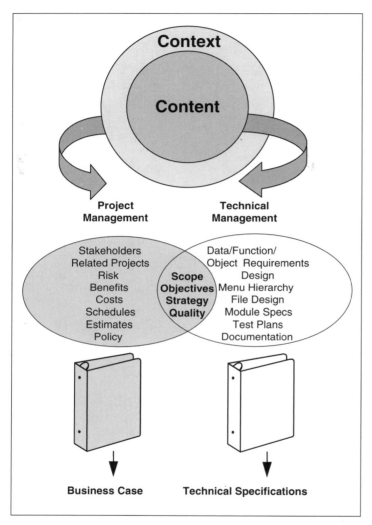

Figure 3.1
Two information sets

LISTEN AND LOOK

The more time you spend listening to, eyeballing, and communicating with your stakeholders the better. Build a relationship with your stakeholders and you will be doing your job: It is all about relationships.

The less the project manager knows about the technical details the better.

In effect, a radical difference between traditional and eXtreme project management is that traditional project management focused downward and inward toward the team and the technical context of the project. eXtreme project management focuses outward and upward toward the stakeholders, project sponsor, and the complex relationships between the project and the stakeholders (see Figure 3.2).[2]

Whole-of-Life Project Management

Traditional project management focused on the development component of the project life cycle. As shown in Figure 3.3, eXtreme project management adopts a whole-of-life perspective.

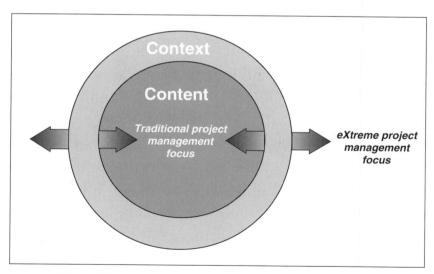

Figure 3.2
New project management focus

---

2. Some folks refer to the black space (content) and the white space (context).

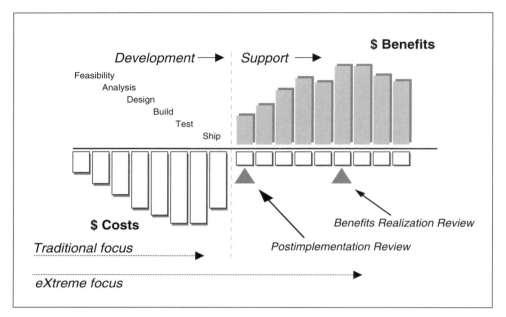

Figure 3.3
Extreme project management perspective

In traditional project management, as the project progressed through feasibility study to implementation, recording of costs, duration and effort, and reporting of these *process* metrics was common. However, after postimplementation review, tracking and reporting mechanisms were stopped as the project was finished.

As a result of this development focus, few organizations accurately tracked either the support costs or the actual realization of benefits. The absence of ongoing measurement in the production cycle has left many business people with little hard evidence of the value added through new products or information systems. It has also enforced the view that many executives have of IT and other project groups as cost centers.

What happens after a project is over is as important as during it.

Moreover, the focus on development effort, cost, and duration often resulted in the compromise of long-term project success (see later) with short-term cost and deadline emphasis. For example, the tracking of development progress reveals that the project is behind schedule and over cost. To get the project back on schedule and to reduce the cost overruns, the project manager and team deliberately degrade quality and de-scope the project's requirements by cutting back on testing and documentation and by dropping what they perceive to be nonessential functionality.

$1 FOR $1

We use a rule of thumb that for every dollar that is spent in development, another dollar is required for support over the production life cycle. Industries such as construction, aerospace, and road building have used this rule for years.

The project is now on schedule and within budget and potential long-term benefits and support costs have been compromised.

The project tracking reports show that the project is now within budget and on schedule, but in reality, the project is back on track for failure. This paradox is explored in later chapters.

Project Manager as Facilitator

As introduced earlier, traditional project management was driven by technically oriented project managers. Further, these project managers worked in the traditional hierarchical culture of the broader organization. As a result, key project management activities such as risk management, estimation, costing, and strategy selection were undertaken *intuitively* (black box project management) and *unilaterally* by the project manager with little involvement from his or her project team members and with no involvement from the business areas. In many cases, the project manager would meet with senior managers and then tell the team how long the project would take and who was to undertake what tasks.

To successfully plan a business project in the contemporary organizational context, you must shift from planning to *facilitating* the planning process.

Using the rapid planning (RAP) process described later in this chapter, you must identify the key stakeholders and related projects and, with the team members, undertake the planning process in an open and collaborative manner using white box project management (see Figure 3.4).

Apart from the advantages identified earlier, the team-driven project management concept ensures that all stakeholders who are service providers to the project

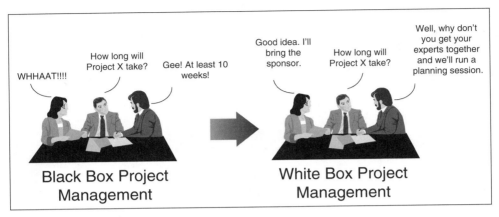

Figure 3.4
Black box versus white box project management

RELATIONSHIP CAPITAL

In his great book, *Mission Critical Leadership* (2001), Paddy Miller developed the concept of relationship capital together with the more conventional concepts of intellectual and financial capital. He argued that the relationships built between an organization, its people, its clients, and its suppliers are critical in the new economy. We agree and our model of project management is all about you, the project manager, building relationship capital with your stakeholders, sponsor, and team members. The more relationship capital you have built, the easier your job will be.

manager and all project managers of key related projects are prepared to support your project's timetables prior to its commencement.

In addition, the internal and external complexity of projects can overwhelm a single person and a collaborative team has a greater capability to ensure that all planning considerations are complete and accurate. For example, in a medium-sized project, more than 100 risk factors will need to be assessed, more than 1,000 tasks will need to be identified and estimated, and more than 100 external relationships will need to be managed. It is clear that a team-driven project planning process involving experts from different backgrounds will have a higher capability of handling this level of complexity.

Apart from increasing the buy-in and ensuring that your key service providers can commit to and be responsible for the proposed project's outputs and outcomes and their service requirements, the values and ideals of participative processes of team-driven and proactive project management are in line with the emerging organization paradigms of empowerment, ownership, and partnership now being implemented in business groups across many organizations.

It should be emphasized that although the preferred team-driven planning approach is based on consensus, you are still the responsible person. It will be common that the team involved in planning will not reach consensus and, in these cases, it remains your responsibility to resolve the issue in conjunction with the project owner or sponsor. How you can manage the balancing of responsibility and participation is covered in more detail later in this book.

The concept of a large group of people meeting together to plan a project may seem costly and risky, but experience has shown that the team-driven process is quicker, less costly, and more accurate than the traditional "expert" project manager approach.

Sponsors as Executive Project Managers

If there is one common theme shared by virtually all 20,000 people who have participated in our project management workshops, it is their relationship, or lack of, with their project sponsor.

The role of the project sponsor is critical in ensuring the success of both IT and business projects. Our research and experience have shown that the effectiveness of the project sponsor role is the single best predictor of project success or failure.

No sponsor, no start.

As a result, for you—a project manager—the relationship that you build with your sponsor is the most critical relationship in your project. Although the identification, prioritization, and approval of projects are critical roles, the responsibilities of contemporary project sponsors or steering committees go far beyond these processes.

As discussed earlier in this book, traditional project sponsors and steering committees tended to find themselves in either a passive or reactive relationship with the project and the project manager. After the approval of the project, the project sponsor and members of the steering committee were inundated with technically oriented reports and basic cost-tracking reports. Often, they were not alerted to major project problems until after they had become critical, leaving few options for the executives in helping the project.

eXtreme project sponsors and steering committees are highly proactive and involved in the management of the project as "executive" project managers. In particular, the following additional responsibilities are essential for senior management to ensure that a project achieves its outputs and outcomes:

THE ONE MINUTE SPONSOR

In extreme projects, every day is significant and every delay is a disaster. We have a rule for our clients called the 1 x 1 Rule. When a decision is required, the project manager must be able to get to his or her sponsor in *one* minute and get a decision in *one* minute.

We thank *Star Trek* for giving us the most powerful model for different types of sponsors. There are the Captain Kirk sponsors who love beaming down to the project planet and getting their hands dirty and are very reluctant to delegate (even to Spock). Then there are the Captain Picard sponsors who love to remain above the project planet and delegate it all to their team while they read Shakespeare (or another consultant report). You need a Captain Kirk sponsor.

- *Active participation in the planning of the project.* Our new approach to project planning is based on highly participative and structured planning sessions. These sessions involve all key stakeholders and, at a minimum, the project sponsor and steering committee members must attend the part of the planning session where scope, objectives, stakeholders, and benefits analysis are being discussed.

- *Assistance to the project manager.* In most projects, the project manager has fairly low levels of organizational delegation and power. In these cases, conflict and disputes will inevitably arise regarding stakeholder involvement, scope, objectives, resourcing, and quality expectations that are beyond the power and influence of the project manager to resolve. It is critical that the project sponsor and steering committee, having being informed of these conflicts, use their organizational power to resolve them.

- *Monitoring of key project variables.* Apart from the traditional concerns of cost and schedules, the focus of project sponsors and steering committees must also be on such factors as these:
  - Has there been any scope or objectives alteration?
  - Have the benefits model or assumptions changed?
  - Are the project risks being managed?
  - Have new project risks emerged?
  - Are the stakeholder involvement and communication strategies in control?
  - Is the approved project development strategy still being deployed?

These factors and the other components of the approved business case (see later) should be reviewed regularly and on demand should any major variations occur between reporting periods.

The other critical role of an eXtreme project sponsor is the management of the whole-of-life dynamic. As we discuss later, the role of the project sponsor in the analysis and realization of project benefits is another element of eXtreme project management.

Scenario Planning

The traditional project planning model was developed during periods of low rates of change and lack of business client power and involvement. It involved a major "one-off" planning process at the beginning of the project and the production of a detailed project plan for all phases of the system development cycle. The extensive use of the "freezing" of client requirements ensured that the plan was locked in (while the client was locked out).

I CAN SEE FOR MILES...

If you can't predict the future with certainty, don't put it in a schedule. All you are doing is creating false expectations.

This approach to planning had parallels in military planning and strategy. As discussed by John Keegan (1992), the concept of *chateau generals,* which involved the planning and management of military campaigns by generals remote from the front line in chateaus, was endemic in military strategy and highly refined by World Wars I and II. The remoteness of the generals led to a loss of real-time intelligence of progress and the evolution of one-way planning. As Keegan noted, this planning approach led to a belief that the plan must be followed at all costs. This concept of remote- and expert-driven planning remained until the Vietnam War, when generals in Washington planned a campaign conducted in a country 10,000 kilometers away.

Real-time planning in the military was developed and perfected by General Norman Schwarzkopf during the Desert Storm campaign against Iraq. In his autobiography, *It Doesn't Take A Hero,* Schwarzkopf (1992) discussed how, in the planning of Desert Storm, "the last thing we want is a repeat of Vietnam where Washington picked the targets" (macro planning) and his insight that "timing is everything in battle and unless we adjusted the plan we stood to lose the momentum" (real-time planning). Using sophisticated feedback loops, Schwarzkopf and others developed a broad four-stage strategic plan for Desert Storm with micro or real-time planning being used to achieve each stage. The plan for each stage was adjusted as events altered the plans. For example, the ground offensive was planned for 100 days and was over in 100 hours.

A DAY IS A LONG TIME

In eXtreme projects, the pace and rate of change are substantially faster than in conventional projects. eXtreme project management is like eating an apple: Daily is better for you.

Peter Schwartz (1991) and others have also developed scenario planning as a strategic planning approach. Again, they argue that traditional linear strategic planning is no longer relevant in today's turbulent business environment.

The L.A. Law Model

Many of the episodes of the TV series *L.A. Law* started with a partners meeting in which the partners discussed the status of the various cases they were involved with.

Real-time planning involves a daily meeting between you and your team (and certain stakeholders) to review the status of your project. In eXtreme projects, events move quickly and the daily meeting (hopefully, with some good coffee, fruit, and Danish pastries) is a key for keeping your team focused on the managerial issues of the project. These meetings should take place when the whole team is together and should not be sidetracked into technical details.

Scenario or real-time planning accepts that requirements, resources, technology, and other variables will alter during the project and, because of organizational turbulence, the realistic window for detailed planning may be less than three months.

In effect, real-time planning identifies major deliverables in the future (as events, not plans) and plans in detail the next achievable point. This concept is also explored later in this book.

Rapid Planning

The concept of team-driven project management leads to the process of RAP sessions. In the early 1980s, AT&T experimented with a technique for systems analysis and design that it termed *FAST*. This technique involved the analysis and design of information systems using key clients and expert systems analysts. By "brainstorming" in an intensive team session (usually less than five days), the process of systems analysis and design could be dramatically shortened with improved quality.

In IT, the FAST technique is now more widely recognized as joint requirements planning (JRP) and joint applications design (JAD). These team-driven techniques, coupled with the use of applications generators and integrated computer-aided software engineering (ICASE) tools, are termed *rapid application development*. A very good description of this development approach can be found in Chris Meyers' (1993) *Fast Cycle Development* and Steve McConnell's (1996) excellent *Rapid Development*.

A similar technique has been applied for a new approach to strategic planning developed by Jacobs and others (1994) in which many people are involved in devel-

(ex)treme project management rule 8

A plan created by one person is another person's nightmare.

oping "bottom-up" strategic plans using participative processes. Like our group, Jacobs found higher levels of buy-in and more achievable plans.

A similar concept can be applied to the planning and managing of projects. You must identify key stakeholders in your project and invite them to a RAP session. Using the project planning steps introduced later in this chapter and covered in more detail throughout the book, you plan the project in an intensive and participative process with the project stakeholders. Guidelines for conducting a RAP session are covered in Part 2.

Experience with more than 500 major projects has indicated that the RAP session approach reduces the time for project plans to be produced, increases the accuracy of the plan, and ensures that all key stakeholders and service providers are consulted and involved prior to "lock in" of the plan. Using traditional project management approaches, for a small project that involves 10 key stakeholders who must review the plan, the review and approval of a project plan could take one elapsed month (allowing only for minimum rework of the plan). A RAP session for a similar project would be complete in one or two days!

In summary, project planning should not be done by one person, should actively involve stakeholders, and should not plan beyond what is predictable.

Virtual Teams

Sometime in the mid-1980s, the type of project team that our group had become used to quietly disappeared. It was replaced by a new form of team that has become the norm for most of the business and IT project teams that we now work with: the virtual team.

The project team in which I learned about teams was formed in 1972. The key members of the team stayed together as a team from 1972 to 1979. We undertook numerous projects and we learned together from each project. We also shared many workshops on building better interpersonal and team processes, as well as the usual technical skill education.

We learned, through a combination of often bitter experience and external facilitation, how to accept the weaknesses of each team member and how to best use each person's strengths. It was a difficult and long journey, but finally we had a real team where the whole was more than the sum of the parts.

Our team was built on the "soft glue" of:

- Loyalty to the team,
- Trust among team members,
- Friendship among team members,
- Shared experience,
- Shared vision, and
- Shared belief systems.

Most important, our team became more effective and efficient as we learned how to become a team. It was a traditional team or whole-of-life team.

As discussed in Chapter 1, "The New Project Environment," the very nature of organizations has changed and teams have changed with them. The typical project team today includes team members drawn from various expert and stakeholder groups. Team members will often be consultants or contractors who work for external organizations. In addition, many team members will have either part-time or ad-hoc commitment to the team and the project. In most cases, the only "normal" (in the sense of full-time and fully committed) member of the team is the project manager.

As a result, the interpersonal process that we believe is essential for building the traditional team is completely absent. In most virtual teams that we have worked with or observed, there is:

- Little or no loyalty to the team,
- Trust among team members that is limited to professional skills,

- No friendship among team members,
- Little shared experience,
- Little shared vision, and
- Varied belief systems.

This is a virtual team, and the management of this type of team is very different from the management of a whole-of-life team. We discuss virtual teams in more detail on our Web site.

It's the Context, Stupid

Throughout our consultancy work and education, one key theme has emerged: **Projects fail because of the context, not the content.**

As we mentioned earlier, the traditional emphasis in project management on the technical issues of the project (content) has led to a legacy of an extremely poor set of tools, techniques, and tips for managing the complex of people, political, and other "softer" issues that make up the context of the project.

On our Web site is an article called "Project Pathology: Causes and Symptoms of Project Failure." It details our conclusions and learning from consulting on over 20 major projects that had failed. All the failures were in managing the context rather than the content.

THE P FILES PILOT EPISODE: THE CONSULTANTS FROM HELL

We attended a briefing session being given by our client for a project development assignment to a number of well-known consulting organizations. As we left, we overhead a partner from one of the global consulting groups whisper to his colleagues, "This contract is a license to print money. They don't have a clue what they want!"

The P Files Team Comment

Welcome to the real world. The statement by the consulting organization partner is evidence of all the poor behaviors discussed in Component 1. eXtreme project management recognizes that, if the client is struggling to articulate requirements, it is not an opportunity to manipulate the client or rip him or her off. It is the professional responsibility of the eXtreme project manager to assist his or her client in understanding its requirements before the project commences.

PART

2

eXtreme Tools

eXtreme Project Management Context

"What we've got here is failure to communicate." ∎

Captain, Road Station 36 (Strother Martin)[1]

In this chapter, we set the basic context for project work. We define some terms and describe the overall eXtreme project management approach.

Two Very Different Types of Work

A project is any activity that changes the status quo. In business, this could involve the development of new products and services and upgrades or enhancements to existing products and services. In computing, this would include the addition of new data, processes, technology, and techniques. Project work also includes development of new business procedures and structures (organization or physical building).

---

[1]. *Cool Hand Luke*, Stuart Rosenberg, Director; Donn Pearce, Frank Pierson, Writers, 1967.

However, all project managers must understand that there are two very different types of work in all organizations. These are:

- Process work or business-as-usual, and
- Project work or business-as-*un*usual.

As shown in Figure 4.1, there are fundamental differences between these two categories of work and, as we'll continue to examine, these differences are the cause of many problems for project managers. As an example, most project stakeholders are paid to do process work, not project work.

Process Work

The most significant attribute of process work is that it constitutes business as usual for the organization. In other words, at the end of a normal day, the bank branch, its people, and its tasks are unchanged. The next day will be the same as the day before and any change is institutionalized as a one-off project and undertaken by experts.

Process work and tasks are the lifeblood of a process culture. The very nature of the work provides consistency and predictability that is also manifest in the organization's structure and control. People know where they fit, where they belong, and what they have to do.

The most significant attribute of project work is that it is designed to change the status quo. The development of a new product or service, the implementation of a new human resource program, and the installation of reengineered work practices are typical organizational change projects that have an impact beyond the project manager and team.

In other words, the project culture is designed for continuous change and the basic organization structure and job design pattern are dynamic and innovative. When a project has implemented the initial product or system, a continuous process of enhancement and refinement is typical. The innovative nature of the project culture also relies on the creativity of people.

The Two Cultures in Conflict

As shown in Figure 4.2, there is an inherent conflict between the relative stability, scope, and predictability of the process work and the instability, flexible scope, and unpredictability of project work.

In a process culture, Executive X is responsible for the people "under" him in his area. Executive Y is responsible for the people "under" her in her area. This hierarchical structure is familiar to all of us. However, Executive Y is the sponsor of Project Y. Project Y's scope includes major impacts in Executive X's area. Stakeholder X

Process work	Project work
› repeats	› unique
› short time-frame	› long time-frame
› documented	› un-documented
› standardised	› not standardised
› easily measured	› hard to measure
› clear performance indicators	› few performance indicators
› variation reduced	› variation amplified
› operates within "status quo"	› changes the "status quo"

Figure 4.1
Two categories of work

reports to Executive X but is also providing critical work for Project Y and Project Manager Y. What if Executive X invokes his legitimate power and moves Stakeholder X to Project X, leaving no substitute for the stakeholder role on Project Y? Welcome to politics.

We explore this critical distinction in more detail in later chapters and in Part 3, "Additional Resources."

The Categories of Project Work

The following categories of work should be treated as projects and managed using project management techniques covered in this book:

- The *development* of new products, services, and information systems;
- The *redevelopment* or *enhancement* of existing new products, services, and systems that involves new functionality, capability, or data and function;
- The *enhancement* of an existing product, service and production system;
- The *installation* of new hardware, telecommunications, operating systems, or development support software;
- The development and implementation of new standards, quality procedures, and so on;

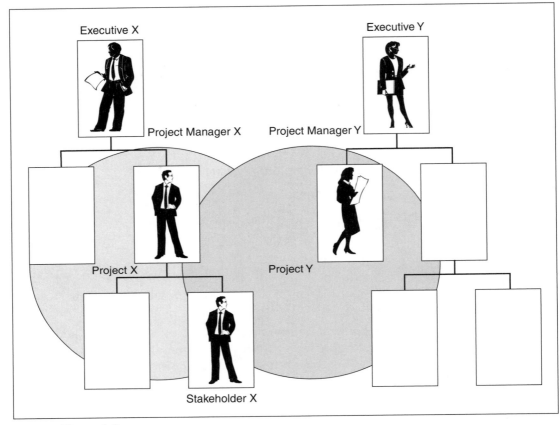

Figure 4.2
Two cultures in conflict

- The *termination* of an existing product, service, or system; and

- *Research and development* activities, strategic planning activities, and human resource development programs.

The other major IT and business work categories include consultancy, production support, and administration. The following categories of IT and business work are, in effect, process work and should not be treated as project work:

- *Consultancy*—The provision of expert advice to internal or external people.

- *Production support*—The maintenance of products, services, applications, hardware, and vendor software at the status quo. Activities involved in production support include defect repair, performance tuning, perfective maintenance, or reengineering of existing code and data; adaptive maintenance, which involves expansion of data size and alteration of calculation variables; help desk and specific system consultancy, and monitoring of hardware and software efficiency and performance.

- The *administration* of the IT and business group and its people (including human resource development).

It is common that these production support activities take generally less than five days in duration.

Many organizations define projects by size or cost rather than the specific work involved. For example, any activity over 30 days in duration or $50,000 is defined as a project. This definition ignores the fact that many significant projects can be undertaken using advanced technologies in less than 30 days. Further, it assumes that the processes of project management are applicable only to major projects.

There is no such thing as a small project.

SIZE DOES MATTER

Large and superlarge projects are completely different from smaller projects. Extensive research has shown that the dynamics of large projects (long time frames, high internal and external complexity, etc.) result in poor estimation, mis-managed expectations, and other dysfunctional results. For more information on the issues in managing large projects, see our Web site.

Although it may appear to be a significant overhead to apply the project management approach to small projects, the process of planning occurs more quickly. As discussed in the next chapter, although the process of project justification and approval may be different for larger projects, the project management process must be applied to all projects, irrespective of size.

Project Size

The most common definition of size of a project is:

- Effort—the number of people, the amount of time, and the costs; or
- Deliverable—the size of the project's outputs; for example, a policy project

being implemented globally in all regions is a bigger project than one being implemented in only one region.[2]

Figure 4.3 provides a basic guide to the sizing of projects. It is important to note that factors such as project risk and the technology used to develop the project can have a major impact on size. For example, a highly innovative medium-sized project should be treated as a large project.

We'll now look at the fascinating area of project initiation, justification, and governance. We also examine the overall project management process.

Minor/Small	Duration:	1–3 elapsed months
	People:	2–3
	Cost:	Up to $100,000
Small/Medium	Duration:	4–12 elapsed months
	People:	3–5
	Cost:	Up to $600,000
Medium	Duration:	13–18 elapsed months
	People:	6–10
	Cost:	Up to $2,000,000
Medium/Large	Duration:	19–24 elapsed months
	People:	11–20
	Cost:	Up to $5,000,000
Large	Duration:	25–32 elapsed months
	People:	21–30
	Cost:	$10,000,000
Superlarge	Duration:	Over 32 elapsed months
	People:	> 30
	Cost:	> $10,000,000

Figure 4.3
Project size

---

2. For IT readers, measures such as lines of code or function points are typically used to define the size of projects. A project delivering 1,000 function points is a bigger project than one delivering 100 function points.

THE P FILES EPISODE 1: THE CASE OF THE LEGLESS PROJECT MANAGER

In one of our workshops, a participant introduced himself as Dr. John. I asked him, "What subject did you get your doctorate in?" He replied, "Oh no! I'm an orthopedic surgeon and I want to become a project manager specializing in the health area." Like the rest of the group, I struggled to understand why Dr. John would want to leave a very highly paid profession after undertaking many years of difficult study. He laughed and said, "Can I let you in on a little secret? I have been performing surgery for 10 years and, after the first 100 legs, they start looking the same. I was taken off-line to do some project work in the surgery and it was a lot of fun. It was so much more creative than cutting legs."

The P Files Team Comment

Process work can be very sophisticated, but it is still routine. Dr. John had discovered the fun of creative project work.

The eXtreme Project Management Model

"I planned a ceiling, he plans a miracle." ■

Pope Julius II (Rex Harrison)[1]

The general structure of projects is shown in Figure 5.1. There is a complex interaction between the project development processes such as feasibility study and analyzing requirements and the project management processes.

Of course, the development of projects, especially eXtreme projects, is rarely as simple and as sequential as shown in Figure 4.3. What is more important is to understand that, whatever model of development you use, the project management process is ongoing throughout the project development process and after, in product support.

Project Management Processes

As shown in Figure 5.2, there are four major processes in the activity of project management:

- Project justification, approval, and review;
- Project planning;

---

1. *The Agony and the Ecstasy*, Carol Reed, Director; W. Phillip Dunne, Writer, 1965.

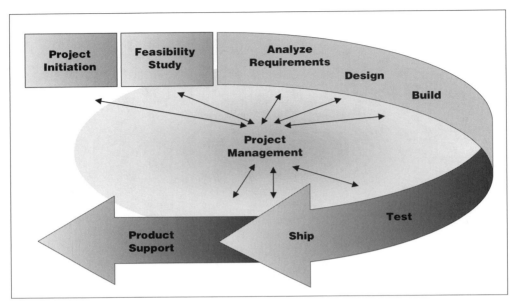

Figure 5.1
Generic project model

- Project tracking; and
- Project reporting.

Project Justification, Approval, and Review

This activity is typically undertaken by senior management. It involves the evaluation of potential projects (projects identified via the strategic planning process and new initiatives), the approval of the undertaking of a project feasibility study, the review of the project's business case (including cost–benefit), and the regular review of the progress of the project in achieving the business case. It is often called project governance.

This is a very complex process and few organizations have really managed to implement it successfully. As we discuss later, the senior management members undertaking this process are rarely educated in the management and governance of projects and, in most organizations, they lack the basic information framework to make effective decisions.

Project justification and approval are supported by the strategic planning process and by the feasibility study activity. The strategic planning process is critical in ensuring that the IT and business projects being undertaken are designed to assist the

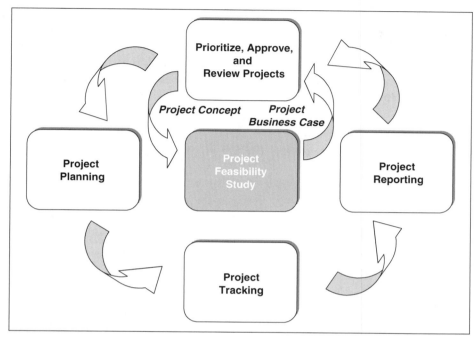

Figure 5.2
Overall project management process

organization in achieving its desired outcomes. As detailed by Peter Keen (1991), Henry Mintzberg (1994), Michael Porter (1985), and many others, the organization's strategic plan involves analysis of the competitive, economic, social, and legislative environment and the internal capability (systems, technology, and human resources) of the organization. The strategic planning process identifies target markets, products, and services and determines major projects that are required to successfully meet these targets.

TOO MANY PROJECTS

Many organizations are faced with too many projects and not enough skilled people to undertake them. The failure of the project prioritization, approval, and review process often leads to existing projects being over-stretched as new projects divert precious effort. The most important key to all of this is the project portfolio. If this information on existing projects was available to the executives then they could decide which existing projects need to be cancelled or delayed to move people to the new or more important projects.

In most organizations, the strategic planning process is undertaken by business and IT people trained in strategic planning techniques such as value chain analysis, market research, information engineering, and problem-solving techniques. Given that the turbulence of the business and legislative environment is increasing, the strategic planning process has also evolved from a process undertaken yearly to an ongoing process similar to the real-time planning concept that applies to project management.

The Critical Information for Project Approval

Typically, the organization's strategic plan forms the framework within which an IT strategic plan can be developed to ensure that the requisite information systems (data and function) and IT infrastructure (technology architecture) are developed and deployed (see Figure 5.3).

In addition, there is a policy framework, which would include new organization policy as well government regulatory changes, occupational health and safety, government and stakeholder reporting requirements, and other mandatory projects.

Finally, the executive team undertaking the project approval process should have access to a project portfolio that contains details of all current projects (e.g., resources, major events, etc.).

The projects identified in these four sets of information are as follows:

- The strategic/IT plan,
- The policy framework,
- The project portfolio, and
- New project requests.

These projects must be evaluated and "ranked" using a common set of information such as the project business case. The relationship between project prioritization and project management is revisited throughout the rest of this book.

Most organizations have a senior management team that includes representatives from all major business groups and IT that drive the strategic planning process and the approval and review of major projects. The interrelationships between strategic plans, feasibility studies, and project justification are covered in more detail in the following chapters.

Project Planning

Project planning is the key to effective project management. Detailed and accurate planning of a project produces the managerial information that is the basis of project justification (costs, benefits, strategic impact, etc.) and the defining of the business

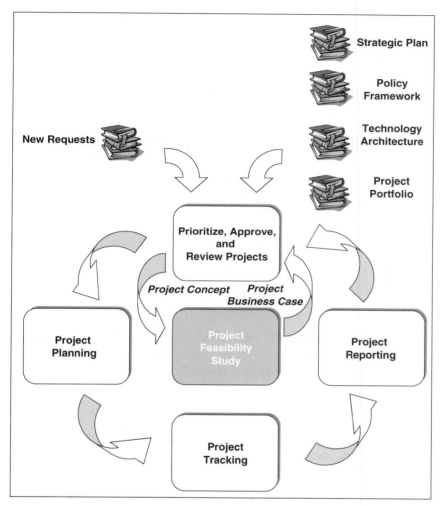

Figure 5.3
Project approval: Detail

drivers (scope, objectives) that form the context for the technical solution. In addition, project planning also produces the project schedules and resource allocations that are the framework for the other project management processes: tracking, reporting, and review.

Planning is work, working isn't planning.

As discussed earlier in this book, traditional project planning tended to focus on a one-off production of a project schedule. The emphasis in eXtreme project management is on the business and stakeholder issues (risk, strategy, service agreements, etc.) that provide the context for the schedule.

Project planning involves 10 interrelated activities:

- Define scope, objectives, stakeholders, and related projects.
- Analyze and develop added-value scenarios and benefits realization.
- Define product quality requirements.
- Select project development strategy.
- Analyze project risk and develop a risk management plan.
- Tailor task lists.
- Estimate tasks and develop a project quotation.
- Develop a project schedule or execution plans.
- Allocate people and develop project staffing agreements.
- Develop cost and return-on-investment (ROI) scenarios.

These 10 activities are undertaken in a structured manner using the RAP sessions and team-driven approach introduced in the next chapter. Techniques and tips for undertaking all these planning steps are covered in following chapters.

Project Tracking

This process involves the monitoring of project success, including actual project progress as compared to the planned progress, the collection of key project metrics (risks, costs, defect levels, etc.), and the monitoring of overall team performance.

It should be driven by the use of PC-based project management tools such as Microsoft Project coupled with task-tracking forms and quality assurance processes. This process is covered in more detail in Chapter 16, "Develop Return on Investment."

Project Reporting and Change Control

This process involves the aggregation of detailed project tracking information into the project reporting system and back into updates of the business case. This system is designed to provide project status, cost, and other relevant information to the project's sponsor, stakeholders, and project managers of related projects.

The project review process also involves the approval of major deliverables and, if required, the approval for the undertaking of further planning sessions. This process is also explored in Chapter 16.

Postimplementation Reviews

There are additional project management processes that occur at the end of the project development process. Following implementation of the product, the processes of postimplementation review, benefits realization reviews, and system support reviews should be undertaken. In many organizations, these processes are not undertaken by the person who managed the development of the product, but instead by some independent team. However, the design and conduct of these reviews are critical to successful project management and are covered in Chapter 17, "Project Tracking and Reporting."

A Note on the Project Initiation and Feasibility Study

As shown in Figure 5.4, the process of project initiation is often simply the process of a person developing an idea and, with little effort, a project is started to fully develop the idea. In fact, the more senior the person is, the easier it is for him or her to be able to do this.

In reviewing many failed projects for clients, we have observed that there was no systematic evaluation of the failed projects before they started.

eXtreme project management requires an investment of effort before the project formally commences. Project initiation is the first filter. This process involves a fairly quick analysis of the potential project's scope, objectives, benefits, costs, and risks.

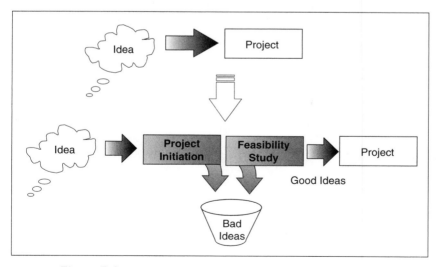

Figure 5.4
The initiation process

Often this is a relatively informal review to eliminate obvious duds. Assuming the potential project passes this first filter, the more formal process of a feasibility study would be undertaken.

 Most projects that fail, failed before they started.

A feasibility study is a hybrid process. It is viewed by many technologists as a technical activity, but it is seen by many business people as a managerial activity. In fact, it is both technical and managerial.

The technical activities undertaken in a feasibility study would involve analysis of the current business and system environment and situation, clarification of the specific business and technical problems that the project is expected to solve, high-level specification of potential business or system solutions, and assessment of alternative technology platforms that could be used in the project.

IT'S ALL IN MY HEAD

We have not met a team that could not tell us all the information about their project. It's just in their heads and they all have slightly different versions of scope, objectives, and so on. The business case is a formal public document that is jointly owned by the team, the project manager, the stakeholders and, most important, the project sponsor.

The managerial activities would be analysis of the scope, objectives, and stakeholders of the project; identification of expected quality requirements; examination of alternative project development strategies; and, using the technical detail being produced in the feasibility study, the development of estimates, costs, risks, and benefit analyses.

In summary, the feasibility study is a critical project management process that involves technical experts (business or system analysts) working with the project manager. In many cases, it involves time, effort, and commitment from senior management.

The Project Charter or Business Case _____

The managerial information outlined earlier in this book is often termed a business case, project charter , or terms of reference.

The contents of the business case would typically include the following:

- Project overview: A brief description of the project and background or business context;

- Project scope/objectives: A detailed model of the corporate, business, project, and system-level objectives;

- Added value analysis and benefits realization plan: A detailed analysis of the expected benefits of the project and a plan for realization of the benefits;

- Quality agreement: A statement of the required quality of the product;

- Stakeholders and related projects: Key individuals, groups, organizations, and projects outside the project manager's direct control on which the project is dependent;

- Project costs: The costs of the project (people, time, equipment, etc.) estimated over the development and support/operational cycle;

- Project development strategy: The overall partitioning of the project into major deliverables, subprojects, and releases;

- Project risk assessment/risk management plan: A formal assessment of potential risks associated with the project and plans for risk management;

- Relevant legislation and policy: A description of government legislation and organizational policies impacting the project;

- Change management: The impact of the project on jobs, workflow, interpersonal dynamic and organizational structure;

- Project staffing agreements: The assumptions regarding skills and experience of the project team;

- Assumptions and constraints: Assumptions or constraints such as deadlines, budget, and technology; and

- Project execution plan: The schedule and interrelationships of tasks.

This set of information is developed during the project planning process and is the basis for all project tracking, review, change control, and postimplementation reviews. As discussed in more detail in later chapters, the business case is a contract between the project manager, project owner, team, and stakeholders.

Most important, the business case is developed for the team, first and foremost. As we discussed earlier, the management of project teams is the management of creativity and, as a project manager, you must have the team build a share in and ownership of the project vision.

The Only Stable Thing Is Change

As we discussed earlier, the average period of stability in contemporary organizations is no more than three months. Your project's business case will change as scope, objectives, risk, team members, stakeholders, and so on shift to reflect the broader changes in the project's business environment.

The process of planning and replanning is continuous in eXtreme project management.

A rough guide is that the higher the risk of your project, the more unstable the business case will be. We look at this issue in more detail later.

THE P FILES EPISODE 2: THE BIG CHEESE SAYS SO SYNDROME

At almost every one of our clients, there is a person who is so powerful (a bit like the Cigarette Smoking Man in *The X Files*) that anything he or she wants happens. Time after time we have discovered really stupid projects that have no benefits, huge costs, and high priority. One great example was a major bank that spent millions on a project to put into their branch offices a suggestion box that could be used while the bank's clients were waiting to be served. Of course over 90% of the suggestions were complaints about the length of the wait. When we asked, "Whose stupid idea was that?" the answer was "G.S.S." "G" was the CEO and "S.S" stood for "said so."

The P Files Team Comment

The fact that a very senior executive wants a project is no excuse to abandon all professional project management. In fact, it is a compelling reason for you to plan the project properly. After all, if it turns out to be a bad idea, you could get thanked for saving everyone's reputations.

CASE STUDY—INTRODUCTION

Smuthe Shifts

Edwina Smuthe owns a small realty group that has offices in four cities. Her team specializes in assisting busy business executives in relocating. By delivering superior service, Edwina has managed to secure an ongoing contract with two major organizations—Big Bucks Bank and Watchout Insurance.

Given the security that these contracts offer her, Edwina has decided to undertake a major upgrade of her office systems. The current business systems are mainly paper-based with some stand-alone PCs. Initially she wants the focus of the projects to be on proof of concept. In a series of interviews with her clients, Edwina has identified an immediate need. Executives at Big Bucks want to be able to visit a Smuthe Shifts Web site and directly communicate with a Smuthe consultant about their requirements for accommodation and so on.

Your consulting company has been hired by Edwina to help her manage this project, which she is calling Project Connext. In effect, Project Connext will comprise a number of smaller projects and your task is to manage and deliver the first of these projects as a pilot project—a Web site for Smuthe consultants to communicate with Big Bucks Bank and with other Smuthe consultants in different cities.

Your consulting group will provide the project management and project integration, but you will subcontract all the technical work to an IT group you have worked with before—

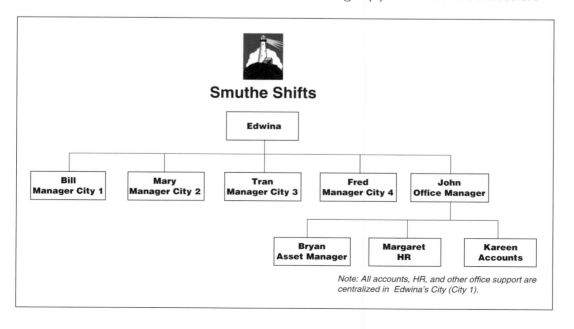

Note: All accounts, HR, and other office support are centralized in Edwina's City (City 1).

No Object, Inc. No Object has a proven track record in e-projects and realtor systems. Their President is Uri Case and their technical guru that you'll be working with is Kim Lee.

Edwina has promised to free up one of her best people—Joan Jette from Edwina's head office in City 1—to work with you on the pilot project. An organization chart is shown on the previous page.

The RAP Process

"If there is something I can do for you, you come, we'll talk." ∎

Don Corleone (Robert DeNiro)[1]

The process of participative planning or RAP sessions is the key to eXtreme project management. As a tool, it encapsulates all the behaviors mentioned in Chapter 3, "eXtreme Concepts." Just to remind you, they are as follows:

- Participative: The management of projects is based on meaningful participation of stakeholders.

- Proactive: Project management is a creative and proactive problem-solving process.

- Open: Everything about the project is shared openly with all stakeholders.

- Outward-oriented: The focus of the project manager is outward toward the stakeholders.

- Trusting: The project team is treated as professionals who are to be trusted.

---

1. *Godfather Part II*, Frances Ford Coppola, Director and Writer, 1974.

In more than 500 RAP sessions for many clients, we have also proven, even to the most skeptical people, that RAPing a project is the most effective and efficient technique for planning and managing a project.

Why Should We Run RAP Sessions?

Almost every project manager has experienced the difficulty of getting key players (stakeholders) in his or her project to agree on important issues such as the scope and objectives.

Project Manager (on phone to key stakeholder Mary):

Mary, hi. I have jotted down some ideas on Project X. You folks in finance are really important and I would like to get your input. When can I see you? Oh! You're away till next week. How about next Tuesday? Fine, see you then.

(Five days later)

Mary, as you can see the objectives as I see them are A, B, C, D. What do you think? Oh, you want to review them with your people. OK, I'll see you next week. Thanks.

(Five days later)

Hi, Mary, I see that you prefer the objectives to be A, B, C, D and E. Thanks. I'll send you a final version after I've checked with Bill in Audit.

Project Manager (on phone to key stakeholder Bill):

Bill, hi. I have reviewed the objectives of Project X with Mary and the finance team. Audits are really important and I would like to get your input. When can I see you? Oh! You're really busy. Next Wednesday? Done, see you then.

(Two days later)

Bill, as you can see, the objectives as Mary and I see them are A, B, C, D and E. What do you think? Oh, you want to review them with your people. OK, I'll see you next week. Thanks.

(Five days later)

Hi, Bill, I see that you prefer the objectives to be A, B, D, E, and F! Aargh.

So, there we are. Seventeen days into the project, your two most important stake-holders cannot agree on the objectives of your project. You are into the good old stakeholder run-around game. What are you going to do?

Faced with this conflict, you have a number of options:

- Give up and make up your own objectives;
- Resign;
- Hire consultants and give them the project; or
- Get Mary and Bill into a room and try to achieve some consensus.

Of course, most project managers select Option 1 and another project from hell has started. The only professional option is Option 4 and, using the RAP process, you can provide a mechanism where the conflict between your stakeholders can be put on the table, recognized, and resolved.[2]

Different Stakeholders, Different Agendas

In all projects, there will be conflicts among your various stakeholders. This is a normal situation, as different people will have different expectations and perceptions of what the project is all about.

There is an old fable about three blind people who are confronted with an elephant. One feels the trunk and declares that it is a snake, another feels the elephant's legs and argues that it is a tree, and the third feels the ears and disagrees, saying that it is a bird. Similarly, in a project, different stakeholders will see different parts of the project and, until they are all together, no one will understand the whole.

As shown in Figure 6.1, the more stakeholders that you have in your project, the more likely there will be differences between the perceptions of scope and objectives.

Clearly, the earlier these differences are identified and resolved, the better. The RAP process and the role of your project sponsor are critical in assisting you in the resolution of these conflicts.

The recognition and resolution of conflicts in expected scope, objectives, benefits, quality, and so on are central to the new project management models, and all the techniques in this book have been designed to assist in both modeling and resolving

---

2. In one of our clients, this looping around with stakeholders had taken more than a year before we RAPed the project in two days.

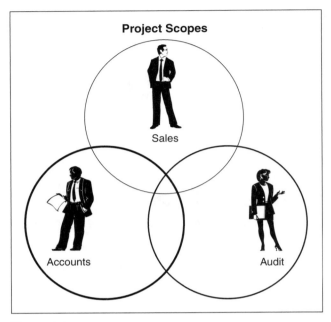

Figure 6.1
Different players, different agendas

SO THIS IS MY PROBLEM. WHY?

The scenario between Mary and Bill is typical of a particularly difficult political game that is played with project managers in all organizations. The key to solving the conflict between Mary and Bill is to undertake the *first step* in solving any problem, which (as noted by Gerry Weinberg in a seminar in 1980) most people skip. Step 1 in solving any problem is to ask yourself "Whose problem is it?" If you ask this question first, you'll often find that it is not your problem. Of course, unless you're careful, the political game quickly makes it your problem. In this case, the conflict is between Mary and Bill—it is their problem. However, unless you get Bill and Mary together where they can see that it is their problem, it'll quickly become your problem. Your job as a project manager is to facilitate the process by which your stakeholders can solve their own problems.

this conflict. Clearly, the greater the number of stakeholders, the greater the potential for conflict.

In addition, as we have discussed earlier, the participative nature of RAP sessions ensures that the team members and project stakeholders are part of building the vision for the project. The complex nature of projects and the need for people to be committed to achieving the success of the project must be based on buy-in and ownership by all participants, whether they are in the team or outside as stakeholders.

Great Idea. . . But I Don't Have a Team Yet

If you do not know who your team members will be at the time of planning, at a minimum see if you can get a colleague and key stakeholders to be involved. When the team members are appointed, you should undertake another RAP session involving them. If for any reason, key stakeholders are not prepared to be involved in the planning of the project (i.e., they don't want to be committed to the plan), then you should raise this with the project owner or sponsor (we'll discuss this more later).

THEY'RE EVERYWHERE

There will be at least 10 stakeholders on every project you do. If you can't find 10, keep looking. They're out there somewhere.

The RAP Structure

It might appear that getting a group of stakeholders together in a room is a high-risk scenario and that the meeting could degenerate into a talkfest, at best, and a rabble, at worst.

Over many years of experience, we have developed a structured process that guides the RAP session and enables the participants to focus on specific project planning issues one at a time. As we'll explain in the rest of this component, we have also developed and refined a series of tools that are used during the RAP session.

Figure 6.2 outlines the basic RAP structure, and we'll go into further detail in the later chapters.

In effect, the RAP process is the project planning process shown in Figure 5.2 broken into a series of subprocesses. As you will see, the RAP follows a particular order; for example, you must get your scope and objectives resolved before you examine benefits.

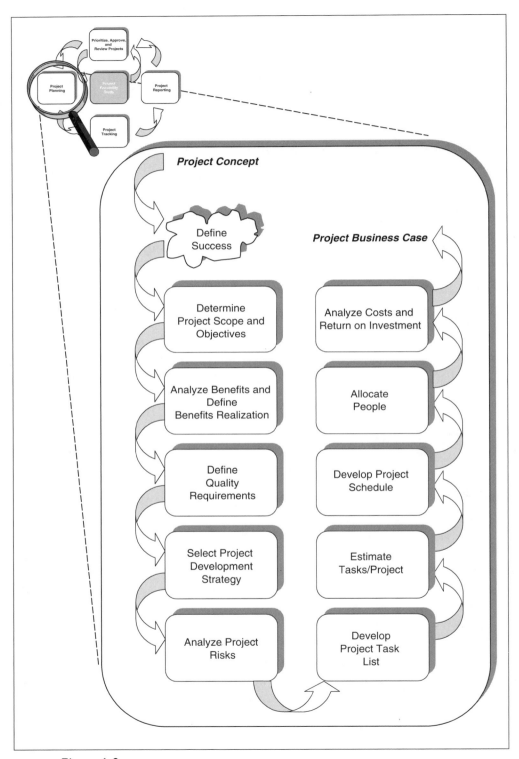

Figure 6.2
The RAP structure

RAP Technology

This is the easy part. After experimenting with groupware, PCs, and various technologies designed to facilitate team meetings, we came to a fairly obvious conclusion: Technology generally gets in the way of the group process.

We have found that electronic whiteboards and good old-fashioned paper are the best way to capture the various outputs from the RAP session. After the RAP session, the project manager and team can clean up the material using the various tools we show you here. The resultant draft business case is then distributed to the RAP participants for review, discussion, and sign-off. A follow-up RAP may be required to include any major revisions to the business case.

How Long Should a RAP Take?

As a rule of thumb, we suggest that you allow between one to five days for a RAP session. For smaller projects (up to three elapsed months), a RAP should take no more than a day. Larger projects can take up to five days to RAP. We once planned a $100,000,000 project in five days of intensive planning.

Another rule of thumb is that the first four steps (success sliders, scope and objectives, added value analysis and quality requirements) take about 50% of the RAP.

THE P FILES EPISODE 3: THE PROJECT MANAGER WHO LOST HER HEART

In a very aggressive merchant bank, we were consulting and introducing our eXtreme project management approach. Although the majority of project managers were excited and supportive of the RAP concept, we met one A-type person who was really outraged with the concept. "This is a waste of time," she declared. "I don't have time to hug the stakeholders. We just can't afford all this hugging crap." Her project failed a number of months later as the stakeholders worked tirelessly to ensure her failure.

The P Files Team Comment

Trevor Boucher, the former Commissioner of the Australian Taxation Office, who is one of the best executives and sponsors that we have had the pleasure to work with, turned the Taxation Office into one of the most efficient and open organizations in the world. One day he shared this great wisdom with me. He said, "After 30 years in this organization, which most clients hate, I have learned that you keep your friends close but you hug your enemies."

CASE STUDY—INITIAL STAKEHOLDER LIST

Let's start by identifying the project stakeholders. Based on our initial information, we can identify these possible stakeholders:

- Edwina Smuthe: Project sponsor
- Joan Jette: Business expert
- Uri Case: President, No Object
- Kim Lee: Tech, No Object
- John: Office manager, Smuthe
- Bill: Manager, City 1
- Mary: Manager, City 2
- Tran: Manager, City 3
- Fred: Manager, City 4

Your team and any related projects happening at either Smuthe or No Object are yet to be identified.

After a discussion with Edwina, you agree that the critical stakeholders are as follows:

- Edwina Smuthe: Project sponsor
- Uri Case: Steering committee member
- Joan Jette: Business expert
- Kim Lee: Tech, No Object
- John: Office manager, Smuthe
- Yourself

Initially, it appears there are no related projects. All parties agree to attend a RAP session.

Analyze Project Success

> "We came, we saw, we kicked ass." ■
>
> *Dr. Peter Veckman (Bill Murray)*[1]

The first step in planning a project using eXtreme concepts is to discuss, define, and negotiate what the measures are for project success.

Traditional project management models start by defining the requirements for a project. In addition, traditional project management defined project success using the so-called iron triangle: to requirements, to budget, and on time. To be fair, recent updates to traditional project management added a fourth factor: quality. The iron triangle has caused more projects to fail than any other project management myth. As we'll show you, it ignores stakeholders, the team and, most important, the added value or benefits expected from the project. Project after project has been constrained during development to meet a budget or deadline, only to fail on implementation.

eXtreme project management takes project success to a more complex and relevant definition of success—meeting client expectations (see Figure 7.1).

---

[1]. *Ghostbusters*, Ivan Reitman, Director; Dan Aykroyd and Harold Ramis, Writers, 1984.

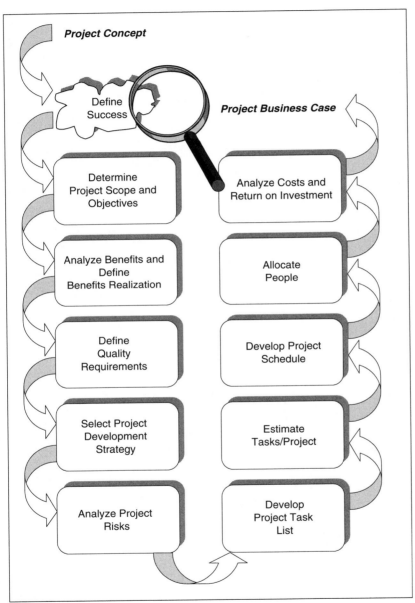

Figure 7.1
Define success

Simply, the question "What are your requirements?" is the wrong question. The right question is "What is your world?" Once the project manager and the team have begun to understand the client's organizational culture, pressures, concerns, and way of working, they can begin to get a clearer idea of the client, making it much easier to understand the requirements.

To understand a client's business system, the project manager and team need to understand the organizational culture, the client's dreams, and the client's expectations.

What Are Expectations?

The word *expectations* has probably been abused and misunderstood more than any other word in the project culture. To many project managers and systems analysts, expectations are simply those elements of the requirements that were not specified by the client. To others, expectations are the difference between what the client wants and what the client really needs. For the battle-hardened project manager, expectations are a wish list that begins a series of hard negotiations to reduce the expectations to minimum requirements. Finally, expectations are a hopelessly vague set of requirements that defy documentation.

However, it is our experience that expectations are a related set of specific factors that can be analyzed and modeled. It's just that data flow, data model, and other system-oriented techniques do not capture all the requirements for a business system.

When business experts talk about expectations, they talk about seven related sets of criteria or drivers:

- Degree of stakeholder satisfaction: How do the clients feel about the project?
- Meeting objectives and requirements: What do the clients want from the project?
- Meeting budget: How much are the clients prepared to pay?
- Meeting deadlines: When do the clients want it?
- Added-value requirements: Why do the clients want the project?
- Quality requirements: How well does the product have to be built?
- Team satisfaction: How good does the team have to feel about the project?

We have discussed this concept with thousands of project and business people and they all agree that this model is superior to the simpler iron triangle approach.

The worst time to define project
success is after it is over.

As we explain later, this model is also a very powerful tool for project planning and negotiation.

The Seven Success Criteria

Each of the success criteria is evaluated independently. However, there is an indirect relationship among them.

Degree or Level of Stakeholder Satisfaction

This is a very controversial success criterion. There are many stakeholders involved in and impacted by a project. In the majority of projects, it is not a requirement for success that all stakeholders are satisfied with either their relationship with the project or the impact of the project on them and their work. For example, the changes being implemented by the project lead to a substantial deskilling, loss of control, or other negatives to the jobs of some people. It would be naïve to expect these people to be satisfied with the results of the project. It is critical for the project manager to determine which stakeholders must be satisfied at the end of the project and to identify those who will be unsatisfied at the end. As we discuss later, both groups of stakeholders are communicated with and different strategies are used for each group.

Meeting of Objectives and Requirements

These requirements deal with the business processes, data, and documents that are the basis of the business or information system. Techniques such as use case, OOA and OOD diagrams, data flows, process mapping, and data models were designed for and, when used properly, are capable of documenting these. In addition, visual development environments such as Microsoft Visual Basic can also be used to capture these requirements through the use of prototypes and early working versions of the product. Again, in most projects not all requirements need to be met for the project to be considered successful.

Meeting Budget

This is a relatively easy success criterion to understand. Budget includes people, equipment, accommodation, and overhead costs. In some projects, the budget is completely fixed and, in others, the budget is more flexible. As with deadlines, budget has tended to be a dominant measure in traditional projects as it is relatively easy to measure (we'll look at how budgets can be manipulated later).

Meeting Deadlines

Again, this is an easy measure of success. The calendar tends to move one day each day. Like budget, this success measure has been used consistently in the past to measure and, in many cases, unfairly condemn projects as failures. Again, as in the case of budget, there are projects in which missing a deadline is critical. There are many other projects in which the deadline is flexible.

Added-Value Requirements

This criterion is probably the most important component of expectations. Traditional approaches to project management and business or systems analysis used extremely crude models of cost–benefit analysis. The common use of intangible benefits such as improved customer satisfaction or management decision making to justify projects and the lack of formal approaches to benefits realization has perpetuated loose and fuzzy concepts of added value. As we show you, techniques such as the added-value chain, the identification of primary and secondary benefits, and stakeholder buy-in can effectively model the business client's expectations of financial benefits from the project. In addition, these techniques also clarify the real business objectives.

DEATH MARCH REVISITED

My friend, Ed Yourdon, wrote a wonderful book on projects where the team was sacrificed to meet deadlines. In *Death March* (1997), he tapped into the terrible experiences of project managers and team members whose working lives (and in many cases, personal lives) were ruined by the pressures of deadlines, shifting requirements, lack of support, and poor project management practices. Clearly, in the organizations these people worked for, team satisfaction was not a relevant success criterion.

Quality Requirements

Quality requirements are often confused with functional requirements, but quality cannot be modeled using standard systems modeling techniques. Quality requirements include attributes such as conformity (functionality), efficiency, reliability, maintainability, flexibility, portability, auditability, security, usability, and reusability. By using techniques such as software quality agreements (see Chapter 9, "Analyze Added Value"), the team can model which quality attributes are required by the clients and stakeholders.

Team Satisfaction

This is, without doubt, the most contentious of all the success criteria. This factor determines whether the team's sense of satisfaction matters for the project. We accept that, in some projects, the other success factors may be more important than the team's emotional state; however, we know that the decision to "sacrifice" the team (see sidebar) must be made openly and at the start of the project. We have seen projects in which the sponsor changed his or her deadline and quality expectations to ensure that a team was allowed to do the best that it could. The sponsor made it clear that he or she wanted the team to "feel good about the project" as the team was needed for another project. We have also seen situations in which the decision was made to drive the project to a deadline, sacrificing both quality and the team's satisfaction. At least the project manager had an open choice as to who worked on the project (e.g., team members with more experience with "tough" projects and a number of contractors).

We now introduce you to our first and probably most powerful eXtreme project management tool.

eXtreme Tool 1: Success Sliders _____

extreme tool

The concept of success criteria provides the basis of our first eXtreme project management tool.

Like all the tools our group has developed to assist project managers, stakeholders and teams, it is both simple and sexy.

We based this tool on the concept of a lightswitch with a dimmer slider. During the RAP session, each stakeholder determines which of the success criteria is either on or off (see Figure 7.2). If the success slider is on for that stakeholder, then there can be a graduation from dim to bright. If a slider is totally on, there is no room for compromise. If the slider is partially on, the stakeholder is saying that there is considerable room to move in meeting that criterion.

Simple is sexy; complex sucks.

If a slider is off, it indicates that that criterion is not significant as a measure of success. For example, if budget is off, it means that the stakeholder is prepared to sacrifice the budget for other more important factors. It is important to note that the budget is still tracked and measured. Everything is negotiable.

By now, it should be pretty clear to you that the chances of 10 different stakeholders agreeing on how to define success for the same project are slim. This is where the project sponsor starts to earn his or her money. As we'll discuss in Part 3, the sponsor has the right to unilaterally override the project stakeholders.

What you have to do is to document the disagreements and then let the sponsor decide where the sliders should be set.

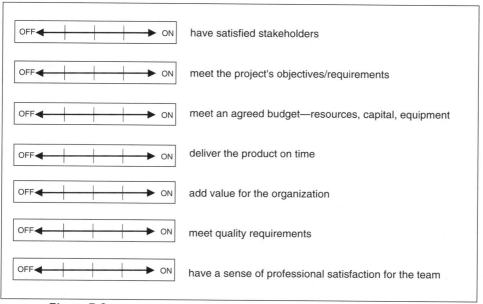

Figure 7.2
Success sliders

The best time to negotiate project success is before the project starts.

LET'S NEGOTIATE

Don't be surprised if a stakeholder puts all the sliders fully on. They are simply negotiating with you by stating their most preferred position (MPP). We have used this tool on hundreds of projects and have never seen a project with all the sliders fully on. People are pragmatic and will trade off.

What is really important is that you have a simple, nontechnical tool to begin the process of negotiating with the stakeholders. More significantly, it is the stakeholders who decide, not you. Even if the sponsor overrides their views, they will know that you are simply providing a mechanism for this to happen.

Don't Panic! It Is Meant to Be Subjective

Some of you may be feeling that the sliders are not precise and quantified. This is the very power of this tool. It has been designed to get a feel for the stakeholders' expectations. We have used this tool on hundreds of projects and it has never failed. The precision and measures are added as you proceed to the other tools in the RAP session. We have more on the power of the sliders in Chapter 23, "The Success Sliders Redux."

Welcome to eXtreme project management.

THE P FILES EPISODE 4: THE WHOOPS FACTOR

We were showing the success sliders to a chief executive officer (CEO) and a number of his direct reports. The chief information officer (CIO) of the company became agitated and stated, "This tool can't work. There are no measures. It is all too subjective!" Meanwhile, the CEO had been quietly completing the slider tool and, raising his head, he replied, "I like this tool. These are my expectations for Project Blaster." As he showed his executive team his slider scores, there was an audible gasp from the CIO. She had completely misunderstood the expectations for Project Blaster, which was already well underway. Her team had been compromising quality to meet the deadline. The CEO had scored quality as totally On and time as 25% On. Needless to say, the slider tool became a critical part of that organization's project management approach.

The P Files Team Comment

This situation is so common that it would be laughable if it wasn't so serious. Make sure that you know which factors matter to your sponsor before you start the project.

Case Study—Success Sliders

You have Edwina and the other stakeholders together in a room and, after a brief introduction by Edwina, you show them the success sliders and explain the tool to them.

Edwina and the stakeholders agree that the majority of people using their Web site must be happy with it (particularly the executives) and that quality is critical. They also agree that the deadline is tight (Edwina would like it quickly) and that the budget is tight (but not fixed). They see that the added value is very important, but the Web site does not have to be fully featured at the initial launch.

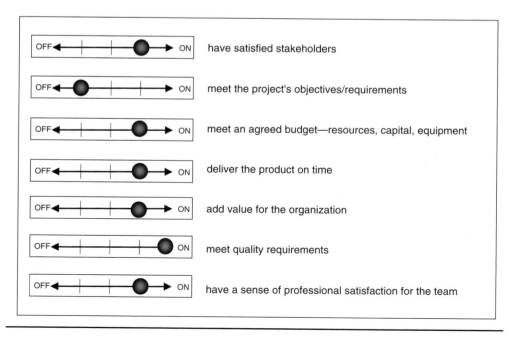

OFF ←——⬤—→ ON	have satisfied stakeholders
OFF ←⬤——→ ON	meet the project's objectives/requirements
OFF ←——⬤→ ON	meet an agreed budget—resources, capital, equipment
OFF ←——⬤→ ON	deliver the product on time
OFF ←——⬤→ ON	add value for the organization
OFF ←———⬤ ON	meet quality requirements
OFF ←——⬤→ ON	have a sense of professional satisfaction for the team

Define Scope, Objectives, and Stakeholders

In this chapter we start getting really dirty. The next step in planning a project is for you to determine as clearly as possible the scope and objectives of the project and to analyze your project's stakeholders and the relationships that you'll have with them (see Figure 8.1). As discussed earlier, it is in this step and the related steps of determining benefits analysis and quality expectations that you'll most likely have the most disagreement, so take it easy and don't panic.

What we face here is one of the most difficult and least understood questions in project management.

What Is the Difference between Scope and Objectives?

The theory states that the scope of a project defines the boundary of the project and the responsibility of the project manager. However, every business project manager has struggled with "how" to state the scope of his or her project. The concept is fine, but most scope statements look like high-level objectives.

---

[1]. *City Slickers*, Ron Underwood, Director; Lowell Ganz and Babaloo Mandel, Writers, 1991.

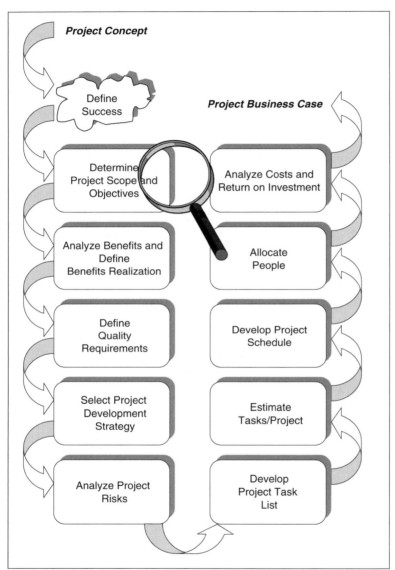

Figure 8.1
Define scope, objectives, and stakeholders

The scope of an information system can be defined graphically using contemporary technical specification techniques such as data flow diagrams and data models. The scope of a building is defined by the physical boundaries such as walls, roads, and so on.

The real issue here is simply that the concept of project scope was borrowed from the construction industry (remember Chapter 2, "Project Management Evolution")

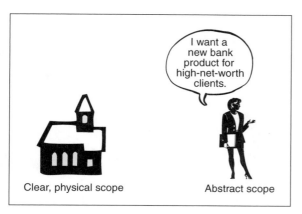

Figure 8.2
Scope? What scope?

where a physical scope makes sense. For decades, business project managers have struggled to apply the concept to abstract business projects (see Figure 8.2). Defining the scope and objectives of a complex policy project or some new software to power the Internet is a completely different problem.

All business and information systems impact the organization and its people in some manner. Often, the successful implementation of a new information system or enhancement will require related job redesign, physical office alteration, new procedures, and new managerial control patterns. In addition, large projects may involve legal issues, financial management, and extensive administrative support such as travel and accommodations. These projects would require a number of noninformation-system activities (often undertaken by business area experts). It is essential that the project scope and objectives reflect the business system objectives as well as the information system objectives.

This leaves you and other project managers with a particularly difficult problem: How can you graphically represent the scope of a project, not a system? This is a serious issue as typical statements of scope look something like this:

Project Scope

To develop a user-friendly system by July 1 to track customer enquiries in head office.

There are some very serious problems with this type of scope statement.

First, it looks suspiciously like an objective. Second, it is very loose in that it is imprecise and fuzzy. For example, does developing the system involve altering any

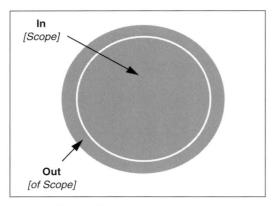

Figure 8.3
The Zen of scope and objectives

business processes? Finally, it contains a date (July 1) and quality expectations (user-friendly), which, as we describe later, aren't either scope or objectives!

What you need is the ability to draw a circle in the sand that clearly defines the boundaries of your project with the objectives you have to achieve inside that circle. As shown in Figure 8.3, one powerful technique is to use the Japanese pottery trick of using the reverse of the circle to make the circle more obvious.

Following this idea, a very useful tool for stating project scope is the modified use of a technique developed by Kepner and Tregoe (1981) for problem statement. As shown in Figure 8.4, this technique involves stating what the scope is, what it is not (could be but), and, in early stages of the project planning, what is not resolved.

extreme tool

Of course, as discussed later, any unresolved issues need to be raised with the project sponsor for clarification as a matter of urgency.

If scope is the boundary of the project manager's responsibility, then the project objectives are what the project manager is accountable for delivering. In the Kepner–Tregoe model, the Is column should contain the objectives of the project and the combination of the Is and the Is not provides a clear definition of the scope.

As we cover later, you'll also notice that the Is not column also contains objectives that become the related objectives that stakeholders and project managers of related projects will be responsible for achieving.

In effect, scope and objectives are the same thing—it's just that some objectives are "in scope" and others are "outside scope." However, both sets of objectives must be met for the project to be successful. This important fact is covered in more detail later in this chapter.

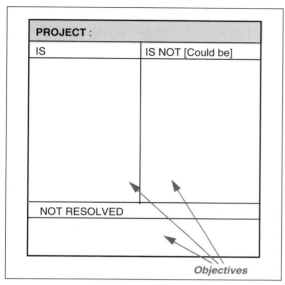

Figure 8.4
Modified Kepner–Tregoe scope/objectives tool

Conflict Is Inevitable

Using the Kepner–Tregoe technique for defining your project's scope and objectives generally leads to some debate among your stakeholders about which objectives are in and which are out.

In addition, the more stakeholders you have, the higher the degree of initial confusion about what your project is going to achieve.

The trick here is to look for a common set of objectives that all your stakeholders can agree are in scope and to see if you can reach consensus on whether each of the remaining objectives should be in or out.

THE TAKE IT AWAY TEST

Another useful test for evaluating the effectiveness of your modeling of objectives is to take the objective away. By taking away an objective such as, "To provide customer enquiry summaries to customer service management" do you make the scope of the project different? If so, then you have a valid objective.

Any remaining conflict should be raised with your sponsor. This is the first example of the Captain Kirk model of project sponsors. As we discuss in later chapters, the sponsor is the person who "owns" the project[2] and, as a result, must have the unilateral right to make the final decision about the scope and objectives of his or her project.

Levels of Objectives

As the objectives for your project evolve, they come in all shapes and sizes. Initially, in your scope and objectives statement, you'll get a grab bag of objectives and other things such as constraints and quality expectations. Don't panic. We'll sort them out step by step.

There will be at least four levels of objectives in any project:

- Corporate: The strategic objectives of the organization as contained in the strategic plans or organization mission statement.
- Department or business: The objectives of each department or business unit in the organization. Clearly, these must reflect the corporate objectives.
- Project: The objectives for the project. These objectives must reflect the department-level objectives of the organization business unit that is sponsoring the project and are contained in the Is column of the scope and objectives statement.
- System: A subset of the project objectives that will be implemented in the information or business system.

All project business cases must explicitly show this hierarchy of objectives to ensure that the project is aligned with the strategic objectives of the organization.

Refining Your Objectives

Objectives should also be specific and measurable. The following process can help you in developing clear and measurable objectives.

For example, the initial objective may be stated as, "To improve management information."

By asking the following questions, the project manager and his or her team will be able to parse the objective to produce a more detailed and specific objective.

- Who: Which managers?
- What: What information?
- When: When do they want the information?
- How much: How much improvement is required?

---

2. The real owners for most projects are the stakeholders and clients.

As a result of these questions, the initial objective can be refined as follows:

To produce statistics on processing time and defect levels in invoice processing daily (5:00 p.m.) for accounts management in the central office.

As discussed later in Chapter 9, "Analyze Added Value," any well-defined objective has an output that has benefits to the organization. This concept also helps you in refining your objectives.

Let's Not Get Physical

A common mistake in many projects is the confusing of project objectives with system objectives. Simply, well-stated project objectives state what has to happen and system objectives state how the system (business and system) will implement the objectives.[3]

For example, "To use the Aardvarker database Release 1.1" is not a project objective, but rather a system objective. System objectives generally are technology or process dependent and project objectives are independent of technology. System objectives are added later as your project progresses through the development cycle.

Don't Fence Me In

Another common mistake is to confuse constraints with objectives. For example, "To implement the system by July 1."

Typically, in projects, you will encounter a predictable set of constraints:

- Corporate: The strategic objectives of the organization as contained in the strategic plans or organization mission statement.

- Deadlines and time frames: Your project must deliver by a fixed date or within a fixed time frame.

- Budget: Your project is limited by a fixed amount of capital or finance.

- Resources: Your project is limited in the number of people or skills.

- Technology: Your project must conform to preexisting or planned technology platforms.

[3.] Many IT people will recognize this as the same as the distinction between logical and physical models. Logical systems are implementation technology independent, whereas physical models are technology dependent.

- Policy: Your project must conform to existing or planned corporate or government policy.

You should never confuse constraints with objectives. Constraints are limits to your capability of achieving your objectives.

In the initial Kepner–Tregoe model developed during the planning sessions, you will probably find that the Is column contains a mixture of objectives (corporate, business, project, and system), quality requirements, solutions, and constraints. As described in this chapter, you can filter out into the various components of the business case during the RAP session. Again, what is important here is to let the stakeholders feel that they are being heard and that the RAP process flows smoothly.

Stakeholders and Related Projects_____

As stated earlier in this book, stakeholders are a critical factor in the eXtreme project management model.

What Is a Stakeholder?

A stakeholder is a person, group, or organization outside your direct control that is involved with your project. Most stakeholders will provide services (requirements, expertise, equipment, etc.) to your project, receive services (data, functions, etc.), or have a two-way relationship.

Stakeholders can be either inside the organization or in another organization. Typical project stakeholders will be IT operations, internal auditing, the organization's business people who will be using the system, IT communications, vendors, project team members, members of the steering committee, the project sponsor, and business analysts.

Related projects are other projects within the organization that have an impact on your project or will be impacted by the current project. As for stakeholders, it is also possible for two projects to be interrelated.

It is important for you to identify which of the project's stakeholders and related projects are essential to the project's success. We have found it useful to triage your stakeholders into three levels of impact:

- Critical: Those stakeholders who can prevent your project from achieving success before or after implementation; in other words, the showstoppers.

- Essential: Those stakeholders who can delay your project from achieving success before or after implementation. In other words, you can work around them, as there will be some alternative stakeholders.

- Nonessential: Stakeholders who are interested parties; that is, they have no direct impact on your project but, unless they are included in your communication, they can change their status to critical or essential.

In all projects, the team members and your project sponsor are by default critical stakeholders.

ABDUCTED BY ALIENS

To determine the right level of criticality for a stakeholder, imagine that they are abducted by aliens during or after your project. This should help you clarify their impact.

As discussed earlier, all critical and essential stakeholders and project managers of related projects must agree to the business case and, where possible, should be involved in the RAP sessions. All critical stakeholders should sign the stakeholder agreement document described later. This document identifies the specific services required from the stakeholder.

Related Projects—A Special Case of Stakeholder _____

With related projects, the types of relationships or services can be easily identified:

- Data, process, objects: One project will be implementing data, process, or objects required by another project.
- Technology: One project is implementing a technology that another project requires.
- Policy: One project is developing or altering corporate policy or government legislation that you require.
- Resources: One project is using people that another project requires or shares.
- Funding: One project is producing benefits (capital) that will fund another project.
- Staff impact: One project is altering processes in a business area for which another project is also implementing changes at the same time.

As with stakeholders, there can be critical, essential, and nonessential related projects. All critical and, if possible, essential stakeholders and related projects must be actively involved in both the planning and tracking of the project. For example, should a project manager of a related project agree to expand the scope and delay the delivery of his or her project, this may have a negative impact on your project. All changes to critical and essential related projects must be reviewed by all related project managers.

WHAT SIGN-OFF?

Never confuse the act of sending a document to someone with the act of their reading it. If you want to ensure that a critical or essential stakeholder has really read key documents such as your business case, you must take it to them and take the time to review it with them.

Nonessential stakeholders and related projects should be kept informed of the status of the project through copies of the project reports and any changes to the business case.

Focus and Communicate

As we have stated many times already and, as is worth repeating, the management of the expectations and relationships between stakeholders and related project managers is the key role of a project manager.

SHOW THEM YOU'RE LISTENING

One simple trick is to start your business case with the relevant corporate objectives that the project is related to. Our experience is that this lets your executives know that their objectives are being implemented and hits their buttons to assist you in getting their buy-in.

The management of stakeholder communications is a key focus for you as a project manager. You can never overcommunicate to your stakeholders. In general, the planning of a formal communication strategy for stakeholders is poorly implemented in organizations. In fact, in our research and experience, one of the major causes of stakeholder problems is the absence of regular and open communications from the project team. In the absence of information, rumors and gossip take over and the management of stakeholder expectations is lost. Remember, if you are not talking with them, they'll assume the worst.

You cannot not communicate.

The general mechanism for stakeholder communication depends on their level of impact:

- Critical: These people must be involved in and approve all changes to the business case and their related stakeholder agreements. Ideally, they should be actively involved in evaluating the impact of the change before it is approved. The primary communication mechanism is involvement in RAP sessions and review and approval of all tracking and reporting information.

- Essential: These people must be informed of and approve all changes to the business case and their related stakeholder agreements. Ideally, they should sign off on all changes. The primary communication mechanism is active review of RAP session outputs and review of all tracking and reporting information.

- Nonessential: These people must be informed of all changes to the business case in a passive manner. The primary communication mechanism is giving them access to RAP session outputs and review of all tracking and reporting information.[4]

To summarize, communication with critical and essential stakeholders must be two-way, and communication with nonessential stakeholders need only be one-way.

Formalizing Stakeholder Relationships

At the end of the RAP session and, after any planning sessions throughout the development life cycle, you must formalize the various service agreements with your critical stakeholders at a minimum.

CHANGES

During your project, certain stakeholders and related projects may change status. For example, during the analysis phases of a project, IT operations may be a nonessential stakeholder. However, during the design phase, they may become a critical stakeholder. You must constantly monitor stakeholder status during the project.

---

4. One of the most interesting developments in stakeholder communication is the evolution of the World Wide Web and intranets This technology provides you with a simple, cheap, and powerful tool for active and passive distribution of key project information to many people.

extreme tool

Figure 8.5 shows a standard partnership agreement that our group has used for many years. It is a very powerful tool and, if used properly, can save you and your project.

The form contains the following information:

- Service: You should agree on and document each unique service required from the stakeholder or that you need to provide to the stakeholder.

- Timing: You should agree on and document the specific timing issues for the service; for example, so many hours per period or a specific date when the service has to be delivered.

- Cost: You should agree on the costs or fees that the stakeholder will incur in delivering the service.

- Contingency: You should agree with the stakeholder about who else can undertake the provision of the service if the stakeholder is not available.

- Person responsible: You should agree with the stakeholder about which member of your team is responsible for managing the relationship.

This is a very important but obviously political document, as it is designed to hold the stakeholder responsible for his or her role in your project. However, our experience is that, provided it is negotiated openly and in advance, you should have no trouble getting agreement. More important, it gives you a clear indicator of the commitment or buy-in of the stakeholder and it gives the stakeholder something to take back to his or her boss.

Stakeholder :				
Service	Timing	Cost	Contingency	Person Responsible

Figure 8.5
Partnership agreement

WHEN THE *@@% HITS THE FAN

The partnership agreement is the only tool that will help you when a stakeholder is moved off your project to another task (we discussed this earlier). When your project has slipped because of the stakeholder's move, you can use the partnership agreement to negotiate with your sponsor.

The agreements must be included in the business case. For small projects, it would be sufficient for the various stakeholders to simply sign off on the business case.

Sponsor Agreement—The Most Important of All

Given the critical nature of your relationship with your sponsor, you should also complete a partnership agreement with him or her. It should focus on the availability of the sponsor for meeting with you on a regular as well as ad hoc basis.

Who Is Your Team?

One of the most difficult issues in your project is determining who are your team members and who are your stakeholders. One simple test is to ask yourself what would happen if you change some of the minor scheduling of your project.

Team members should have no problem rescheduling their work, as you are their boss in the formal organization sense. Stakeholders will have to ask someone else— their boss. In effect, they are reporting to someone else even though they are working for you on the project. The virtual team lives.

THE P FILES EPISODE 5: THE LONE DISSENTER

One of our favorite movies is Monty Python's *The Life of Brian*. In that movie there is a running gag about the lone dissenter. Remember the scene where Brian, falsely mistaken as the Messiah, extols his followers, "You don't need me. You are all individuals." Hundreds of his followers shout in unison, "We are all individuals!" One wild-looking character at the front of the mob looks around confused and says, "I'm not." We were reviewing a major project that had been in development for 18 months. We met the team and the project manager and showed them the Is/Is not tool. The team were quite annoyed that they had to restate the objectives. "We have been doing the project for 18 months. We know the #@@!!@ objectives," they said. However, we persisted, and within 10 minutes the team was replaying the scene from *The Life of Brian*. They all agreed that training was outside scope except for two team members, who argued that training was in scope. So it went for another hour. At the end of the session, the team agreed that they had no agreement at all as to what the objectives of the project were. The project manager went to the bathroom.

The P Files Team Comment

It is never too late to plan your project. If you haven't replanned your project in the last month, do it now. Try the Is/Is not tool.

CASE STUDY—SCOPE, OBJECTIVES, AND STAKEHOLDERS

At the RAP session, Edwina and the stakeholders agree on the following objectives.

Corporate Vision

- To take our client's problems away.

Corporate Objectives

- To be the best relocation service in the region.
- To provide superior service to busy executives.
- To provide a caring, family environment for Smuthe consultants and employees.

Business Objective

- To place the right client with the right house.

Project Objectives

- To capture extended client personal details.
- To capture more comprehensive client requirements for accommodation.
- To enable internal access to all client information for Smuthe consultants in all sites.
- To distribute more details on available accommodation to clients.

Your team uses the scope and objectives tool and the result is as follows:

Project: Project Blastoff	
IS	**IS NOT [Could be]**
To capture extended client personal details. To capture more comprehensive client requirements for accomodation. To enable internal access to all client information for Smuthe consultants in all sites. To distribute more details on available accomodation to clients. To determine hardware requirements.	To accomodate Watchout Insurance requirements. To acquire hardware. To market new Web site accomodation to clients. To handle any Smuthe financial information (i.e., fees).
NOT RESOLVED	
To train Smuthe consultants. To train Big Bucks clients. To support Web site.	

Edwina agrees to think about the unresolved objectives and get back to you in a couple of days.

Because all the stakeholders are present you can proceed to develop the draft partnership agreements. The following is the one you develop for Joan Jette.

Stakeholder: Joan Jette

Service	Timing	Cost	Contingency	Person Responsible
Requirements for client and accomodation data	*8 hrs/wk*	*$100/hr*	*Other Smuthe consultants available but with delay*	*Project Manager*
Review of requirements/ prototype	*2 hrs/wk*	*$100/hr*	*Other Smuthe consultants available but with delay*	*Kim Lee*
Data capture	*By October 1*	*N/A*	*Jeff Brown*	*Kim Lee*
Communication with Smuthe consultants about requirements	*2 hrs/wk*	*$100/hr*	*Project Manager*	*Project Manager*

What is interesting about your arrangement with Joan is that she is clearly an essential stakeholder, as a backup for her is available.

Most important, you get an agreement with Edwina that you can meet with her weekly for at least an hour and, if required, daily at 8:30 a.m.

There are a number of related projects, including the acquisition of hardware, that are being undertaken by No Object.

Analyze Added Value

"Show me the money." ■

Rod Tidwell (Cuba Gooding, Jr.)[1]

This chapter provides you with a very powerful yet simple approach to modeling and analyzing the financial benefits and other added-value factors in your project (see Figure 9.1).

Like all the eXtreme project management tools, the roles of your stakeholders and project sponsor are key to ensuring that your project not only is delivered but, more important, delivers the benefits expected.

The State of the Art

The prevailing approach to cost–benefit analysis in business and IT projects reflects all the problems with traditional project management.

In the worst case, no effective cost–benefit analysis is undertaken and there are a series of excuses that are offered as justification. These excuses include a belief that

---

1. *Jerry Maguire*, Cameron Crowe, Director and Writer, 1996.

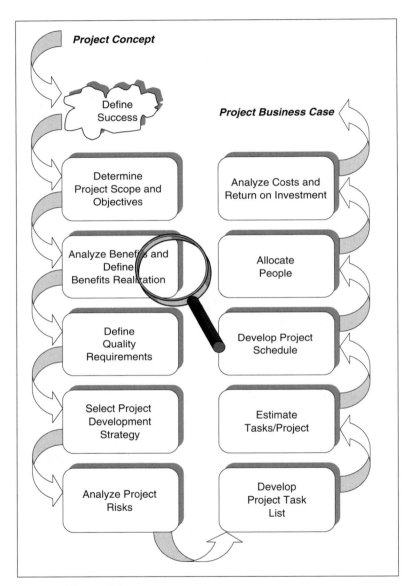

Figure 9.1
Analyze and develop added-value scenarios

the application of technology automatically leads to benefits or that a senior manager, politician, or client has demanded the system or that a competitor has a similar system or product that must be matched to maintain competitive advantage. In the best case, traditional cost–benefit analysis was nothing more than an exercise in mathematics. The projected cost of the new system is simply offset by a reduction of people, but there is no effective mechanism for garnishing the benefits.

These token approaches to cost–benefit analysis have placed many business and IT groups in a difficult situation. Many are now seen as cost centers; that is, the internal IT group does not add value per se, but rather consumes costs and provides a service at a cost. Any benefits gathered by the service are attributed to the client group receiving the service. This model is very common in Australian and U.S. organizations and further separates the service delivery and IT people from their business clients. At worst, the service delivery and IT groups are placed in a position where their costs are being measured reasonably accurately and the benefits are left for the business groups to identify and calculate, with little capability for the IT groups to be involved in determining the benefits of their services and products.

BENEFITS, THEN COSTS

Benefits are the result of the changes being implemented by the project. The benefits of a project are fixed by its scope and objectives. The costs of a project depend on the solution chosen. Typically, there are many alternative solutions. A great paradox is now revealed: A project has fixed benefits and variable costs.

The inevitable result of these poor approaches to cost–benefit analysis was recently summarized by senior management of an Australian bank: "We spent $500,000,000 on IT last year and have managed to identify only $50,000,000 in benefits. IT are dropping the ball." From this perspective, the organization lost $450,000,000 in investing in their IT group (clearly a candidate for outsourcing). However, in that organization, the business groups are responsible for identifying benefits and justifying projects, so the failure to effectively realize benefits is a business client problem for which IT is blamed.

This issue and the following problems of traditional cost–benefit analysis have led to our group's development of a new approach to cost–benefit analysis that is explored in this chapter.

Problems with Traditional Cost–Benefit Approaches

As discussed in earlier chapters, the poor quality of most project management processes has led to serious problems in cost–benefit analysis.

Limited Economic Focus   Most traditional approaches to IT projects focused on a limited economic model of cost avoidance. This approach argues that the analysis of added-value benefits is complex and open to manipulation, so the only way to justify IT and business projects was to examine the projected costs of the current situation and compare these against the proposed costs of the new IT system. If the new system was cheaper than maintaining the status quo, then the project was justified.

This approach ignores any added benefits associated with the new technology and system and forces a focus on cost reduction, generally through staff reductions. The cost-effectiveness model has probably been the most widely used in computing and, although useful for functional replacement projects (see later), is not suitable for the new generation of IT and business projects.

Intangible Benefits   The de facto endorsement of intangible benefits has been widespread, especially in very competitive industry segments. Projects have been justified on fuzzy benefits such as improving competitive position, being aligned with a vendor's architecture strategy, improving company image, or improving global reach. The problem with intangible benefits is that they remain intangible and unmeasured. In effect, the use of intangible benefits encourages the nonmeasurement and quantification of benefits that, if measured, would significantly improve the organization's understanding of their business, their clients, and their environment.

Fuzzy benefits lead to fuzzy projects.

More important, the analysis of intangible benefits using the techniques covered later offers significant areas of financial benefits for projects. The use of shadow pricing and contingent valuation techniques, which have been developed over the past decade, can provide dollar values for benefits that were previously treated as intangibles.

Lack of Benefits Realization Planning   As discussed earlier, the traditional approach to cost–benefit analysis (and project management, in general) did not involve business clients in any meaningful manner. The arms length model of project areas such as IT as a service provider left business people alone to determine and garnish benefits. As a result, through lack of education, effective cost benefit analysis models and accountability, many business people have sponsored projects that eventually did not provide the benefits expected. A typical example of this is justification of a project on the elimination of five staff positions, but no one is accountable for the redeployment of the five people currently in the positions.

The process of benefits realization planning is critical to advanced project management and involves a partnership among the IT service providers, the business clients and, in many cases, external stakeholders.

Early Commit   One of the paradoxes in cost–benefit analysis is inherent in the nature of the system or product development process. As shown in Figure 9.2, the analyzing of benefits is associated with the objectives of the project, which are often identified at the beginning of the project initiation and business analysis phases. As a result, it may be possible to both identify and quantify the proposed benefits for a project during project initiation.

However, the estimation of costs depends on the selection of the design options for the system and, in most cases, this will not be known accurately until the end of the requirements analysis stage (at best) and the end of the design phase (at worst). In other words, the estimation of costs and benefits occurs at different stages of the development process.

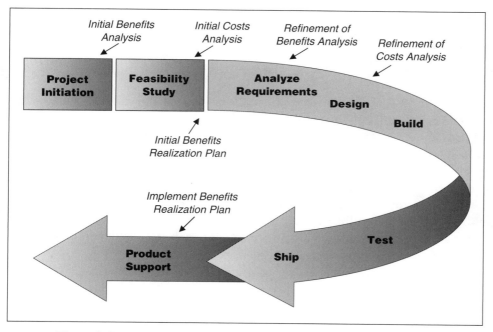

Figure 9.2
Cost–benefit analysis

However, it is expected in most organizations that both the costs and benefits are calculated at the beginning of the project. This approach reflects the engineering background of traditional project management where the costs of a building or appliance can be identified through accurate historical project metrics. The reality in many IT projects is that the technology is so dynamic and estimation metrics are so poor that even if there could be some estimates made of costs during the feasibility study, new technology and design options would probably emerge during the development process. Put simply, benefits can be estimated early but costs can only be estimated later.

Poor Costing Models   This is a serious problem in all projects. There are a number of major problems with the mechanisms used to track costs. These include the following:

- Inadequate on-costing (nonsalary costs);
- Early commit for cost estimates;
- The noncosting of unpaid work;
- The noncosting of business expert effort;
- The noncosting of system or product support; and
- Distorted or falsified time sheets.

These are covered in more detail on our Web site (www.Thomsett.com.au).

The Ultimate Fiddle

Probably the most serious issue in traditional cost–benefit analysis is the lack of the whole of life model that is the basis of our eXtreme project management approach. As we discuss in more detail in Chapter 18, "Postimplementation Reviews," the lack of inclusion of the support costs in a cost–benefit analysis is a major fiddle. For example, assume that the project is going to cost $10,000,000 in development. The estimated benefits are $15,000,000. In many organizations, the analysis of costs and benefits would simply involve the development costs ($10,000,000) being subtracted from the benefits ($15,000,000), leading to a profit (return on investment) of $5,000,000. However, the whole-of-life model in eXtreme project management would require the product support costs to be included in the virtual financial analysis.[2]

In our example, assuming that support costs were $10,000,000, then the whole-of-life costs would be $20,000,000 (not $10,000,000). This would mean that instead of a ROI of $5,000,000, the project would suffer a *loss* of $5,000,000.

---

2. As we detail in Chapters 16 and 19, the rule of thumb that we use for estimating support costs is that they will be the same as the development costs.

Added-Value Analysis_____

The concept of expanding traditional cost–benefit analysis to address the problems detailed earlier has been explored by many experts. Of note is the work of David Osborne and Ted Gaebler (1992), who expanded the linking between project outputs and organizational outcomes, and Marilyn Parker, Bob Benson, and Ed Trainor (1988), who developed a comprehensive model of business value for IT projects. In addition, the IRACIS model and the use of primary and secondary benefits first developed by our group in 1984 is critical in developing an integrated approach to determining the added value from investments in business and IT projects.

SHOW THEM THE MONEY

It is amazing how quickly people become interested in a project when you focus on the benefits early in the RAP process. Too many projects get caught up in costs before they really get to look at the benefits. Positives should always come first.

Some of the key concepts and principles are given in the following sections.

The Added-Value Chain

The concepts of primary or direct and secondary or indirect benefits have proven effective in clarifying the real benefits of projects. This model is similar to concept of a value chain or value linking also documented by M. Schumann (Parker et al., 1988) and by Osborne and Gaebler (1992). As shown in Figure 9.3, the value chain in projects can be followed in two directions: horizontally and vertically.

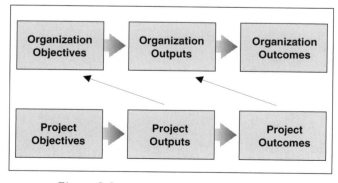

Figure 9.3
Benefits or value chain

extreme tool

Using the Osborne and Gaebler model, an organization's objectives lead to specific outputs (products, services, etc.) and these outputs lead to outcomes that the organization desires.

For example, a government department of transportation may have an outcome of maintaining road safety. One of the strategic objectives to meet this outcome is to ensure that registered cars are roadworthy and safe. The output is to reduce the number of cars with mechanical faults. The outcome of this objective is a reduction in traffic accidents caused by mechanical failures.

A project is identified to redesign car registration and inspection procedures. One objective of this project is to redesign the inspection processes. The output of this objective is new inspection processes including more detailed mechanical inspections, and the outcome is safer cars. The project outcome is aligned with the strategic objectives, outputs, and outcomes.

In other words, there should be a link between the project's objectives, outputs, and outcomes and the organization's objectives, outputs, and outcomes. It becomes apparent that not only should this link exist, but the organization cannot achieve its outcomes without the project succeeding. This is a clear example of added value from the project.

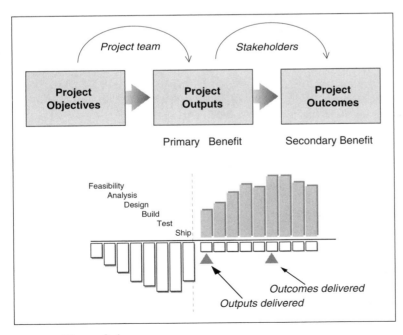

Figure 9.4
The linked value chain

The second link is horizontal and is implicit in the relationship among objectives, outputs, and outcomes. In our example, the meeting of the objective "to redesign inspection processes" leads automatically (assuming the project is successfully completed) to the output "redesigned inspection processes," which is a primary or direct benefit from the project. If these redesigned inspection processes are used properly they will lead to an outcome of fewer accidents, which is a secondary or indirect benefit.

In effect, as shown in Figure 9.4, there is a linked if–then test in which the primary objective directly leads to a primary benefit and, in the case of the improve service objectives and benefits (see IRACIS later), there is a link between the primary and secondary benefits.

This value chain can then be evaluated using the IRACIS model (expanded later) to develop project savings or benefits.

The Polaroid Test   One useful technique to identify the value chain is to use the Polaroid test. When analyzing the benefits chain, ask yourself this question: If I took a Polaroid of the situation before and after the project, what has changed? This can avoid claiming outcomes (secondary benefits) as outputs (primary benefits)—a very common mistake. For example, in an office automation (OA) project, the savings of management time in using the OA software (avoided costs) is claimed as a savings. However, the Polaroid test shows that after the project, the management have only received the OA hardware and software as the direct primary benefit (improved service). It is not until the managers use the primary benefit (i.e., the new technology) that the secondary benefit (avoided cost) is achieved. In the Osborne and Gaebler model, the delivery of the OA technology is the output and the savings of time is the outcome.

Projects don't realize benefits, people do.

It should also be noted that some objectives will have multiple outputs and outcomes that also need to be identified and modeled as shown later.

The IRACIS Model

The IRACIS model was first described by Gane and Sarson (1979), who argued that there were only three classes of benefits:

Table 9.1
Application of the IRACIS Model

Objective	Output	Outcome
To redesign inspection procedures	Redesigned inspection services	Reduced accidents caused by mechanical failure
	Improved service (to vehicle inspectors and car owners)	Avoided costs (estimated % reduction of accident incident and cost)
	Avoided costs (more efficient inspection process)	

- Increase revenue (IR): The objective directly leads to an increase in revenue.

- Avoid costs (AC): The objective directly leads to a decrease in cash outflow or costs.

- Improve service (IS): The objective directly leads to a quantifiable improvement of service to the organization's internal or external customers or organizations.

There are a number of benefit taxonomies (for example, Appendix C in Parker et al. (1988) lists more than 100 specific benefits), but use of the IRACIS model in numerous IT and business projects has confirmed that all benefits can be expressed in the simpler IRACIS model.

The IRACIS model can be applied in our transport example, as shown in Table 9.1.

Assuming there is a cause and effect of safer vehicles having fewer accidents, the saving of the costs of accidents caused by unsafe vehicles can be claimed as a secondary benefit.

It is important to remember that the financial analysis of the outcome or secondary value link or chain should only be applied to improve service or primary benefit objectives as increased revenue and avoided costs or primary benefits can be financially quantified at the primary benefit level.

Provided that stakeholders are held accountable for the secondary benefits, this model can eliminate the use of intangible benefits (see "Benefits Realization" later).

Actual Versus Notional Costs

One issue with the avoided costs class of benefit is the difference between actual and notional or potential costs. For example, in Figure 9.5, the projection for rises in staffing levels in a branch is mapped against transaction volumes in the branch

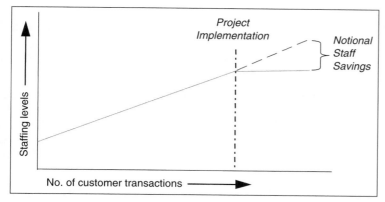

Figure 9.5
Notional cost avoidance

office. When a new IT system or redesigned business process is introduced, the traditional growth in staff numbers is reduced while transaction rates increase. Although there are no actual cost savings (staff size was not reduced), the potential savings of staff can be estimated and the extrapolated savings can be claimed as a notional avoided cost (often called cost avoidance).

Given that the sustained use of IT over the past 20 years to automate manual and older technology systems has resulted in many organizations gaining most avoided cost-type benefits, there is an expectation that the demand for improved service-oriented projects (client relationship management) will increase and, as identified by value chain analysis, the concept of notional savings will become critical.

It should be noted that some traditional accounting and finance people would not allow this approach, as "real" money is not saved. We come back to this concept later.

Shadow Pricing: Hedonic Costing and Contingent Valuation

These techniques have been developed to assist in the quantification of intangible benefits. In general, shadow pricing involves determining whether other organizations or areas have a similar service and product and determining the "market" price or value for the proposed service or product using the market or shadow price as an implicit cost benchmark.

Shadow or Hedonic Costing   This technique was developed to assist in quantifying the value of complex variables such as the value of land and houses. Any person who has purchased a house understands the hedonic model. It is a well-known adage in real estate that there are three important factors in considering to buy a house: location, location, location. Clearly, the location of a suburb or a house in a suburb has some implicit but definite value, which through the use of shadow pricing or contingent valuation can be measured. In effect, the hedonic model breaks a house into certain factors such as size, location, size of garden, proximity to transportation and facilities, and so on, and places a financial value on the components.

PROOF OF CONCEPT

In many projects, especially those involving innovative technology or procedures, the development of a realistic benefits and cost analysis can be difficult. If there are no similar projects that could be used to develop shadow costs or prices, the organization may need to fund a pilot project to prove the concept and, more important, provide data for a more accurate ROI analysis. This approach is common in other industries where new products are trialed in limited and controlled environments. In addition, it will be common that surveys, interviews, use of focus groups, time analysis, and other investigative processes may be required during the feasibility study phase to develop data for avoided cost and improved service objectives.

Peter Sassone and Perry Schwartz (1986) modified the hedonic model to analyze the benefits of OA and their model is extremely useful in evaluating certain avoided cost benefits.

Sassone and Schwartz linked the hedonic model with work profile analysis, where people use diaries to analyze and determine the relative amount of time they spend on various categories of work, typically classified as follows:

- Nonproductive: Waiting, searching for information, rework, traveling, and so on;

- Clerical/administrative: Time recording, typing, general meetings, and so on;

- Professional: Systems analysis, basic research, programming, and so on; and

- Expert professional: Project management, complex data and function analysis, and so on.

Using both the work profile and hedonic analysis techniques, the avoided cost class of benefits can be more accurately and realistically quantified.

Contingent Valuation   Contingent valuation involves the use of focus group or a representative sample of the project's clients. The members of the group are asked what they would be prepared to pay if the proposed service or product was available. There are really two questions that are explored in a contingent valuation process. The first is the people's willingness to pay (WTP) and the second is their willingness to accept (WTA) what they will accept doing without. Some experts argue that WTP can be distorted as a result of equity. For example, a poor person may not have the same WTP as a rich person. Using WTP, the focus group is asked, "How much are you prepared to pay for safe vehicles?" Using WTA, the focus group would be asked, "What lowering of government fees would compensate for having unsafe vehicles?" Clearly, WTA would tend to provide higher figures than WTP. In general, WTP would be a better approach provided the issue of equity (in this case, equity of ability to pay) was understood in the focus group. The WTA approach is more useful in projects where government services such as clean water, lower pollution, parks, conservation, and so on are involved.

For example, a project is proposing to integrate some information into CD-ROM technology and sell the CD-ROM with the information presented in multimedia format. Using a contingent valuation approach, a focus group of target clients would be interviewed and asked to place a value on the information and the CD-ROM packaging. Other packaging options could also be valued in the same process.

Then, using the implicit value gained from the focus group, a search could be made to see if similar products exist in similar markets and the shadow price could be compared against the contingent valuation price.

Let's assume that a competitor sells similar information in floppy disk (text-only) format for $4.50 a disk. The focus group puts a WTP value of $6.00 on the CD-ROM version. Given the difference between the multimedia version and the text-only version, an implicit value has been determined for the multimedia option ($6.00–$4.50 = $1.50) and there is confirmation of $6.00 as an estimated benefit (increased revenue).

Benefits Realization

It should be clear to you that all contemporary approaches to added-value analysis involve stakeholder and client involvement. The determination of both costs and benefits must be expanded to include client and stakeholder costs and the benefits that the clients and stakeholders expect for the project.

More important, the use of the added-value chain to determine primary and secondary benefits must involve clients and stakeholders, as they will generally be the major recipients of the benefits and, as a result, must be accountable and responsible for the garnishing of the benefits.

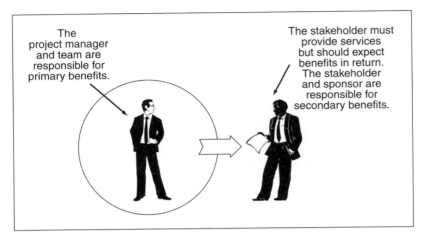

Figure 9.6
The benefits responsibility model

In our example of the vehicle inspection objective, the primary avoided cost benefit of the reduction of time in inspections must be realized by:

- The project team delivering the redesigned process, and
- The vehicle inspectors and police effectively using the redesigned process (these are stakeholders).

The secondary avoided cost benefit of reduction in costs through reduction in accidents can only be realized by the car drivers, insurance companies, and police.

This expansion of the benefit chain is another strong argument for total involvement of the project's clients and stakeholders in the participative planning process (RAP sessions).

As shown in Figures 9.4 and 9.6 you and your team are responsible for the primary benefits and your project sponsor and stakeholders are responsible for secondary benefits. The critical issue here is that stakeholders must be held accountable for the changes required to realize the outcome (secondary) benefits.

Cost-Effectiveness Model

As discussed earlier, traditional cost–benefit analysis was often an application of cost-effectiveness models.

This model ignores benefits and focuses on costs and risks only. In effect, the process is relatively simple. As shown in Figure 9.7, the costs of maintaining the status quo or base case are estimated over an agreed-on period of time.

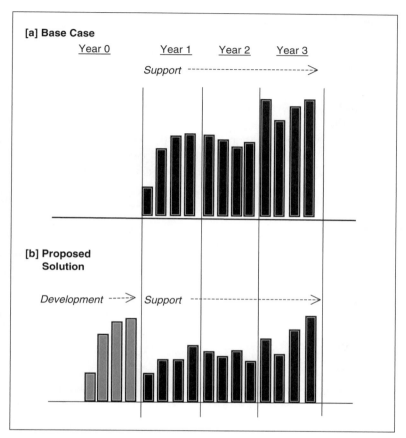

Figure 9.7
Cost-effectiveness

The development and support costs of the proposed solution are also estimated over the same period and, if the total development and support costs of the proposed solution are less than the ongoing support costs of the base case, then the project is viable. Typically, there would be a requirement for at least two alternatives to the base case.

This approach is particularly useful for projects that are functionally replacing an existing technology or process. For example, it could be used for local area network (LAN), hardware, and other technology projects. However, it is only viable when the new technology or process replaces the existing technology or process. Any additional benefits from the proposed solution should be ignored to avoid double-counting. Otherwise, the project value analysis approach should be used.

Another Form of Double-Counted Benefits

It is common that a number of project objectives and, more interestingly, a number of projects may have different outputs but the same outcome.

For example, an organization may be concerned about loss of existing clients to competitors. A number of projects are initiated, such as a project to improve formal written communication with existing clients and another project to increase direct personal contacts with the clients. In both projects, the outputs are different (revised letters, more phone calls) but the outcome (reduced client turnover) is the same. To avoid double-counting the outcome benefits, these two projects should be combined as a single program as shown in Figure 9.8.

Additional Added-Value Drivers

Many organizations use other factors to assist in the difficult area of project prioritization. The factors that our client companies use include these:

- Strategic alignment
- Technology impact
- Competitive advantage
- Organizational impact

The use of a simple scoring system such as 0 (the project has no relationship to the corporate strategic plan) to 5 (the project is an integral component of the corporate strategic plan) can be used to rank projects. We have a full example of this approach on our Web site (www.Thomsett.com.au).

In addition, using a concept developed by McKinsey & Company, some of our clients also consider competing projects using the concept of innovative *horizons:*

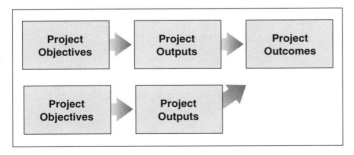

Figure 9.8
Two projects, same outcome

- Horizon 1: Projects developing products in an existing portfolio; for example, a bank is developing another bank product.

- Horizon 2: Projects developing products in a proven portfolio, but not one with which the organization is operating. The bank decides to develop insurance products.

- Horizon 3: Products that are totally innovative and unproven. The bank decides to develop artificial intelligence (AI) salespeople.

This model ensures that the organization is creating a project portfolio that balances risk, innovation, and growth. There are different governance guidelines for projects in different horizons. For example, Horizon 3 projects, which are inherently more risky, would have a more tight and regular governance.

All these added-value factors are analyzed during the RAP session.

A Final Note on Added-Value Analysis

Although the adoption of added-value analysis ensures that the project justification process is professional and equitable, it should not be forgotten that undertaking this process is a vital element in ensuring that the project manager and team understand the client's expectations for the project. It is true that many of the initial estimates used to develop the added-value analysis will be incorrect and based on assumptions that eventually are proven incorrect.

By undertaking an added-value analysis with the stakeholders and team members, the project manager is also building a team that shares a set of common expectations for the project based on business rather than technical drivers.

THE P FILES EPISODE 6: THE MISSING BRAIN

One of the scariest terms that has entered contemporary business, thanks to Bill Gates, is the term *no brainer*. We consulted on a project that had already commenced. A senior manager told us, before we met the team, that the project was a "no brainer." What he meant was that it was obvious to the management team that the project would be highly beneficial to the organization and that everyone believed this to be true. After a few hours of looking at the project's outputs and outcomes, it was obvious to everyone at the review that the outputs would not lead to any of the expected outcomes. Worse, none of the outcomes had any benefits at all for the organization. There was no stakeholder buy-in and the budget was 300% larger than the one management had approved. We reported back that indeed the project was a no brainer. As we reported, "We couldn't find any evidence of any brain being applied to the project at all!"

The P Files Team Comment

If you are working on a no brainer, then don't switch off your brain just because everyone else has. No brainer is too often an excuse for avoiding any proper project management.

CASE STUDY—ADDED-VALUE ANALYSIS

Edwina returns to the RAP and resolves that Smuthe office consultants will train Big Bucks clients but you have to train Smuthe people. Smuthe will acquire all the technology based on your team's recommendation and the support of the new systems is outside scope; in effect, another contract. The revised objectives are:

Project: Project Blastoff	
IS	IS NOT [Could be]
To capture extended client personal details. To capture more comprehensive client requirements for accomodation. To enable internal access to all client information for Smuthe consultants in all sites. To distribute more details on available accomodation to clients. To determine hardware requirements. To train Smuthe consultants.	To accomodate Watchout Insurance requirements. To acquire hardware. To market new Web site accomodation to clients. To handle any Smuthe financial information (i.e., fees). To train Big Bucks clients. To support Web site.
NOT RESOLVED	

You can now turn to the added-value analysis.

We'll use one objective to show how the added-value analysis is applied.

Objective	Output	Outcome
To capture extended client personal details	More information about the client's family, lifestyle, and accommodation preference for Smuthe consultants	More appropriate placement for clients
	Improved service (to Smuthe clients and Smuthe consultants)	Increased revenue (increase in fees for faster service)
	Avoided costs (less research required for consultants, fewer accommodation showings)	Notional avoided cost (reduced level of potential clients loss)

This is an example of different outputs leading to the same outcome as all objectives and outputs lead to the same outcomes.

What is revealed during the added-value chain analysis is a number of operational problems that Edwina and her team are facing. The first is that by not having up-to-date and complete details of potential clients (i.e., Big Bucks executives) Edwina and her team often suggest inappropriate accommodation, which leads to multiple site visits by Smuthe consultants and clients. In addition, there are some Big Bucks executives who have found that dealing with Smuthe is time-consuming and these people have chosen not to use the service.

In addition, Edwina has negotiated a premium fee arrangement for clients who use the company's Web site.

Edwina agrees to gather some data to estimate the financial information and improved service measures.

In addition, you discuss these added-value issues:

- Strategic impact;
- Technology impact;
- Organizational impact; and
- Competitive advantage.

You agree with Edwina that Project Connext is ranked as follows:

- Strategic impact—5

The project is an integral component of the corporate strategic plan.

- Technology impact—4

The project is deploying technology that is an integral component of the corporate strategic plan.

- Organizational impact—3

The project is driving change that impacts a significant component of the business process.

- Competitive advantage—4

The project is delivering a product that is ahead of similar products in the competitive area.

Define Quality

"You know we're sitting on four million pounds of fuel, one nuclear weapon, and a thing that has 270,000 moving parts built by the lowest bidder. Makes you feel good doesn't it?" ∎

Rockhound (Steve Buscemi)[1]

In this chapter, we introduce you to another powerful project management tool that we have developed and refined over many years. Our approach to modeling your clients' quality expectations is probably the most radical of all our techniques (see Figure 10.1). You will need to take some time here.

The tool we use was developed from the quality function deployment (QFD) approach pioneered by Yoki Akao (1990).

Project Quality Deployment

Ever since Edwards Deming (1986) and Joseph Juran (1989) expanded the debate about quality from their pioneering work with Japanese manufacturing companies in the 1950s to the broader application of total quality control and management in all industry and service sectors, the debate has always recognized the interaction between

---

1. *Armageddon*, Michael Bay, Director; Robert Roy Pool, Writer, 1998.

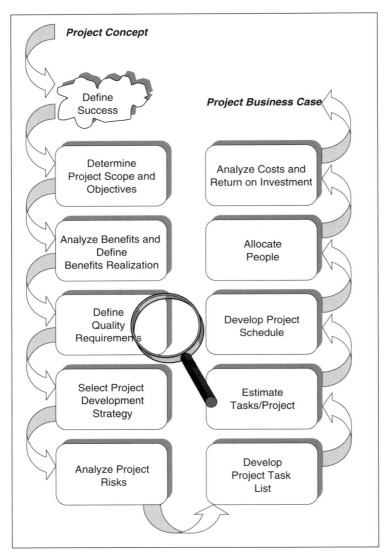

Figure 10.1
Define quality requirements

the product development process and the intrinsic quality of the product. However, over the past 10 years, there has emerged a philosophical gap between the advocates of process improvement and those concentrating on product improvement.

Following Deming's assertion that 80% of all quality problems can be attributed to failures in the system (process) rather than individual worker-induced defects, much of the total quality management (TQM) thrust has concentrated on process improvement.

In the industry, quality standards such as the ISO 9000 series and more, in software, models such as the capability maturity model (CMM) are similarly oriented toward improvement and standardization of the software development process.[2]

Although these process improvement initiatives are clearly valid, they beg a critical question: Does product development process improvement result automatically in improvement of product quality?

Although this assumption is, in the main, true, it accepts that the required quality of the product is both understood by the development group and that the required quality is designed into the product development process. As a simple example of this problem, Superb Sausages Pty Ltd., a sausage manufacturer, determines that its customers require a gourmet chicken and strawberry sausage. Using their standard sausage design methodology, the sausage designers determine the ingredients, volumes, and so on required by the new sausage. They produce a sample batch and after a successful taste test begin mass production. However, after mashing up 1,000 kilos of chicken and strawberries, the mashing machine clogs up, as it was not designed to process a soft fruit. The sausage (product) has the required quality specification but the sausage mashing machine (development process) failed to implement the required quality.

In the area of business project development, the same problem regarding process and product quality exits. Does the installation of a standard development methodology, quality assurance procedures, and rigorous project management processes guarantee the development and shipping of quality systems?

It is revealing to note that in the vast majority of quality-oriented books, articles, and "packaged" total quality control (TQC) methodologies, the need to tightly couple the product development process and the product quality is *completely* ignored.

Linking Product and Process Quality: QFD

In Japan, the coupling of process development to product quality is achieved through a technique that has little exposure in the populist quality push in the United States and Australia. QFD was developed by Yoki Akao (1990) and others in the late 1980s specifically to address the linking between product development process and intrinsic product quality. Recently, articles by John Hauser and Don Claussing in the *Harvard Business Review* (1988), by Rich Zultner in *American*

---

2. The CMM is an appraisal model used to measure the degree of rigor and repeatability of software development processes.

QUALITY IS A SET OF ATTRIBUTES

When you shop for a loaf of bread, what makes you choose one brand or type over another? Is it that you prefer whole-grain to processed bread? Is it that you prefer brown bread to white? Do you like thick slices or thin? These are all different attributes that bread possesses. What is really interesting is that each person prefers a different set of attributes that is entirely *subjective*. However, we match the specific loaf of bread to our preferred attributes *objectively.*

Programmer (1992), and books by Bob King (1989) and Lou Cohen (1995) have begun to draw attention to the use of this powerful technique in manufacturing and software development.

In essence, QFD is a rigorous and highly structured process involving the precise definition of required product quality and the deployment of tailored processes designed to embed the quality requirements throughout the product development process. QFD provides the missing link between process and product quality and it is a major factor behind the impressive growth in Japan's quality reputation.

The traditional approach to attempting to link product and process improvement is the use of formal quality plans. The standard procedure included in most project management approaches is to require the project manager to detail the process that he or she is going to use to assure quality. This would include what project or system development tools, technologies, and support are to be used in the project and what external quality assurance reviews are to be conducted. In many cases, these quality plans are nothing more than a simple checklist of the development processes that should be followed, similar to those loved by traditional auditors. Such checklists are important but they ignore a fundamental question: What is the required quality for the product or system? For example, when conducting a quality review of a system design, what does the review team look for? Do they check whether the design is efficient, follows the organizational standards, is compliant with the company's policy or IT architecture, or has inherent defects?

As in QFD, any process for assuring system quality must start with an unambiguous statement of the required system quality.

What Is a Quality?

The IEEE and ISO 9000 define quality as "fitness for purpose," which mirrors Philip Crosby's (1979) widely accepted definition of quality as "conformance to requirements." However, for a project manager planning a new project, the ISO 9000[3] definition does not provide a detailed basis for software quality planning.

Although many people seem comfortable accepting these definitions, they miss an important related question: Whose requirements and whose purpose?

Based on Jim McCall and Mike Matsumoto's (1980) work, our group has been using the following definition of business product and software quality. Quality is an agreed combination of the following quality attributes:

- Conformity: Does the product or software have all the data, process, or functionality specified?

- Usability: Is the product or software easy to use and understand from the client's perspective?

- Efficiency: Does the product or software use the people, business process, hardware, database or other support software efficiently?

- Maintainability: Is the product or software easy to maintain and support?

- Flexibility: Is the product or software easy to modify to include or add new functions and data?

- Reliability: Does the product or software perform reliably and is it free from errors?

- Portability: Can the product or software easily operate in different physical, business, software, or hardware environments?

- Reusability: Does the product or software require reuse for a different purpose or application?

- Security/auditability: Is the product or software secure from unauthorized access and modification and can the software be easily audited and does it include adequate controls?

- Job impact: Does the product or software affect the existing workflows, control, and autonomy of the business area?

As in many other quality models, the various attributes can be positively or negatively related. For example, although improving maintainability does improve

---

3. Recently, ISO has released a new standard, ISO 9126, for software. This refines the definition of quality into attributes similar to those used by McCall and our group for the past 14 years.

flexibility, the improvement of efficiency can lead to a lowering of usability, maintainability, flexibility, security, and auditability. The positive–negative relationship is identified by the fact that many of the quality attributes share common criteria. For example, flexibility and maintainability share four common criteria. As discussed later in this chapter, you and your team must identify potential conflicts in the product's quality requirements and resolve them before the project begins.

Some pragmatists also add deadlines and cost as a measure of software quality. However, these are constraints, not quality requirements. Many business people

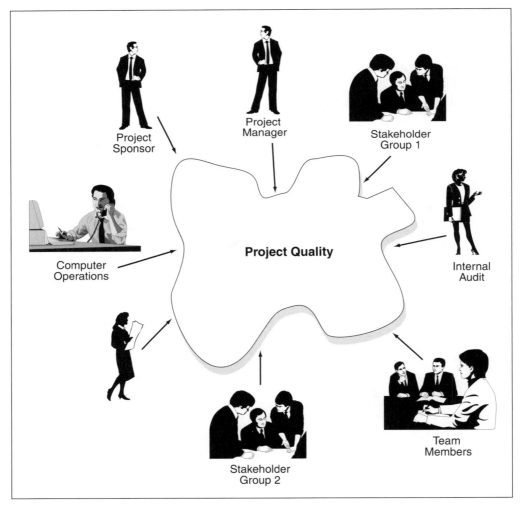

Figure 10.2
Product quality: A conflicting client community

faced with cost-reduction pressures and increasing competition based on market windows have been prepared to sacrifice the software quality attributes just listed to simply get a low-quality software solution on time and in budget. Cost and deadlines clearly have a negative relationship with all other software quality attributes.

Although Crosby's admonition that "quality is free" is true in respect to the costs of rework, many computer people have learned that certain software quality attributes are very expensive. The development of a GUI system with full online help and extensive manuals for users, administrators, and power users could incur 50% to 100% additional effort when compared to a similar data and function requirement with a minimum requirement for usability.

In other words, the formalization of software quality attributes reveals the fact that software quality has inherent conflicts. These are exacerbated by the existence of many external people or groups (stakeholders) that have differing views on the required quality for a particular software system. As shown in Figure 10.2, these groups have specialized and often narrow views of the required software quality.

For one particular system, the internal audit department may be concerned about controls and audit trails, whereas the data center may be concerned with reliability, efficiency, and maintainability. Communications may be concerned only with network efficiency and standards may be interested in the following of development standards during the system life cycle. Senior management is focused on deadlines and the business people want usability and reliability. Faced with conflicting quality requirements, it is understandable for project managers and the teams to simply ignore the conflict and impose their own quality requirements on the project!

The process of product quality planning must recognize these conflicts and provide two structured and negotiated outcomes: What is the required quality and what processes are to be in place during the development process to ensure the negotiated quality is delivered. This is the essence of project quality deployment (PQD).

Toward an Effective Quality Plan: PQD in Action_____

Using the modified McCall product quality definition, you can use a three-step process to plan the deployment of the required quality through the development process.

extreme tool

Once the PQD process has been applied to the overall product requirements, the product is partitioned into subcomponents and the process is repeated for each subcomponent. For a software system, the components would usually be subsystems such as front-end and back-end processing.

	Stakeholder				
Attribute					
Conformity Does the product/software have all the data, process, or functionality specified?					
Usability Is the product/software easy to use and understand from the client's perspective?					
Efficiency Does the product/software use the people, business process, hardware, database, or other support software efficiently?					
Maintainability Is the product/software easy to maintain and support?					
Flexibility Is the product/software easy to modify to include or add new function and data?					
Reliability Does the product/software perform reliably and is it free of errors?					
Portability Can the product/software easily operate in different physical, business, software, or hardware environments?					
Reusability Does the product/software require reuse for a different purpose or application?					
Auditability/Security Is the product/software secure from unauthorized access and modification, can the software be easily audited, and does it include adequate controls?					
Job Impact Does the product/software affect the existing workflows, control, and autonomy of the business area?					

Figure 10.3
Quality agreement

Step 1: Define the Product Requirements

This step would usually be undertaken during the project feasibility study and, in more detail, in the requirements analysis phase. Typically, the RAP process would provide enough information for the stakeholders to reach an initial agreement.

Step 2: Negotiate Product Quality Attributes

This step is the most crucial in the quality planning cycle. Given the potential for conflict in quality expectations between your various stakeholders in the project and the conflict between the various quality attributes, you must identify the quality requirements of your critical stakeholders, identify any conflicts, and negotiate an agreed quality requirement, the quality agreement (see Figure 10.3).

Step 2.1: Determine and Review Stakeholders' Ranking
Preferably in a group session, interview each critical stakeholder and review and determine their quality requirements using the form in Figure 10.2. It is important that you are patient here, as some stakeholders will simply say, "They're all on." Remember, they will generally be stating their MPP.

DON'T GET TOO COMPLEX

You may be tempted to use more sophisticated scoring mechanisms than the simple on/off ones that we propose (e.g., mandatory or not applicable). You may feel that using scales such as mandatory, desirable, and not applicable could be more useful, but our experience is that the simpler scales always work better. By getting too into the ranking process, people get focused on what the ranking means (i.e., what is the difference between a 6 and a 7?). Remember, simple is sexy. Complex sucks.

Step 2.2: Derive Final Ranking
Evaluate all mandatory quality attributes, looking for a majority agreement between the team and stakeholders (say, where 50% or more of the stakeholders agree, the attribute is mandatory for the project). Also, evaluate the rankings for any potentially conflicting mandatory quality attributes. For example, efficiency has a negative relationship with maintainability, flexibility, and portability.

Step 3: Review Quality Attributes with Your Sponsor

The final rankings should be reviewed with senior management, including your project sponsor, and any unresolved conflicts in the stakeholders' rankings should be resolved by senior management.

Your own project's quality agreement can then be used to develop broad quality baseline drivers and review points across the system development process. This development and use of quality baseline drivers is the key to quality planning and deployment.

Repeat Until . . .

As described earlier, for larger projects, the PQD process would be repeated for individual subprojects broken into major modules. As the project progresses through the system development life cycle, the quality agreements would become more detailed. For example, by the design phase of a software project, the quality agreement would be platform-specific.

Quality Index

If the relevant software attributes and criteria have been scored, then they can simply be added together to provide a simple, yet powerful numeric indicator of the relative quality of the product or system.

The simple approach is to use Table 10.1, which is based on just scoring the quality attributes.

Table 10.1
Quality Index

Conformity and/or maintainability and/or flexibility and/or auditability/security	1
Conformity and/or maintainability and/or flexibility and/or auditability/security and any **one** of portability, efficiency, usability, reliability, reusability, and job impact	2
Conformity and/or maintainability and/or flexibility and/or auditability/security and any **two** of portability, efficiency, usability, reliability, reusability, and job impact	3
Conformity and/or maintainability and/or flexibility and/or auditability/security and any **three** of portability, efficiency, usability, reliability, reusability, and job impact	4
Conformity and/or maintainability and/or flexibility and/or auditability/security and any **four** or **more** of portability, efficiency, usability, reliability,reusability, and job impact	5

The quality index provides a reasonable baseline to adjust project productivity measures or metrics and also to measure the quality of production systems. For example, two teams may have reported the same delivery productivity rates, but one team has delivered a system with a quality index score of 5 (very high quality requirements) and the other has delivered a system with a quality index score of 2 (low). Clearly, the first team has been more productive.

Quality in Action

Once the quality agreements have been agreed to and documented, these provide the basis for the proven quality assurance techniques, such as technical reviews, inspections, and walkthroughs.

Given that the quality agreement defines the required quality attributes, it enables the project team to review all critical deliverables from the specific quality requirement for the system.

If you haven't defined quality, you can't measure it.

The quality agreement also provides a vehicle for the postimplementation evaluation of product quality and project change control. In particular, with a clear and negotiated definition of product data and function requirements and quality assurance, any change to agreed-on quality attributes or criteria should be treated as a request for change and processed using standard change control procedures (discussed later in this book).

The use of PQD as a vehicle for project quality planning provides a vital link between the software development process and the required product quality.

The quality assurance of the specific components of the service, product or system involves team-driven techniques. External support groups such as development support and data administration would act as facilitators for these techniques rather than being involved in the actual assessment of product quality. The majority of the product assurance techniques have developed from the work of Gerald Weinberg (1971) and others in the early 1970s. With the exception of the system testing techniques, all quality assurance techniques follow a common set of rules, as follows:

- The producers determine when the product is ready for review.
- Everything new should be reviewed.

- Quality assurance starts when the project starts.
- Reviews should be short (one or two hours), sharp (small deliverables), and regular (daily).
- Reviews raise problems but don't resolve them.
- The product is commented on, not the producers.
- Reviews should involve people external to the team (i.e., stakeholders, operations, etc.).
- Formal reviews should produce reports and be conducted by a designated chairperson.
- Quality assurance reviews should focus on major issues.

Within this framework of common rules, there are a number of different quality assurance review techniques that are appropriate for different products and different stages of the development cycle.

Technical Reviews   Technical reviews involve a small team representing stakeholders, dependent projects, support groups, and project team members examining the product without the producer present. Experience has shown that these reviews are the most rigorous, as they require the product to stand on its own and avoid the defensive and selling behaviors that often mar walkthroughs. Technical reviews are ideal for documentation, analysis, and design specifications.

Walkthroughs   These reviews, often called structured walkthroughs, are similar in structure to technical reviews but the producer steps, reads, or walks through the product with the review team. Walkthroughs are the most widely implemented of the quality assurance techniques, but they can be reduced in effectiveness by interpersonal behaviors such as selling, arguing, avoidance, and so on. As a result, this technique is most effective when a strong chairperson is conducting the review. Walkthroughs are most commonly used for detailed design, program, and testing documents.

Inspections   Inspections are either walkthroughs or technical reviews that are driven using an inspection or checklist. These inspection lists highlight common errors and critical components that the quality assurance group should be evaluating in the product. Inspection lists are available for analysis, design, coding, and other system development deliverables (Freedman and Weinberg's 1977 book contains a number of excellent inspection lists). Inspections are ideal for all types of deliverables, provided the inspection lists are available for the specific deliverable.

Speed Reviews   This review technique can involve larger teams than the other product review techniques. Speed reviews are ideal for reviewing large deliverables that have not previously been subject to the other quality assurance techniques and that the review participants have not had an opportunity to preread or review. A typical speed review would require 10 or more people. A chairperson would partition the product into segments that could be read in a 10- to 20-minute session. As review members read the document, they mark errors or comments directly on the product. At the end of the session, a summary is made of the individual comments and the process is repeated until the entire product is reviewed. Speed reviews can take up to a day and are ideal for documentation and other textual material.

Feature Chiefs   This review technique is a modified version of all the review techniques already discussed where the participants are selected to represent a specific area of expertise. For example, in a feature chief review, the data administration representative would be restricted to raising issues relevant to data administration.

All these review techniques can be conducted either formally or informally. Formal quality assurance reviews must produce a review summary including a decision to accept or reject the product, together with a list of errors and issues to be resolved by the producers. Informal reviews do not produce any management documentation.

The other forms of product quality assurance review techniques are generally included in the approaches of product or system testing. System testing techniques are not covered in this book.

Quality Assurance Drivers

Using your project's quality agreement provides you, your team, and stakeholders with a baseline for determining whether your project is delivering the agreed-on quality.

In effect, the quality agreement is used to determine which specific quality attributes should be reviewed in each deliverable. For example, if usability is required, then usability problems would be identified as serious defects. If usability is not required, these problems would simply be noted, not corrected.

GOOD ENOUGH

There is an on-going debate between software people, in particular, about the issue of quality. One school is the CMM and ISO group, who believe that quality is perfection. The other school is the "good enough" school, who believe that quality is whatever the client perceives as good enough for their need. The quality agreement tool clearly belongs to the "good enough" school.

Our experience has shown that this approach ensures that the quality assurance reviews do not get into wasteful arguments about whether a product is "correct" or not.

It all depends on the client's requirements.

Quality Assurance Principles

The techniques involved in quality management vary depending on whether the focus is on the process or the product. However, there is a common set of principles in all the techniques:

- The people producing the product, service, or system are responsible for the quality.
- The techniques of quality management and assurance are participative and team driven.
- Quality cannot be inspected in—it has to be built in.
- Quality starts with senior management.
- Quality is in the details.
- Quality improvement is achieved incrementally through small changes.
- Quality improvement requires resources and expenses that are paid back in the long term.
- Quality improves productivity and morale.

Quality, Estimates, Costs, and Risks _____

The negotiation of a quality agreement provides a process for defining the quality expectations of the stakeholders, and it also is a critical process in understanding and improving the project estimation and risk management processes.

Put simply, the higher the quality expectation, the higher the costs and risks of the project will be.

The Impact of Quality

Let's assume that you have negotiated with your stakeholders that, for their project, conformity, reliability, and job impact are the only mandatory attributes. Clearly, you would take these attributes into consideration when the RAP session undertakes project risk assessment and estimation. However, during the project, your critical stakeholder group decides that usability is also important. Clearly, the impact of this change in the quality agreement is significant. Experience has shown that adding usability to the expectations could double the effort and cost of the project. In addition, you may need to recruit a new team member who is an expert in GUIs and the relevant technical tools. This results in a higher level of project risk.

The Hot Buttons

Experience and some supportive data from Capers Jones (1994) have shown that the following quality attributes are very expensive to implement:

- Usability,
- Reliability,
- Efficiency,
- Job impact,
- Portability, and
- Reusability.

We'll revisit the cost issues of quality later in Chapters 13, 15, and 23.

A Final Note on Quality for Now

As noted by Philip Crosby, quality is free and poor quality costs. One of the less documented aspects of a poor quality environment is the dysfunctional effect of poor quality on the morale and sense of professionalism of the people producing the system, service, or product. Not only will a quality agreement reduce costs and increase productivity, but it will improve the morale and satisfaction of all people working in the organization.

THE P FILES EPISODE 7: THEY DESERVE IT

As one of our workshop participants put it, "Quality is like religion. Everyone believes in it. Only a few practice it." Quality has remained the last escape clause for many project team members. We were showing a project team the quality agreement tool and the team members were very excited about the fact that they could finally agree on what quality really meant for their project. We then pointed out that the stakeholders have the final say on what the quality should be for their project. One of the team members was stunned: "You mean we show this to the users!? They don't know anything! If we let them decide the quality, they'll be happy with crap. We can't let them do this. They deserve great quality and we will build it for them. I hate this tool."

The P Files Team Comment

Open project management means the stakeholders drive the project. If they want poor quality (as long as they are prepared to pay for the clean-up later), then that's what they get. It is always interesting to see traditional technical people struggle with this concept.

CASE STUDY—QUALITY AGREEMENT

You discuss the various quality attributes with Edwina and the other stakeholders at the RAP. The quality agreement is completed and Edwina is prepared to pay the additional cost and risk so that both Kim and Joan get the additional attributes that they expect, as shown here.

This gives you the following quality index:

Conformity and/or maintainability and/or flexibility and/or auditability/security	1
Conformity and/or maintainability and/or flexibility and/or auditability/security and any **one** of portability, efficiency, usability, reliability, reusability, and job impact	2
Conformity and/or maintainability and/or flexibility and/or auditability/security and any **two** of portability, efficiency, usability, reliability, reusability, and job impact	3
Conformity and/or maintainability and/or flexibility and/or auditability/security and any **three** of portability, efficiency, usability, reliability, reusability, and job impact	4
Conformity and/or maintainability and/or flexibility and/or auditability/security and any **four** or **more** of portability, efficiency, usability, reliability, reusability, and job impact	5

Attribute	Stakeholder				
	Edwina	Kim	Joan		
Conformity Does the product/software have all the data, process, or functionality specified?	✓	✓	✓		
Usability Is the product/software easy to use and understand from the client's perspective?	✓	✓	✓		
Efficiency Does the product/software use the people, business process, hardware, database or other support software efficiently?	✓	✓	✓		
Maintainability Is the product/software easy to maintain and support?	✓	✓	✓		
Flexibility Is the product/software easy to modify to include or add new function and data?	✓	✓	✓		
Reliability Does the product/software perform reliably and is free of errors?	✓	✓	✓		
Portablility Can the product/software easily operate in different physical, business, software, or hardware environments?					
Reusability Does the product/software require reuse for a different purpose or application?		✓			
Auditability/Security Is the product/software secure from unauthorized access and modification and can the software be easily audited and does it include adequate controls?					
Job Impact Does the product/software affect the existing workflows, control, and autonomy of the business area?		✓			

Select a Development Strategy

"We aren't in a rush. We want to get there in a hurry." ∎

Benjy Benjamin (Buddy Hackett)[1]

Following the definition and negotiation of the project's scope, objectives, stakeholders, and related projects, the next step in planning your project is for you, your team, and your stakeholders to analyze and select the appropriate project development strategy (see Figure 11.1).

The choice of project development strategy is one of the most important decisions that you make during the planning sessions. As we also discuss when examining risk assessment, the choice and, in some cases, alteration of project strategy has generally been made covertly and intuitively by the technical experts in a project. It is a key concept in our new approach to project management that issues about project development strategy are made public during the planning process and that the final choice and approval of project strategy is made by your project sponsor and stakeholders.

---

1. *It's a Mad, Mad, Mad, Mad World*, Stanley Kramer, Director; Tania Rose, William Rose, Writers, 1963.

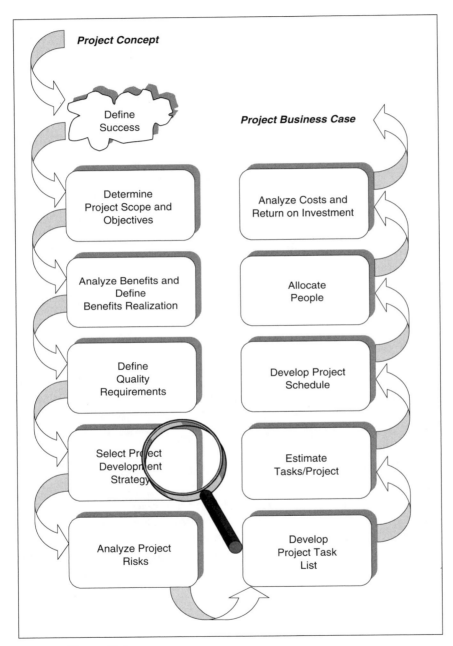

Figure 11.1
Select project development strategy

Strategy Ain't Methodology

Project development strategy is about the overall game plan of how you plan to undertake the project. For example, you may be planning to develop the whole product in one hit or alternatively, break up the product into subproducts and develop the subproducts as independently as possible.

The most common misunderstanding about project development strategy is that strategy is often confused with methodology or task lists. As we discuss in Chapter 12, "Analyze Risk," projects move through a number of development phases, steps, or tasks (often called *methodology*). In a software development project, we may commence with a phase involving analyzing requirements (a similar phase would be found in developing a new insurance policy, e.g.). The analyzing requirements phase may involve lower level tasks such as interviewing clients and so on.

The project development strategy is independent of the particular methodology being used for your project. For example, as we discuss later in this chapter, if you are using a sequential release strategy in your project, you'll undertake the analyzing requirements phase (and its related subtasks) for as many releases as you are developing.

The first mention of project development strategies that we are aware of was in the famous NATO Software Engineering Conferences in 1968 and 1969. During a chaired discussion in 1968 on large projects and lessons learned from them, John David from Bell Labs indicated that it was Bell Labs' experience "that any software system that cannot be completed by some four or five people within a year can never be completed."[2] Fred Brooks (1975) also indirectly discussed project development strategies in his classic book *The Mythical Man Month*, discussing lessons learned from IBM's OS/360 project development. However, in 1976, Paul Melichar from the IBM Systems Science Institute wrote a great paper, "Management Strategies for High-Risk Projects."[3] In this landmark paper, Melichar clearly identified three project development strategies and provided some excellent guidelines on what type of project would be ideal for each of the strategies.

Since that paper, our group has further developed and refined Melichar's original model. As we discuss in this chapter, strategy is critical to planning your project and in managing changes in scope, objectives, quality, and risk during your project.

[2.] Of course, it is amazing to us (though it shouldn't be) that in 1995, some 27 years after Bell's comments, the concept of 6×6 and 3×3 projects became very popular with some new-breed IT gurus (*NATO Software Engineering*, Naur & Randell, 1968, p. 84).

[3.] This paper was an internal IBM document and, to our knowledge, was never published.

The Four Development Strategies

To help understand the impact and power of project development strategies, we assume that you have a simple set of system requirements, as shown in Figure 11.2.

In our example, there is a requirement for four processes, A, B, C, and D. There are four stakeholders, A, B, C, and D. The system processes use two sets of data, Data A and Data B.

There are four basic project development strategies, explained in the following sections.

Monolithic or Waterfall

As shown in Figure 11.3, this strategy involves developing the system or product as a whole with each phase as a stand-alone activity, and subsequent phases are not commenced until preceding phases are complete; that is, design is not commenced until analysis is complete. In effect, the waterfall or monolithic strategy treats system and product development as an assembly line.

It is probably the oldest of the strategies, and computing and business borrowed this strategy from the building, engineering, manufacturing, and defense industries in the early 1960s. I was taught this strategy as the only way to build systems in the

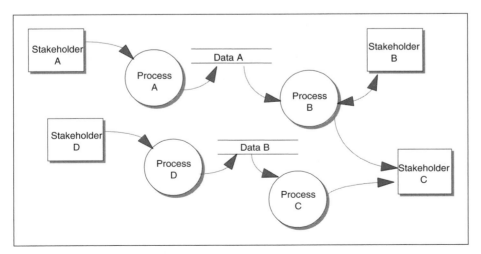

Figure 11.2
Sample system requirements

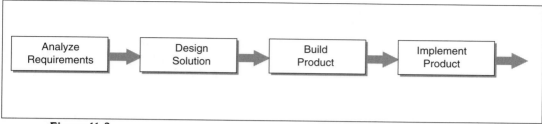

Figure 11.3
Monolithic/waterfall strategy

late 1960s. Until the mid-1990s this was mandated as a standard for the U.S. defense industries[4] and many IT organizations.

In our example system, all the processes (A, B, C, D) and all the data (Data A and Data B) would be implemented in one big bang on the delivery date. Each phase of the development cycle would be completed before the subsequent phase commences.

Strengths and Weaknesses   The strengths of the waterfall strategy are its simplicity and ease of scheduling. Scheduling tools such as Microsoft Project are well-suited for this strategy. Given the longevity of this model, this strategy is the basis of most traditional software engineering approaches and texts and, as such, has become the intellectual framework for many IT people and the universities that train them.

The weaknesses of this strategy are substantial. It is poorly suited for the chaotic and client-driven business environment of the 21st century.

FRED BROOKS' REVISION

In the 20th anniversary edition of his classic *The Mythical Man Month*, Fred Brooks [1975] admitted that the waterfall model, which had been integral to his view of systems development, was totally wrong, citing the same weaknesses that we have found over the past 25 years. We have also been advising our clients to avoid the waterfall for all but small, low-risk projects over the same period.

---

4. William Perry, a former Secretary of Defense, sent a memo to the U.S. Defense Department clearly abandoning the waterfall strategy as the only way to build systems in the early 1990s. The waterfall strategy had been embedded in DOD-STD 2167, which was a standard that all defense projects had been forced to follow for many years.

First, the business clients and stakeholders will not see any of the product until they see the whole product, so if the quality of the product or the functionality is not as expected, it is too late to find out after the product has been delivered. As we discussed earlier in this book, in traditional project management and system development approaches, the users were remote from the development effort and, as a result, often didn't really get a chance to determine whether their requirements were going to be met until late in the development cycle.

Second, it is totally inadequate for handling requirements changes. As shown in Figure 11.4, if a requirement change occurs during the design phase, there are only two viable choices. The first is to effectively ignore the change and schedule it as an enhancement after the initial delivery (this choice was widely used in the era when computer people and other experts controlled the development effort). The second is to loop back into the analysis phase to examine the requirements change. The allowing of looping back to earlier phases effectively destroys the strategy and research has shown that with backward looping allowed, the final phase of the development cycle is always the longest, as the team loops backward to all subsequent phases, attempting to eliminate as many errors and changes as possible.

This looping often resulted in a bizarre phenomenon—analysis paralysis—where the team continually loops either within the analysis phase or between analysis and design as requirements continually change. This failure of the waterfall strategy is well illustrated in an Australian Department of Defence project, Supply System Redevelopment (SSR), where after more than 10 years of systems analysis, no firm requirement had been produced.

The third problem with the waterfall strategy is simply that it takes too long. There is considerable evidence that project team members experience a "midproject slump" as they begin to question whether they will ever produce a working system or product. It is also very difficult for the project manager to keep the team focused for long periods when they are beginning to question whether the project will ever

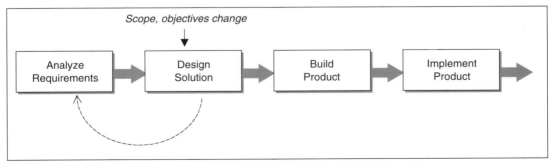

Figure 11.4
The failure of the waterfall strategy

end. In addition, the pressures for faster delivery cycles from business (discussed earlier in this book) demand alternative development strategies. Finally, long projects are more exposed to changes from external areas than shorter projects.

Release, Version, or Incremental

This strategy attempts to address some of the shortcomings of the waterfall strategy by shortening the development life cycle. There are two variations of this strategy.

Sequential Release   This variation involves breaking the system into semi-independent subsystems or subproducts and then producing and implementing an entire operational subsystem or product as Version 1 or Release 1, then a second subsystem as Version 2 or Release 2, and so on, as shown in Figure 11.5. For example, Release 1 of the new banking product may not have all the features, but it is an effective stand-alone product. Release 2 adds some additional noncritical features.

DON'T BUY VERSION 1

Cynics among our readers will recognize the concept of releases of products. Who remembers Microsoft Windows 3.0 or the first "portable" computers?

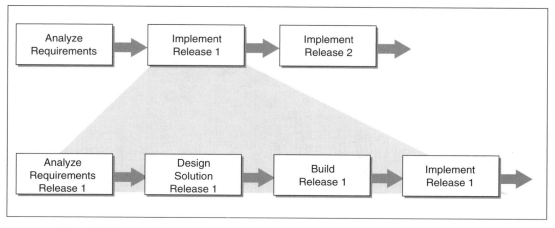

Figure 11.5
The sequential release strategy

In our example, let's assume that we break our system into two releases as shown in Figure 11.6. Processes A and B with their related Data A are partitioned into Release 1 and Processes C and D are treated as Release 2. Note that each release has different stakeholders (this is very important and we spend more time on this concept later).

Strengths and Weaknesses   Clearly, the sequential release strategy addresses the major weaknesses of the monolithic strategy by providing the capability of shortening the life cycle and delivering working product quicker. In addition, the sequential release strategy enables smaller teams (which, as we discuss later in this book, are more efficient and easier to manage) to develop big systems and products. In sequential release projects, the team is still focused on one specific group of functions (and data), which also helps team cohesion.

The weaknesses of sequential release are centered around the fact that you have to break up the system or product into subsystems or subproducts that are as independent as possible. Of course, the nature of systems and products is that they consist of interlinked subcomponents and it is the links that are the problem, not the components.

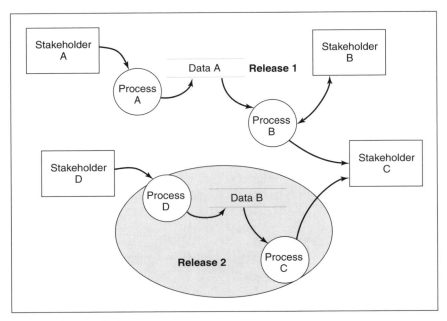

Figure 11.6
Partitioning into releases

If you are using either the sequential or concurrent release strategies, you must ensure that the shared data (or links) between Release 1 and Release 2 is carefully managed. For example, using sequential release, after Release 1 is implemented Data A is being used in the production system. The support team, who are supporting Release 1, and the development team, who are working on Release 2, must communicate effectively and review each other's work. When the shared data (e.g., the format, content, and structure) is changed by one team, the other team must approve of the change and change either their system or design accordingly. The lack of management of the interfaces between releases has caused serious problems in many projects.

MINIMUM DELIVERABLE

One of the key considerations when you are planning a project, especially during the discussion about project development strategies, is for you and your project sponsor to negotiate the *minimum deliverable* or core functionality. There are a couple of ways that you can identify the core functionality of the system. The simplest way is to ask your sponsor and critical stakeholders, "If everything goes wrong in this project and, as you know things tend to go wrong, what is the minimum that has to be implemented by the deadline?" Clearly, the minimum functionality or core functionality should be scheduled for Release 1.

Concurrent Release   This strategy is another variation on the release approach where, as shown in Figure 11.7, the releases are scheduled concurrently.

The concurrent release strategy offers the best of all worlds. It enables bigger teams (broken into subteams by release) to work together to produce the entire system in a relatively rapid manner. In our example, one team would develop Release 1 while, concurrently, another team would be developing Release 2.

The key to understanding this version of the release strategy is that various components of the system or product each go through the development life cycle (methodology) independent of the other releases. In other words, Release 1 could be in the design phase while Release 2 is still in the analysis phase.

Strengths and Weaknesses   Clearly, this strategy has all the strengths and weaknesses of the sequential release strategy. In addition, as mentioned earlier, it has the additional advantage of being able to deliver more functionality in a relatively quick manner.

However, the issue of managing the interfaces or links between the releases is even more difficult in this strategy. In large and complex projects, it is possible that many releases could be under development concurrently and a change by one

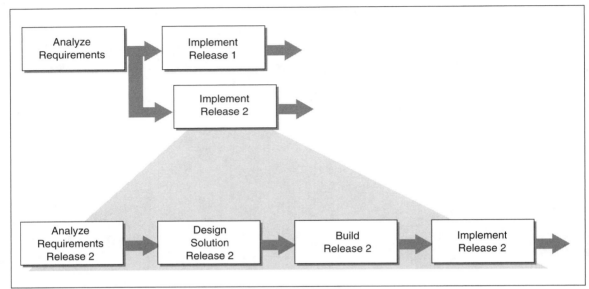

Figure 11.7
Concurrent release strategy

subproject manager and his or her technical experts in shared data or interfaces could ripple across a number of interrelated releases, causing major disruptions to the project. In addition, whereas in the sequential release strategy you are focused on one release, the concurrent release strategy involves focus on multiple releases. Each has its own scope, objectives, stakeholders, risks, and so on. In effect, you have an overall business case for the project and a series of subproject business cases, all of which have to be coordinated.

The concurrent release is not for first-time project managers, and our experience is that concurrent release strategy projects require higher levels of both project management effort and experience.

Fast Track, Evolutionary, or Production Prototyping

This involves producing a production prototype of the system as quickly as possible. It is better understood when you understand that the "street language" title of this strategy is the *quick and dirty* strategy.

Paul Melichar (1976) identified this strategy, and for many IT and other project professionals, it is seen as a covert and unprofessional strategy. Much of this view

A DIRTY LITTLE SECRET?

In hundreds of project management workshops, we have observed thousands of business and IT project managers struggling to admit that they have used the fast track strategy. In fact, many feel a little nervous that our group explains this strategy to business stakeholders and senior management. In other words, this strategy is a dirty little secret. This is paradoxical as, in other areas such as construction and manufacturing, fast-tracking is common.

can be blamed on the majority of academics and quality assurance and software engineering gurus, who are still focused on the more professional and engineered strategies.

The key to understanding this strategy is that the whole requirement is developed as quickly as possible with careful and planned degradation of quality. This can be achieved by minimizing adherence to standards and by use of application generators or high-level languages (e.g., Visual Basic, etc.). The first operational prototype is shipped into production. Often in the fast track strategy, training, documentation, and testing are compromised (see Figure 11.8).

The initial version of the system or product is then redeveloped through a series of reengineering projects that include additional functionality.

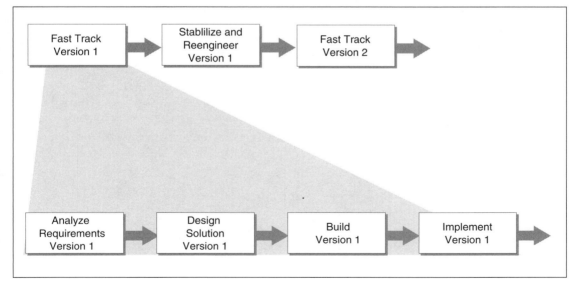

Figure 11.8
Fast track strategy

As the pressure to be first to market and to beat competitors increases in many sectors of business, the use of the fast track strategy will grow, and it is our experience that fast-tracking is already the most commonly used strategy. Perfect examples of this justification of lower quality systems and products to gain market share by being first to market are the highly competitive area of World Wide Web browsers and the pharmaceutical industry. In amazing articles in *Fast Company* (both available on Fast Company's Web site at *www.fastcompany.com*), Eric Matson ("Speed Kills (the Competition)")[5] and Tom Steinert-Threlkeld ("Can You Work in Netscape Time?")[6] clearly show how companies such as Netscape and Quintiles have refined the fast track strategy and have used it to gain significant market positions.

A COUPLE OF SECONDS OF NETSCAPE TIME

In the *Fast Company* article on Netscape there are some wonderful examples of the issues surrounding the fast track strategy. The issue of fast to market is highlighted by the fact that for each week Netscape delayed in shipping Navigator, their major competitor Mosaic was shipping 600,000 copies! As Jim Clark, the co-founder of Netscape comments, "If we had been 6 months later we would have been lost in the noise." The success of early shipping of a bug-ridden Netscape [PQD in action] was proven when, 6 months after shipping, Netscape commanded 75% of all browser traffic and Mosaic's share had fallen from 60% to 5%. One of Netscape's core principles is "fast enough never is."

Strengths and Weaknesses   The strengths of the fast track strategy are its sheer speed and that the entire product is built rather than a subcomponent, as in the release strategies. In addition, the fast track strategy is a highly charged, entrepreneurial, creative, and exciting strategy. More important, because of the schedule compression associated with the strategy, it is less exposed to changes (in some cases, the product is delivered before the requirements change) and well suited for high-risk projects (see later).

THE DOWN-SIDE OF FAST TRACK

While the concept of rapid implementation using fast track is appealing to a business executive looking to beat competitors to market, our research has shown that the support costs of fast tracked products can be 5 times higher than for higher quality products. These support costs need to be considered before fast-tracking is approved.

---

5. "Speed kills the competition," Fast Company, Issue 4, August/September 1996, pp. 84–93.
6. "Can you work in Netscape time?," Fast Company, Issue 1, November 1995, pp. 86–92.

Given the potential for this strategy to involve long hours and degradation of quality, it is critical that the team members are highly skilled and experienced.[7] This is very important as the use of fast-tracking with inexperienced teams can lead to disaster. Also, because the delivered quality is typically low, the project sponsor and stakeholders must be prepared to support and fund the review and reengineer activities (see Figure 11.8). Without planning and implementation of the cleanup, fast track projects are simply excuses for putting quick and dirty systems into production. Finally, the fast track strategy requires very sophisticated and professional project management, including real-time planning as discussed in this book.

Hybrid

The hybrid strategy is a variation of concurrent release. The hybrid strategy really involves a series of concurrent releases or subprojects with each subproject or release using a different development strategy.

In our example, let's assume that Release 1 (Processes A and B with Data A) is a high-risk release, as Stakeholders A and B are likely to change their requirements and they have a relatively low quality expectation (as determined by our quality agreement). Release 2 (Processes C and D and Data B) is a lower risk, as Stakeholders C and D are more sure of their requirements and have very high quality expectations. In this case, the hybrid strategy would be ideal, with Release 1 being developed using the fast track strategy and, concurrently, Release 2 developed using either the monolithic or the sequential release strategy.

The hybrid strategy is very powerful and is the most common in large or super-large projects.

Rapid Application Development (RAD), Agile, and Other Variations_____

There are a number of interesting variations of the four basic development strategies, including those explored in the following sections.

---

7. It is interesting to note that Microsoft and other "fast track" companies prefer Generation X people for these intense projects because of their youth, lack of "outside" lives, flexibility, ability to multitask, and stamina. Experience may thus need to be tempered with physical fitness and total focus.

RAD or Time-Boxing

The partitioning of a system into small releases between three and six months apart, which are then developed using sequential or concurrent release strategies, has been termed RAD by some vendors. RAD is essentially a variation of the sequential release strategy. It is also important to note that some technology vendors claim that sophisticated development environments such as high-level programming languages, application development tools, and support technology (computer-aided software engineering [CASE] tools and such) are required for RAD. Although these tools are useful, they are not necessary.

Radical Fast Track

This strategy is highly controversial and dangerous, yet within certain constraints, it can be very effective. It is the fast track strategy taken to the extreme. Whereas in the fast track strategy the normal project management processes described in this book are still used, especially the active involvement of stakeholders, in the radical fast track strategy a SWAT team or "skunk works" team is formed and given substantial freedom and power to get on with it. The team focuses totally on delivering, with any processes that would slow development avoided. For example, there would be limited or no involvement of stakeholders and no need to follow any corporate standards and technology architectures. In effect, the team is free to break whatever rules they need to enable delivery ASAP. This strategy was used effectively by IBM in developing the personal computer (though the deal that the IBM team made with Microsoft has become the stuff of legend and changed the future of IT) and by Lockheed's famous Skunk Works group.

However, this strategy mandates the existence of a very powerful sponsor or champion who can provide the requisite corporate support and funding. It can only be undertaken by highly skilled teams.

Microsoft's Daily Build

This strategy is a highly refined and effective variation of the release strategies that is more suited for IT projects. It is described in detail in Cusumano and Shelby's *Microsoft Secrets* (1996), Steve McConnell's *Rapid Development* (1996), and Pascal Zachary's *Showstopper* (1994). Basically, after determining the functionality of the system, small teams of developers and testing experts using very powerful development tools build a working version of the system day by day with the testing experts working in partnership to test the daily build. Microsoft used this strategy to build Windows 2000 and Windows XP with great success. Again, this strategy depends on state-of-the-art development technology, highly skilled and motivated developers and testing people, and a creative working environment.

Agile, Lite, or Extreme Methods

These are relatively recent variations of strategy and, like many radical project management models, they had their origins in IT. There are many packaged versions of this approach, but the basic concept was developed by Beck and Fowler (2001). XP, lite, and agile approaches use concepts such as team programming; very small time frames (generally less than eight weeks); and surprisingly low-tech concepts (e.g., requirements as stories on small 3 × 5 cards) coupled with very high-tech development tools.

Mixing and Matching

Of course, you can mix and match the four basic strategies, giving you almost unlimited options in planning your project. For example, you can undertake the monolithic strategy for the analysis phase and then partition your product or system into releases for the design and build phases, then recombine the releases for a monolithic implementation phase. You are limited only by your imagination and the project constraints (ahem).

Partitioning Guidelines_____

The power of the process of analyzing and selecting the project development strategy, in conjunction with your team and stakeholders, is best understood when we examine the various factors that you need to consider when partitioning your system or product. There are three key perspectives to consider, as discussed in the following sections.

By Function or Data

This is the most obvious and, in general, the perspective most favored by technical experts. Using the well-understood guidelines of coupling (interfaces of data or technology) and cohesion (the logical or functional complexity of subunits), this partitioning perspective breaks the system or product into subcomponents with minimum coupling and maximum cohesion. In our example, the partitioning into Release 1 and 2 leaves no interfaces and would be an ideal partition from this perspective.

By Stakeholder

This perspective is more radical but, in some cases, it can be very powerful and, in the new client-focused environment, it is increasingly important. Instead of partitioning by function or data, you discuss with each critical stakeholder which project objectives are critical to them. Then, you partition the system by the stakeholders and the functions that meet their requirements. In our example, Stakeholders A and C are critical stakeholders so you would partition the system (using the concurrent release strategy) to deliver Processes A and C with the relevant data from Data A and Data B. The downside of this strategy is that, in many cases, complex technical work will be required to build temporary data and interface functions to support subcomponents with messy interfaces.

LOW-HANGING FRUIT

When analyzing your project development strategy, you should always look for quick wins or "low-hanging fruit." That is, you should try to see if there are any easy or low-risk deliverables that you and the team can build quickly. By choosing the easy parts of the system first, you can build credibility with your stakeholders and prove that you and your team can deliver. In addition, you provide a strong motivational boost for your team and, in many cases, a positive environment for building cohesion.

By Benefits

This is a variation of partitioning by stakeholder (remember that objectives and benefits are related). The key perspective here is that you focus on which objectives or functions provide the highest benefits and, by using sequential, or concurrent, or fast track release strategies, you partition the system or product to deliver benefits earlier. The same concerns regarding the need to build interim interfaces and so on apply to this partitioning approach as well.

Strategy Selection

Should the release or hybrid strategy be chosen, there are typically three primary points at which the system can be "packaged" into releases:

- At the end of the project feasibility phase,
- At the end of the detailed analysis phase, and
- At the end of the design phase.

It should be emphasized that prior to partitioning the system into subsystems, you should develop a representation of the system or product, (e.g., data flow, flow chart, mechanical drawings, or structure chart) sufficient to ensure that the interfaces are understood. The earlier the system is partitioned, the higher the risk that the subsystems may not be partitioned cleanly.

Strategy as a Change Control

It is also essential to recognize that for many projects, the strategy may change at various stages of the development process. For example, the project may have a high-risk requirements analysis phase requiring the use of the fast track strategy (which may involve the developing of prototype screens, etc.). However, once your client's requirements are determined, the project may move to a low-risk design, development, and implementation stage. For the remainder of the project a more conservative strategy, such as sequential release or monolithic, may be implemented.

In another project, a new requirement emerges that is critical and must be implemented by the deadline. Your project is currently using the sequential release strategy. By splitting up your team (maybe with some additional people), you can alter your approach to the concurrent release strategy with a new release focused on the new requirements.

As discussed further in Part 3, changing your project's development strategy is a major lever for you to keep your project under control. Of course, as with all project management processes, the selection or alteration of the project development strategy must be negotiated with senior management and clients.

It is essential that the selection of the project development strategy be undertaken in an open and participative manner. Each strategy has a different impact on the major deliverables and on the stakeholders and related projects. Remember, as in all major project decisions, the final choice of the strategy must be undertaken by the project sponsor and stakeholders.

Strategy and Risk Assessment

There is a very important relationship between the project development strategy, the development length, your team size, and the risk (see next chapter) of the project. In general, the higher the risk of the project, the more likely strategies such as fast track and hybrid would be used. Generally, with a team size of greater than five to seven people, the project would have to use one of the variations of the release or hybrid strategies.

extreme tool

IT'S COUNTERINTUITIVE

It is in the nature of many people that, when faced with a risky project, their inclination is to be conservative in approaching the choice of strategy. It is counterintuitive, but the higher the risk of the project, the more risky your strategy should be. In other words, for a high-risk project, the best strategy is either fast track or hybrid. Think of your project as a bed of hot coals. Would you rather walk slowly or run over the coals?

Figure 11.9 shows the suggested relationship between the risk of the project (see next chapter), team size, duration, and project development strategy. The table should be treated as a guide only, as there may be projects where the specific nature will require a particular strategy. For example, the use of the monolithic strategy should be avoided for large projects. However, the ultimate choice of strategy is dependent on the business drivers of your project.

As a final note on strategy, it is important to recognize that IT and other professionals have tended to keep the strategy analysis and selection hidden from their business clients. This is partly due to the use of strategy as a mechanism for managing changes in project requirements (see Part 3). By opening up the process of strategy analysis and selection, you will find that your business clients and stakeholders will have a better understanding of their project and some of the options available to them.

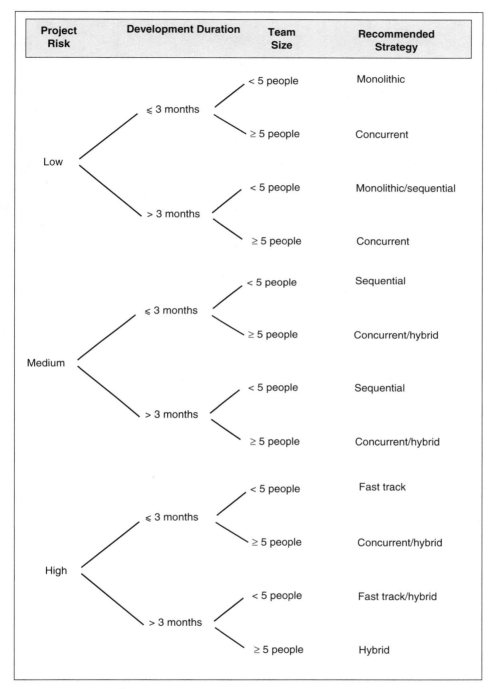

Figure 11.9
A guide to strategy selection

THE P FILES EPISODE 8: THE ONE-MINUTE MANAGER

We were asked to address a senior management team (including project directors) in a major telecommunications company. Their CEO had mandated that all projects would use a RAD strategy of 6 × 6. That is, all projects had to be partitioned into components that could be built by six people in six months. The senior management wanted us to give them some ideas on how to get this to work, as they did very large projects and the 6 × 6 arrangement wasn't working very well. We made the point that, although we agreed with the concept, our experience with extreme projects was that the sponsors often were unavailable for quick decisions. This leads to serious delays in projects. It would certainly compromise rapid delivery. To deliver projects in 6 × 6, we recommended that senior management adopt a 1 × 1 sponsor model. What we said was, "If senior management want 6 × 6 delivery, the project manager must be able to see his or her sponsor in one minute and get a decision in one minute." The project directors all agreed. The senior management looked at us in a strange way. We weren't invited back. The company continues to see its share price drop and its turnover rate increase.

The P Files Team Comment

Strategy is about culture as much as it is about projects. It is not acceptable for senior management to fall in love with a new development fad such as RAD, agile, or object-oriented without understanding how the new model affects their role in projects. All strategies have their strengths and weaknesses and all strategies impact the project management process.

CASE STUDY—SELECT PROJECT STRATEGY

Although you have not completed a formal risk assessment with the stakeholders, you and the RAP participants decide that a sequential release strategy is suitable for the project.

Edwina agrees that there will be three releases:

- Release 1: The complete functionality working in City 1 only.
- Release 2: The new system working with access in each city restricted to Smuthe consultants.
- Release 3: Big Bucks clients have complete access.

She wants to test the waters first. Kim is happy with the strategy, as it enables her to ensure the quality is acceptable before external clients get access. It also enables you to train the Smuthe consultants.

Sliders Revisited—eXtreme Project Management in Action

Based on the quality agreement and the selected strategy, Edwina revisits the success sliders and agrees to ease off on the time frame.

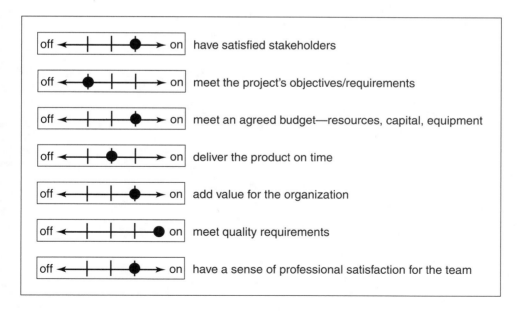

off ←——┼——┼—●——→ on	have satisfied stakeholders
off ←——●——┼——┼——→ on	meet the project's objectives/requirements
off ←——┼——┼—●——→ on	meet an agreed budget—resources, capital, equipment
off ←——┼——●——┼——→ on	deliver the product on time
off ←——┼——┼—●——→ on	add value for the organization
off ←——┼——┼——┼—● on	meet quality requirements
off ←——┼——┼—●——→ on	have a sense of professional satisfaction for the team

Analyze Risk

"Risk is part of the game if you want to sit in that chair." ∎

James T. Kirk (William Shatner)[1]

So you're getting there. You have your scope, objectives, stakeholders, benefits analysis, quality agreement, and project development strategy negotiated and agreed to by all your project partners. You're looking good!

However, the next step of the planning process is where you begin analyzing what can go wrong with your project (see Figure 12.1) and—here's the good news—what can be done to prevent disaster.

In his book *Against the Gods: The Remarkable Story of Risk*, Peter Bernstein (1996) described how organizations have been practicing risk assessment and risk management since the 1700s. For example, in the financial sector, there is a highly formalized process of risk assessment and risk control in lending. On receiving an application for a loan, the loans manager would undertake a risk assessment based on the applicant's current financial position, length and stability of employment, credit rating, amount of money requested, proposed term, proposed security, and so on. Risk control (reduction or containment) would then be applied to the loan,

---

1. *Star Trek: Generations*, David Carson, Director, Rick Berman, Writer, 1994.

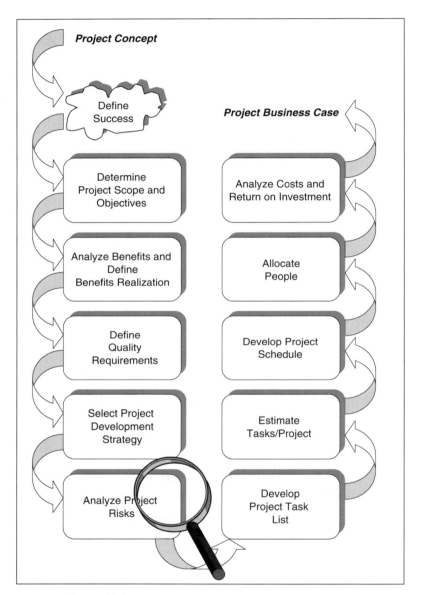

Figure 12.1
Analyze project risk and develop risk management plan

including offloading the loan, loan insurance, monitoring of payments, late payment patterns, and so on.

Managing risk is one of the most poorly understood aspects of project management. In the late 1990s, Accenture (Andersen Consulting) released a study that showed the majority of senior management did not understand the issues of project risk at all.

Project Risk Assessment Overview

However, despite the long history of risk management in broader business areas, the practice of risk management in business and IT projects has a less than remarkable[2] history. It is still too common for our group to find multimillion-dollar projects with no systematic and formal risk assessment and management process. As we outlined in the Project Pathology paper (see our Web site, www.Thomsett.com.au), one of the most interesting aspects of the major project failures we have reviewed is that most team members understood the risks of these projects before they started but the organization either had no mechanism or—worse—no willingness to address the risks. We come back to this issue later in this chapter.

In general, the management of risk involves four related processes[3] as shown in Figure 12.2. On analysis, it turns out that these processes are part of our normal lives, and risk management is simply a formalization of a day-to-day activity.

The first is generally termed *risk assessment* or *risk analysis*. This process involves the identification of risk factors that are intrinsic in the activity being undertaken. For example, in the activity of commuting from home to work, we face a number of risks:

- Is the family car working?

- Are the trains, buses, or other public transportation on time?

- Do we have to drop the kids off at school?

- Are the kids ready?

- What is the weather like?

---

2. Unless we use the word *remarkable* in a more negative light, as in it is remarkable because it has been so awful.

3. It should be noted that some experts such as Barry Boehm (1989) and others treat risk management as a separate component from risk assessment, although most experts see risk management as the overall process.

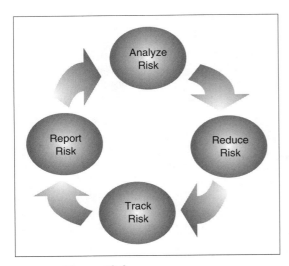

Figure 12.2
Risk management cycle

Clearly, the more risk factors involved in the activity, the higher the risk of the activity and the lower the probability of success (i.e., getting to work on time and unstressed). If you lived in an apartment next to the building in which you work, the risk involved in getting to work on time is much lower than that facing a person with a 20-mile commute that involves driving to the station, getting kids to school, taking a prework study course, and using public transportation.

The second process in risk management is the process of risk control, risk reduction, or risk containment. This process involves planning and taking action to reduce the risks and, if that is not possible, to introduce strategies to minimize the impact of failure.

To manage the risks in our commute, we could reduce them by moving closer to work, obtaining flexible working hours, or undertaking community and political action to improve public transportation.[4]

Risk management also involves the evaluation and management of the impact of failure of the activity. This is typically called risk transfer or risk impact. For example, what is the impact of failing to get to work on time?

- You will be fired.
- Your pay will be deducted.

---

4. Of course not having children would also lower the risk of your commute!

- You may miss an important meeting.

- Nothing.

Clearly, the greater the impact of failure, the greater the need for positive risk management processes. At the same time as we are attempting to reduce the risks, we could limit the impact by establishing a good reputation at work, negotiating performance agreements not linked to being at work on time, and so on.

The third activity in risk management is the constant activity of monitoring and tracking risks. This involves keeping a watch on the risk factors you have identified in analyzing the risk and, as we show later in this chapter, tracking of the indicators that show the risk is impacting your project.

The fourth component of risk management is the risk monitoring and reporting of the status of risks (particularly high risk factors), the identification of new risk factors that have emerged during the project, and reports on the effectiveness of containment strategies. This is very important, as many organizations undertake risk assessment at the beginning of projects but do not continue to monitor existing and new risks as they emerge. In the turbulent environment of today's projects, it is normal for projects to change (scope, objectives, etc.) and, as a result, for the risk of the project to also continue to change. Therefore, risk management must be an ongoing, integrated component of the management of your project.

Many Classes of Risk

Many of the books and standards on risk do not distinguish among a set of different classes of risk. For example, there is insurance risk, lending or credit risk, audit risk, gambling risk, foreign exchange risk, trading risk, and so on. In our approach to risk management we focus on two classes or types of risk:

- Project risk: The factors inherent to a project that may cause it to fail.

- Business risk: The exposure of the organization if and when the project fails.

In projects, there are two different but completely related risk considerations. The first is the inherent risk of the project that is being planned, or *project risk*. The second is the exposure or impact that the company undertaking the project faces on project failure, or *business risk*.

For example, a bank may be undertaking a project to implement new credit controls demanded by government legislation. During the RAP, the project risk is assessed by the project manager as being high because the new legislation involves complex changes to sophisticated existing information systems. The business risk is also assessed as high because if the bank does not implement the new credit controls by the deadline, it will face possible fines, loss of its trading license, and substantial public scrutiny through the media.

Simply put, the higher the project risk, the higher the probability that the project will fail and that the organization will be exposed to business risks. In addition, the higher either the business or project risks associated with the project are, the higher the level of governance should be.

The assessment of project risk and business risk requires consideration of different risk factors, but the control and management of both areas of risk is similar.

Project Risk Management

IT and business project risk management is a subset of the broader processes of business risk management. However in the past, the process of project risk assessment in business and IT projects has tended to be intuitive and hidden.

As shown in Figure 12.3, whenever a software or business guru is asked to estimate how long a project will take, he or she undertakes a most amazing process. In essence, the expert intuitively assesses factors that he or she has learned from bitter experience will influence the length of the project, assesses the impact of those factors depending on the specific tasks, adjusts the estimates by the relative weights of the factors, assesses the probability of the factors actually occurring, and then calculates an adjusted guesstimate. No wonder project people are considered clever!

Figure 12.3
Risk assessment: Mysterious and covert

In effect, project risk management is the formalization of a process that has been covert and subjective. As a result, it has been poorly understood and practiced. (Most contemporary project management texts do not even mention risk management.) Worse, this approach is totally dependent on the project manager's experience.

A Little Risk Test

You are having your first meeting with your project sponsor. Your sponsor says, "We are very excited about this new product. It is going to kill our competitors and they will take so long to match us that, by the time they have it out, there'll be no market left. As you are probably aware, I am very busy with a takeover of another company, but I'll be right behind this product. Our suppliers have promised us some new supersecret technology to help us. So, the sooner you get started the better."

How would you feel about your new project?

Of course, because the process of risk assessment and risk management has remained intuitive and covert, most business people and senior management have no idea of project risk assessment and the need for managing risks. The fact that project risk assessment has been a covert process is one of the major reasons so few organizations have adopted a formal approach to project risk management—they just don't know about it.

Project Risk Assessment

The risk of a project can be assessed by considering the following broad risk categories:

- System or product complexity (risk),
- Client or target environment (risk), and
- Team environment (risk).

Each of these categories considers different risk factors and should be treated as independently as possible. The overall project risk is the aggregation of all three risk categories.

RISK TEST ANSWER

If you have any experience in projects at all, the words of your sponsor should have struck fear in your heart. Your intuitive "risk antenna" should have gone wild when you read the test. You have a project with an aggressive sponsor who is busy on other projects, you'll probably have a fixed deadline, and you'll be using new and probably unproven technology. Get another job (unless you're a masochist).

Product or System Risk   It has long been understood that the complexity, size, degree of innovation, and other variables of the system or product being developed are a key factor in risk, estimation, and sizing. For software projects the complexity and therefore the risk of a system can generally be evaluated by considering its data complexity; that is, how many inputs, outputs, enquiries, logical internal files, and shared files are involved in the system. For business products, the internal complexity of the product and the size or organizational impact would be indicators of risk.

Other factors that affect system and product complexity are as follows:

- Function, process, and algorithm complexity;
- Complex control, decision exception, policy considerations, and mathematical operations;
- High performance requirements;
- High quality expectations;
- Innovative technology or processing requirements; and
- The degree of change implicit in the product.

A MUSEUM OF WONDER AND HORROR

It is useful for you to imagine a Museum of Modern Products that displayed all systems and products, teams, and client groups in Perspex cubes for public appreciation (or horror!). In this context, consider your system or product in comparison with others that you or your organization has undertaken. Then compare your team and your client group with others that you and your team have had experience with. Putting it all together gives you the overall project risk.

By evaluating the intrinsic system or product complexity, the person or team undertaking risk assessment can predict the risk associated with the product: Is it low, medium, or high risk? As mentioned earlier, it is important that this assessment is undertaken only by considering the software or product, not the team or target environment categories.

Client or Target Environment   For many projects, the most difficult area of risk is the target area or client group for whom the product is being developed. Many of the risks associated with this category are beyond the team's scope of control and, as we discuss later, many of the risk factors in this category defy any form of measurement.

The complexity and risk of the target or user environment are related to the following factors:

- The number of sections and departments, agencies, branches and installations (client sites) involved in developing, implementing, and using the system;
- The level of client knowledge and participation in the application and the project development process;
- The degree of support for the project from the business groups;
- The priority and impact of the application within the client area; and
- The need for physical restructuring of offices, development of new sites, and so on.

Again, as for the other risk categories, when considering the risks associated with the client area, it is important for the project team to consider the client area as independently as possible from the product risks and team risks.

Team Environment   The final category of risk involves the intrinsic risks associated with the project team. As documented by Larry Putnam and Ware Myers (1992), as well as by Boehm (1989) and Jones (1994), the most significant factors affecting project productivity, risk, and effectiveness are the capability, morale, and experience of the team members.

The complexity or risk of the team environment is related to the following factors:

- Schedules, whether fixed or flexible;
- The experience and likely stability of the project team;
- The development and estimated time frame of the project;
- Use of outside vendors or contractors; and
- The physical team and project environment.

Subjective Versus Objective Risk Assessment

Given that there are at least 100 factors that can be included in a risk model, it is difficult to gather objective measures for many of these factors. In the subjective approach, the complexity of the software is determined as simple, average, or complex, depending on the group's experience. However, for example, in a software project, the use of function points (this is a technique for estimating the size of software based on counting inputs, outputs, interfaces, enquiries, and internal files) can provide an objective measure of software complexity where there is an agreement that simply means < 100 adjusted function point (AFD); average means 100 to 1,000 AFP and complex is > 1,000 AFP.

THE DANGERS OF STATISTICS

In his book, *Programming Productivity* (1994), Capers Jones identifies 45 risk factors, which he claims account for 90% of the variance between projects. This appears impressive. However, as you probably know, there are a couple of animals that share just over 95% of the same genetic stuff as us humans. So next time you have a look at a pygmy chimpanzee or an orangutan, think about 10% variance.

METRICS—THE HOLY GRAIL

Computing has been measuring various risk factors (e.g., the difference between the productivity of highly experienced and inexperienced programmers) for over 30 years. Significant progress has been made in the objective measurement of these factors. The work of Capers Jones and his group (op cit) is particularly impressive. Put simply, there are good measures for system and team categories of risk. However, the target or client risk factors remain difficult to objectively measure. Worse, in the area of business projects, almost no measures are available.

Unfortunately, many of the risk factors are not practically measurable. For example, the risks associated with developing software for four different client groups who are engaged in advanced political warfare are clearly much higher than those associated with a product for one supportive client. To quantify such factors and their impact is beyond the practical limit for most organizations.

A sensible approach is to quantify the factors that are easily measured and use subjective group agreements for the remaining factors. We have found that this combining of subjective and objective assessment works well.

As Bernstein (1996) stated, "Both objective measurement and subjective degrees of belief are essential; neither is sufficient by itself" (p. 100).

The Risk Assessment Process

The process of risk assessment involves the same participative process as we use in all our planning and project management processes. You as the project manager, your team members, and your critical project stakeholders complete a risk questionnaire and, through a series of open discussions, you discuss the ranking of each risk factor and achieve an overall risk assessment for the project.

What is important is the discussion undertaken during the risk assessment process between team members and stakeholders. It is a powerful process for bringing into the open assumptions and different views on the project.

In our experience, it is unlikely that a team will agree on the risk ranking of all factors. Depending on their skills and background, different team members will see the project differently. If after discussion, there is still no agreement, then a voting technique where the majority wins is the best approach. If the votes are tied, the worst case is used for the risk assessment.

When planning a project, it pays to be paranoid.

Ideally within each organization, there should be a standard risk assessment questionnaire for each class of project (e.g., in-house software, package, communications, and operations). However, if there is no standard risk model for your organization, it is reasonably simple to develop one by gathering your most experienced project managers for a brainstorming session in which all factors that have caused their projects trouble are listed, discussed, ranked, and scored by level of impact. The resultant questionnaire can then be compared to the various factors discussed by Jones, Boehm, and others for confirmation of impact.

A simple and very useful risk questionnaire is shown in Figure 12.4.

It is very important that you use the short risk assessment questionnaire only for small projects (i.e., shorter than three months). For larger projects, use this model as a starting point and brainstorm with the RAP participants any additional risks that may apply to your project.[5]

---

5. There is an online version of this questionnaire available on our Web site (www.Thomsett.com.au).

Project :

PRODUCT/SYSTEM RISKS	LOW	MEDIUM	HIGH
1. Overall system/service/product	Simple	Average	Complex
2. Logical data (include files)	Simple	Average	Complex
3. I/O and enquiries or organisational impact	Simple	Average	Complex
4. Interfaces to other systems/services/products	Simple	Average	Complex
5. Functions and processes	Simple	Average	Complex
6. New business procedures/alterations	None	Some	Extensive
7. Stability of requirements	Stable	Average	Unstable
8. Performance requirements (including quality)	Low	Medium	High
9. Technology requirements	Simple	Average	Complex
10. Level of technical innovation	None	Some	Innovative

TEAM RISKS	LOW	MEDIUM	HIGH
1. Intrinsic team skills (general skills)	High	Average	Low
2. Relevant skill level with application/product	Extensive	Some	None
3. Project manager experience	Extensive	Some	None
4. Project staffing level	1 - 5	5 - 10	over 10
5. Use of contractors/part-time members	None	Some	Extensive
6. Project development length	1 - 3mths	4 - 6mths	Over 6mths
7. Schedules/deadlines	Flexible	Firm	Fixed
8. Priority of project for team	High	Average	Low
9. Team experience with hardware/software or technology	Extensive	Average	Some
10. Project team physical/support environment	Excellent	Average	Poor

ENVIRONMENT/TARGET RISKS	LOW	MEDIUM	HIGH
1. Level of client/user support	High	Medium	Low
2. Client experience with product/system	Extensive	Some	None
3. Client Project Sponsor support	High	Medium	Low/None
4. Impact on client operations (new technology, policy, etc.)	Low	Medium	High
5. Client/business expert participation	Full-time	Part-time	Ad-hoc
6. Key (Critical and Essential) stakeholders	1-2	3-10	Over 10

OVERALL PROJECT RISK	LOW	MEDIUM	HIGH

Figure 12.4
Project risk assessment: Short model

Open or Closed Voting?   If there is a high degree of trust among you, your team, and your stakeholders, you can undertake the evaluation and ranking of each risk factor in a open, free-wheeling discussion. If not, then each participant in the

ZIP YOUR LIPS

It is pretty likely that during the risk assessment process with your team and your stakeholders you'll personally disagree with many of their rankings. Just zip your lips. Remember, you will be more experienced than your team, so what they see as a high risk you may see as low (because it's easy, right?). Well you must ask yourself this question: Who is doing the project? You have a right to see if there is anything that can be done to help the team lower the risk but, if not, you must go with their assessment.

planning session completes the questionnaire privately and then you have the open discussion. This generally reduces the likelihood of groupthink.

Overall Project Risk Assessment

At the conclusion of the risk assessment process, there will be an assessment of the risk level associated with the product, the team, the target environment, and the overall project:

- Product: Low risk
- Team: Medium risk
- Target: High risk
- Overall project: Medium risk

In addition, the team will have identified a number of high risk factors that place the project at risk. It is here that the second process of risk management, risk control (or containment), is undertaken.

Risk Containment or Reduction _____

extreme tool

In many cases during the risk assessment process, the project manager and the team will be able to identify strategies to minimize or eliminate the risk factors. For example, if the team is perceived to be a high risk because of lack of experience in the development platform, the recruiting of experts or hiring expert contractors can control the risk. All high risk factors that cannot be con-

FALSE SCIENCE

Some approaches to risk assessment use probability and other scientific approaches. For example, you get assessments such as probability of risk occurring (.2) and so on. We believe that this is still a subjective technique and the use of indicators such as .2 gives business people a false sense of science and rigor. It is still all a series of guesses.

High Risk Factor
List the unresolved risk factor
Risk Factor Impact [if unresolved]
Document the impact on the project if the risk is unresolved and "hits" the project
Risk Minimization Actions
Document the possible actions available to the team, stakeholders, or the sponsor to eliminate the risk or reduce its impact
Person/s Responsible   *Identify the person/s responsible for the action*
Contingency Plan
Document the possible actions available to the team, stakeholders, or the sponsor if the risk minimization fails

Figure 12.5
Risk memorandum

strained or eliminated during the risk assessment sessions should have a risk memorandum developed for them, documenting the risk, the impact of the risk on the project, what actions the steering committee and project sponsor can take to assist in reducing the risk, and, for high-impact risks, a contingency plan. Figure 12.5 shows a sample form for this purpose.

By estimating the costs (people, dollars, time lost) of noncontainment of the risk factor, the project manager can often help focus executives on the added value of proactive risk reduction.

BEAM US UP, SCOTTY

It is really important that you identify the contingency or fallback position for all high risk factors. What you will generally find is that the contingency will be similar for all high risks (e.g., to fall back to a minimum or "quick win" deliverable; remember the previous chapter). You should never start a project without the ability, when things get too tough, to be "beamed up."

The proactive reduction or elimination of risk in a project is a classic case of win–win. The project's sponsor and clients win as they have a higher chance of success, and you and your team win because you have a higher chance of success and a lower level of pain in the project.

What is significant is that many project managers face risks in their projects that are beyond their capability (organizationally, politically, and financially) to control and manage. The technique of risk memorandums enables the people within the organization with the right level of power to assist the project manager in managing the risks.

For larger projects, you may need to go even further than risk memorandums and, with the help of your team and stakeholders, you should develop a risk management plan.

Risk Management Plans

A risk management plan is an extension of the concept of risk memorandums. The model that we use is basically a text document that details for each unresolved high risk factor the following points:

- Risk factor
- Risk impact
- Date by when the risk impact should be evident
- Risk containment strategies

- Person responsible for implementing strategy
- Date or timing for implementation
- Cost of containment strategy
- A time line or schedule for risk action (optional)

Risk Tracking and Reporting

The final process of risk management occurs during the project. Having identified the high risk factors and implemented the proactive risk reduction strategies before commencing the project, you, your team, your project sponsor, and the project stakeholders must regularly monitor and report on the following:

- The effectiveness of the implemented risk reduction strategies;
- The emergence of any new risk factors;
- The elimination of existing risk factors; and
- Any change of status of existing risk factors, for example, a medium risk factor becomes high risk.

This monitoring would typically occur during the normal project tracking and review meetings and reviews undertaken throughout the project. However, it is important that you and your team constantly adopt a risk perspective and keep your collective "risk antenna" tuned for any early warning signs of new risks or changes in the level of existing risks. For example, during a team meeting with stakeholders, a new requirement emerges. Although the impact of the new requirement would typically be assessed from an effort and time perspective, the impact of the new requirement on risk should also be carefully evaluated and reported to the sponsor and stakeholders.

Risk Management Committee   In larger projects, it is useful to convene a risk management committee. This committee is usually a subset of the project steering committee and would include the project sponsor, the project manager and a representative from internal and, in some cases, external auditing. We suggest that after each project steering committee meeting, the risk management committee has its meeting. The risk management committee would review the risk management plan and the risk reporting documents.

Shooting the Messenger

Often, the process of risk management is perceived as negative and, in fact, it does focus on what can go wrong rather than what can go right. However, it is important for you and your project sponsor to realize that proactive reduction of risk before the project starts is more effective and less expensive than reactive reduction of risk impact during the project.

We have found that in many companies, there is a tendency to see the process of risk assessment, risk memorandums, and so on as "wimpy" and "butt-covering." Although we find this attitude unbelievable and unprofessional, in the macho, go for it, cracking-an-all-nighter culture of many companies, we can certainly see why such a view exists.

In our workshops, we use the example of Indiana Jones running down numerous tunnels, ducking the horrible things that spring out of walls, leaping over pits, and mixing with spiders, snakes, rats, and so on as the exemplar of the project hero. However, we also make the point that in Indy's projects, his team often ends up impaled, the precious artifact he went into the tunnel after is either lost or stolen by his enemies, and, most important, the most interesting archeological find—the tunnel itself—is destroyed. As we discussed in the last chapter, in the real world, these projects fail. It's just in the movies that they work.

Don't be an Indiana Jones. Analyze your risks before going into your project, take some protection with you, and have a "beam me up" mechanism. You owe it to your team, your stakeholders, and your company.

THE P FILES EPISODE 9: INDIANA JONES IS A WUSS

We had been contracted to assist an organization in managing a huge $1 billion project. We were meeting the elite project managers whom the company had assigned to the project. Throughout the meeting, all eyes kept turning to Clint (the alpha manager of the mob) to see how he was reacting to what we were saying. He wasn't happy. Finally, he couldn't hold it in and he burst out, "Look, you fancy consultants might know a lot about managing projects. But, in this organization, we know a lot about surviving them!!!" Everyone cheered.

The P Files Team Comment

Clint's reaction reflects a common view about project risk management. It has been said to us many times by hard-nosed senior managers that they pay project managers to deal with risk. Why should the senior managers bother with risk management? This is a serious issue for you and you must be firm in engaging executives to assist you in managing the risks in your project. Remember, a great project manager knows when to ask for assistance.

CASE STUDY—ANALYZE RISK

You explain the concept of risk to Edwina and the RAP participants and together you complete the following risk assessment:

Project: *Connext*

PRODUCT/SYSTEM RISKS		LOW		MEDIUM		HIGH
1.	Overall system/service/product	Simple	✓	Average		Complex
2.	Logical data (include files)	Simple	✓	Average		Complex
3.	I/O and enquiries or organizational impact	Simple	✓	Average		Complex
4.	Interfaces to other systems/services/products	✓ Simple		Average		Complex
5.	Functions and processes	✓ Simple		Average		Complex
6.	New business procedures/alterations	✓ None	✓	Some		Extensive
7.	Stability of requirements	✓ Stable		Average		Unstable
8.	Performance requirements (including quality)	Low		Medium	✓	High
9.	Technology requirements	Simple	✓	Average		Complex
10.	Level of technical innovation	✓ None		Some		Innovative

TEAM RISKS		LOW		MEDIUM		HIGH
1.	Intrinsic team skills (general skills)	✓ High		Average		Low
2.	Relevant skill level with application/product	✓ Extensive		Some		None
3.	Project manager experience	✓ Extensive		Some		None
4.	Project staffing level	✓ 1–5		5–10		Over 10
5.	Use of contractors/part-time members	None	✓	Some		Extensive
6.	Project development length	1–3 months	✓	4–6 months		Over 6 months
7.	Schedules/deadlines	✓ Flexible		Firm		Fixed
8.	Priority of project for team	✓ High		Average		Low
9.	Team experience with hardware/software or technology	✓ Extensive		Average		Some
10.	Project team physical/support environment	✓ Excellent		Average		Poor

ENVIRONMENT/TARGET RISKS		LOW		MEDIUM		HIGH
1.	Level of client/user support	✓ High		Medium		Low
2.	Client experience with product/system	Extensive		Some	✓	None
3.	Client project sponsor support	✓ High		Medium		Low/None
4.	Impact on client operations (new technology, policy etc.)	✓ Low		Medium		High
5.	Client/business expert participation	Full-time	✓	Part-time		Ad hoc
6.	Key (critical and essential) stakeholders	1–2	✓	3–10		Over 10

OVERALL PROJECT RISK	LOW	✓ MEDIUM	HIGH

You review the high risk factors and complete the risk memorandums.

High Risk Factor *Client experience with the system*
Risk Impact *The Smuthe consultants are not familiar with using the Internet or Web sites for business.*
Risk Minimization Actions *The Smuthe consultants will be trained extensively using Release 1.* *Use of prototypes to gain early familiarity.*
Contingency Plan *Hire experienced consultants from real estate area who are familiar with Internet and Web-based business.* *Delay launch of site to Big Bucks.*

The contingency plan causes some debate in the RAP session.

Develop Task Lists

"I don't see any method at all, sir." ■

Captain Willard (Martin Sheen)[1]

Well, it's time to relax, as the next step in developing your project plan is probably the easiest of all the steps.

Develop Project Task Lists

Although this planning step is often considered a no-brainer,[2] it is a very critical step, as forgetting a task in a project can be a catastrophe in the estimation and risk process (see Figure 13.1). In fact, forgetting project tasks is one of the more common reasons for poor estimation and project slippage.

The process of developing a task list for your project is fairly straightforward:

- If your organization has a standard work breakdown structure, project development cycle, or methodology, you use that as a starting point.

[1.] *Apocalypse Now,* Francis Ford Coppola, Director; John Milius and Francis Ford Coppola, Writers, 1979.
[2.] Remember our concerns with the concept of "no brains."

175

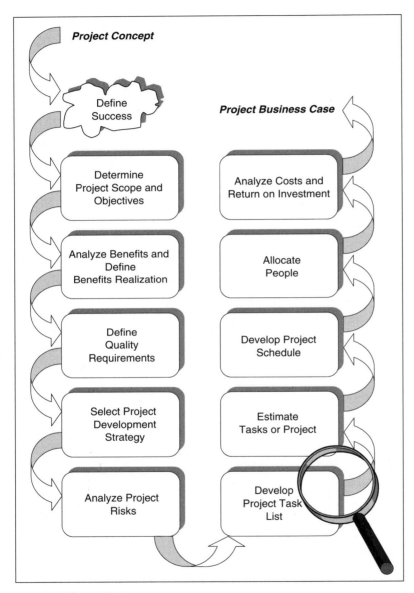

Figure 13.1
Developing a task list

- If not, you brainstorm the tasks required for your project using your technical team members, business and support experts, and stakeholders.

- If you have a methodology, you still need to fine-tune your methodology by brainstorming any new tasks (i.e., any that are not in your standard methodology) and any standard tasks that you can delete for your project's task lists.

- Review your task list with as many experts as possible.

- Repeat the process, breaking up the tasks into smaller subtasks (work breakdown).

Clearly, if you are using the RAP process that we have been discussing throughout this book, you'll have your team and your critical stakeholders planning the project with you. You'll have all the people you'll need to do the task listing without a problem.

Methodologies: A Brief Introduction

The computing profession has had access to very comprehensive packaged sets of work breakdown structure or task lists or, as they are more commonly termed, methodologies since the early 1970s.

However, all project or system development approaches are based on a long understood and commonsense approach to solving problems that we first saw in Kroberg and Bagnall's (1974) wonderful book, *The Universal Traveller.*[3] This step-by-step approach is also well suited to the monolithic or waterfall project development strategy that we explored in Chapter 10. Kroberg and Bagnall's model is overviewed in Figure 13.2.

All packaged methodologies provide a framework of development phases that are broken into subphases that, in turn, are further broken down into tasks, and so on. This partitioning or leveling of tasks into smaller subtasks is the essence of work breakdown. The breaking down of tasks into smaller units is essential for estimation and scheduling, as we discuss in later chapters.

1. Tailor Methodology

The easiest way to do this activity is for one of the participants in the planning session to read aloud the major phases and subphases contained in your organization's standard methodology. If your project needs the task, list it on a whiteboard or a public document. If anyone in the planning session doesn't understand what is

---

[3.] Kroberg and Bagnall's book was originally written for architectural students.

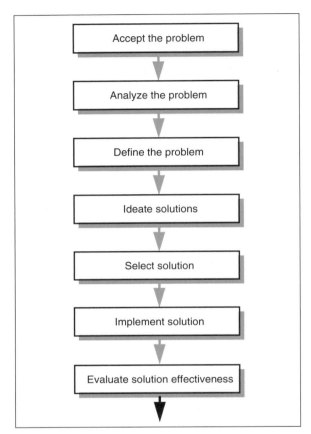

Figure 13.2
The universal traveler approach

involved in the listed task, have the reader get more information from the supporting documents associated with the methodology.

2. Brainstorm Project Tasks

If you do not have access to some predeveloped task list, you'll need to develop one for your project using the experience of your team and as many other project experts as possible. It is also useful to see if you can access other project plans or task lists from other project managers. In addition, there are fairly good task lists available in some of the books we have already referenced in this book.[4] In fact, any book on a

---

4. Christopher Myers (1993) is a good source for basic task lists for business projects.

DON'T GET TOO LINEAR

A good tip here is to avoid the sequencing or scheduling of tasks while you are brainstorming task lists. You can schedule or sequence the tasks later in scheduling the planning process. Too much focus on sequence of tasks can get you into linear thinking that often limits the flow of the brainstorm. Let the creative juices flow when you are listing tasks and don't eliminate tasks too quickly.

new technique such as object orientation or visual development tools will give you the basis for a methodology.

3. Fine-Tune Your Methodology

Even with a "packaged" methodology, you'll generally need to add new tasks that reflect the uniqueness of your project. Be careful here, as many methodologies are focused on system development and often miss tasks associated with the clerical, policy, and business process redesign associated with many projects. By having your business stakeholders at your RAP session, you should have this issue well covered.

4. Review with Other Experts

Even in a RAP session you probably won't have all the experts you need in your project. It thus makes sense to check your "first cut" task list with as broad a group of experts as you can. In many projects, you should also check with your external suppliers and vendors. In one project, our client was having trouble developing a task list for a highly innovative project. They engaged a consultant recommended by a vendor. Within two days, a complete and, as it turns out, very accurate task list was created. In our opinion, this was a very wise investment.

5. Repeat the Process

This step breaks or partitions the "first cut" task list into smaller subtasks as shown in Figure 13.3. As we discuss later in this chapter, there are a number of considerations when creating a more detailed work breakdown structure. However,

TAKE A BREATHER

Once you have developed your task list, take a break. Have a coffee or, better still, do something completely different, such as walking outside and listening to some Megadeth or Mahler (both are good for getting in the project mood). After the break, go back to your task list and you'll find some new tasks. Remember, you can't be too careful here—double-check and re-double-check.

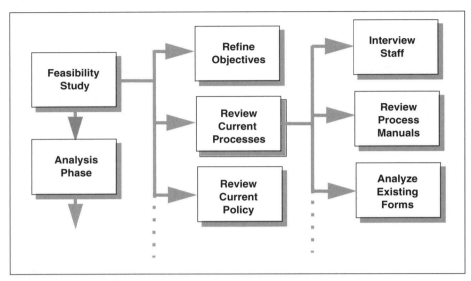

Figure 13.3
Work breakdown structures

the overriding consideration here is that by breaking up higher level tasks (e.g., requirements analysis) into smaller subtasks (e.g., interview business experts, review current business processes, etc.), you get a better understanding of what is required to complete the task and this improves the accuracy of your estimates.

Simply put, the better you understand what you have to do, the better your estimates will be.

The Amazing 5/10 Day Rule

One of the long-held beliefs in traditional business project management is the concept of partitioning or breaking down into subtasks of 5 to 10 days in duration. On reflection, this rule reflects the process culture view of the world (remember Chapter 4?) and has little or no relevance to the project world. The concept of 5- to 10-day tasks with associated deliverables has a lot of appeal in a world driven by hourly, daily, weekly, and monthly processes.

DON'T SWITCH OFF YOUR BRAIN

Every time someone chants a mantra such as "All tasks must be 5 days. No more. No less," ask them, "Why?" You'll often be amazed by the answer. Typically it will be a variation on "I don't know. I think someone told me years ago."

In reality, the degree to which you can partition a task depends on the nature of the task, not the calendar, as we discuss later in this chapter.

DON'T BECOME A NAG

If you agree with a team member that the task will take 10 elapsed days, don't check everyday how he or she is going. Just think how you would feel if your manager was "nagging" you every day. Trust the person. You can't do much else when you really think about it.

The real issue here is how often you need to track tasks for completion. As shown in Figure 13.4, Task A is 10 days in duration, Task B is 6 days, and Task C is 4 days. As we cover in more detail in Chapter 17, the process of task tracking should be driven by the "0/100%" approach (either the task has not started or it is finished). In this case, the tracking cycle is 10 days for Task A, 6 days for Task B, and 4 days for Task C.

The smaller you partition the tasks, the finer the granularity of the tracking process. You really need to consider this, as it determines the cycle of your project tracking.

However, as you break down tasks into smaller tasks you need to consider the guidelines presented in the following sections.

The Risk of the Project or Task

Clearly, the higher the risk of the project, the smaller you should partition the tasks. The justification for this guideline is fairly obvious. The higher the risk of the project, the more likely it will be subject to variances in requirements, scope creep,

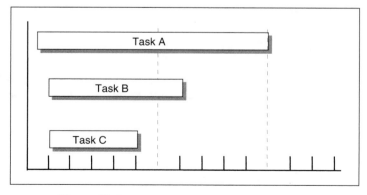

Figure 13.4
Task size and tracking granularity

unexpected problems, and estimation errors. By partitioning into smaller tasks, you increase the tracking granularity and this should give you greater control. You can apply the same guideline to tasks, as some tasks are higher risks than others.

The Nature of the Task

There are some tasks for which breaking into smaller units simply doesn't make any sense. For example, at one of our clients, some un-informed managers attempted to break project tasks into deliverables of half an hour. This resulted in some bizarre situations. In undertaking the systems analysis of some complex business processes, the natural cycle was to examine each business process in turn. On average, the modeling of the process and the related business rules involved a minimum of 5 days' work and more than 10 days in some cases. The systems analysts were forced to create "abstract" deliverables of half an hour in duration. We finally suggested that they report in the form:

Reporting time: 9:00–9:30 am   Deliverable: Half a thought

Reporting time: 9:30–10:00 am   Deliverable: Rest of the thought

It made the point and the system was abandoned with significant embarrassment to the managers.

The Experience of the Team Members

The more experienced the team members, the higher you should make the level of partitioning. For example, for a new and inexperienced team you might want to partition the tasks into the smallest units you can. The more experienced the team, the larger and longer you can leave the tasks. For an experienced team, you could leave the tasks at up to three months in duration and expect that the team would partition the three-month task at their own discretion.

The Degree of Trust

The more you trust your team, the higher you can leave the partitioning. By breaking tasks into about five days in duration, you are giving a hidden message to the team that you will be "checking up" on them regularly. You need to examine the different messages, relating to trust, between leaving a team with 15-day tasks rather than 5-day tasks.

If you can't trust your team, get one you can.

To summarize, it is difficult to give simple rules when partitioning tasks into smaller tasks. You'll have to use your judgment here and hopefully the preceding guidelines will help you here.

A Moral Dilemma

The process of task listing also points out an interesting effect of the spectacular growth in technology and technology options.

In the 1960s and 1970s, the choice of development options (i.e., what technology was going to be used to implement the system) was extremely limited. Usually the choice was binary: COBOL[5] on the mainframe or manual. As shown in Figure 13.5, in the 1990s, development options are virtually unlimited.

In Figure 13.5, the team is concurrently analyzing the requirements for the system while they are evaluating alternative package solutions. The system requirements are then compared with the initial evaluation of package system options.

Matching the requirements against the package software functionality provides at least three development options. Scenario 1 is that there are no packages that fit the requirements and the team will develop a tailored in-house solution (there are a number of suboptions within this option). Scenario 2 is that the package "fits" the requirements perfectly and the development is a package installation. Scenario 3 is to modify the package to fit the requirements.

As you can see, each scenario has different tasks involved; hence the dilemma.

Until the team members have both understood the requirements and evaluated alternative packages, they cannot professionally eliminate any of the scenarios. In addition, until they have eliminated all unsuitable scenarios, they cannot estimate how long the project will take! This dilemma is becoming even more complex as development scenarios proliferate through new technology and languages.

There are a number of additional implications of this dilemma. First, the process of task listing does not make much sense beyond the "if" test.

Of course, you should recognize this as an example of the real-time or scenario planning approach we introduced in Chapter 3. The solution to the dilemma is to estimate the worst case scenario (usually tailored development) using the techniques we cover in the next chapter with a more accurate estimate to the "if" test. Then, once you have decided which option is the most viable, you can provide a second estimate for the remainder of the project. This is often called *two-stage quotation*.

---

5. For purists, Assembler and FORTRAN were other language options.

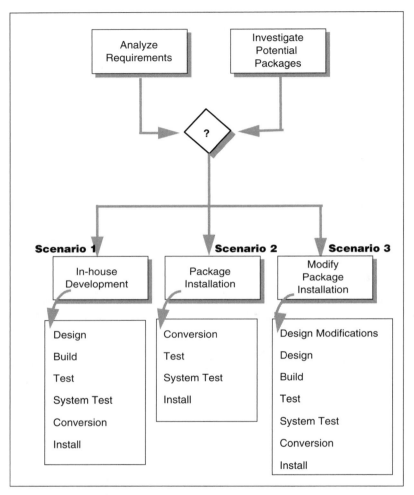

Figure 13.5
Task listing dilemma

Where Is the Moral Dilemma?

The moral dilemma is clear. The easiest route to take in solving the existence of multiple development options is to eliminate them early, choose the option that is of most interest to you, or hide them from your project sponsor and stakeholders. You choose whether you go with the good side or the dark side.

Scenario and Real-Time Planning _____

The situation just raised is now the most common in extreme projects. The increasing rate of technology innovation and the rate of turbulence in the project environment mean that it is increasingly rare for you to be able to predict in detail all the tasks required to complete a project.

Even if you could, the rate of change in your project would condemn you to a fate worse than death: the dreaded reschedule and reprinting of the hundreds of pages that make up your schedule, only to have to repeat the effort the following week!

The solution is to start considering your project as a journey with a clear endpoint. However, the journey to that endpoint is made up not of tasks, but a series of scenarios (alternative routes). Each route has a different series of events that mark a major point in that route. An event could be any of the following:

- A deliverable,
- An agreement (e.g., stakeholders agree to support the project),
- A proof of concept,
- A working prototype, or
- The arrival of a key person.

Each project and each scenario has different events and the people at your RAP session will have to help you identify the relevant events. Then, as we show in

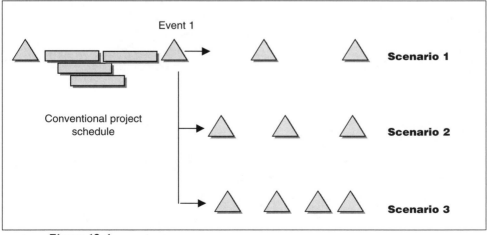

Figure 13.6
Scenario planning

Figure 13.6, the conventional process of task lists and scheduling is only undertaken for the first event.

This eXtreme technique is more suited to the contemporary project environment. Indeed a number of our clients use this model for project funding as well. For example, a project might be budgeted in the worst case scenario for $10,000,000. However, the only committed budget is the $100,000 required to get to Event 1 of the project. If it is clear that, for example, Event 1 reveals that the project is no longer viable, the remainder of the $10,000,000 is available for other projects.

We can now move on to a very interesting and controversial planning step: estimating your project.

THE P FILES EPISODE 10: THE INSIGNIFICANT TASK

Probably the worst project we have ever seen was a project for a major government department. A newly appointed project director saw the project with fresh eyes. She knew immediately that the project was in trouble. It had been going for nine months and the team was working 60-hour-plus weeks to meet a deadline three months away. Some 5,000 business people were dependent on the project and, worse, had already given up people to pay for the project. The project was capturing sensitive information on more than one million people. The sponsor had promised the minister that the project would be live on the deadline. After a brief review, we agreed with the director's assessment that the project was in serious trouble. We convened a meeting with the project managers, critical stakeholders, and the sponsor (a deputy secretary). The deputy secretary had promised his minister that the project would be live on the deadline. As we gently tried to explain the situation, the sponsor went nuts. He started to plan the project, on the fly, to try and meet the deadline. "OK, OK," he said, "What do we need to do? Yes, we need to scan all the data. OK, let's get all the data entered by the end of next week." A hand went up from the data administrator: "Errr, boss, we don't have a database management system yet. We must have missed it in the plan." Three months to go and the team had forgotten to buy a mainframe database management system! That task took seven months and ended up in litigation. The sponsor and many of the project team members lost their jobs. We'll have more on this bizarre case later.

The P Files Team Comment

We tend to overlook the criticality of getting the right tasks right. It is one of the easier processes in planning, but it should never be done by one person and it should always be reviewed, reviewed, and reviewed again. Missing a task is a case of instant "out of control" for your project.

CASE STUDY—TASK LISTING

You begin to focus on the tasks required. Using scenario planning, you, Kim, and Joan identify the major tasks required to develop the Web site that will run only in City 1 (Release 1, shown in the following diagram). You do not identify detailed tasks for Releases 2 or 3.

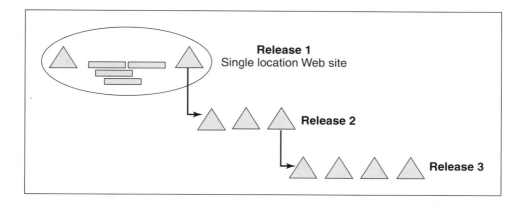

Initial Task List, Release 1

- Analyze data requirements.
- Develop basic data design.
- Design database (client and accommodation).
- Analyze Web content.
- Design Web content.
- Prototype screen design (look and feel).
- Design basic Smuthe training requirements.
- Determine hardware requirements.
- Analyze site performance requirements.
- Build HTML.
- Build database.
- Test Web site.
- Train City 1 Smuthe consultants.
- Design new work processes for consultants.

Kim and Joan agree to discuss and review the initial task list with their stakeholders.

Estimate Tasks

"I don't know. I'm making this up as we go." ∎

Indiana Jones (Harrison Ford)[1]

This is where the rubber hits the road. All the work you have now done in the RAP session leads to this point—the estimation of the project (see Figure 14.1).

Poor project estimation causes organizations and project sponsors to make decisions based on poor information. The business case is clearly dependent on accurate estimates of both the costs and benefits of the project. Most important, how you approach the process of estimation is the true measure of your professionalism.

Causes of Estimation Error

As revealed by Jones (1994) and many other experts, both IT and business project teams have an extremely poor track record in the area of estimation. However, unlike many other experts, we believe that IT people, in particular, are very good at

---

[1] *Raiders of the Lost Ark,* Steven Spielberg, Director; George Lucas and Philip Kaufman, Writers, 1981.

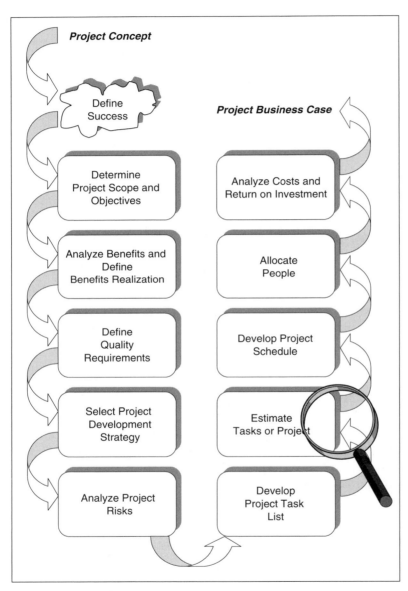

Figure 14.1
Estimating tasks and developing project quotations

estimating. Other factors just confuse the estimation process. In fact, it is our experience that the factors covered in the following sections are the most significant causes of estimation error.

Misestimating the Scope

This is such an obvious problem that it is amazing it still is a problem in business and IT projects. As shown in Figure 14.2, Barry Boehm's (1989) research shows that the *average* estimation error in estimates made before the project's scope and objectives are clarified is +400% to –400%. Yet many IT and business experts are constantly expected to provide estimates at the early stages of projects before any detailed understanding of the project's scope and objectives is gained.

Misestimating the Stakeholders' Effort

This has already been covered throughout this book when examining the role of stakeholders in projects. The process of estimation involves you making assumptions about your critical stakeholders' commitment (time and effort). For example,

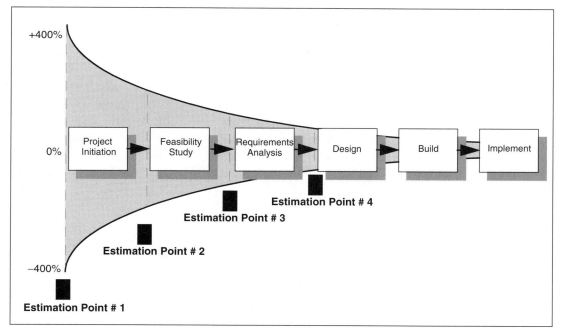

Figure 14.2
Project estimation points

you may have gained an estimate and commitment from another project manager of five days to modify an interrelated system from which your project is going to get vital data. However, the related project manager is pressured by another stakeholder to deliver a different change. As a result, the system interface takes 15 days instead of five days. Your project is 10 days behind schedule, your estimates look bad, and you look bad.

 Most estimation errors occur before you estimate.

Misunderstanding the Quality

This is one of the major estimation errors made in projects. Without the negotiation of a formal quality agreement (Chapter 10), you are making assumptions that have a serious impact on your estimates. For example, in making your estimates, you have assumed that your critical stakeholders do not require full system documentation. However, halfway through your project, you get a new requirement that full system documentation, including online tutorials, is required. Your original estimate is now wrong by at least 100%.

Miscalculating the Project Risk

Miscalculating or missing a major high-risk factor can result is massive estimation errors. As we discussed in Chapter 12, project risk assessment examines over 70 factors that can cause problems in your project and contribute to estimation errors. In developing your original estimate, you and your team assume that you will have access to a room in which you can all work together. However, that room is not available and your team is split across two building levels. You can add more than 30% to your original estimates.

ESTIMATION IS POLITICS

The process of estimation is also heavily influenced by a series of well-understood and private political "games" such as The Low Bid, where a project manager or sponsor believes that the organization will not be prepared to fund the project. The Low Bid game involves a deliberate lowering of the estimates to get the project approved and started. The whole game works when the organization is not prepared to stop the project once the real costs are revealed. This and many other estimation games are discussed on our Web site (www.Thomsett.com.au).

Forgetting Tasks

We covered this in Chapter 13. Forgetting a task that will take 40 days of elapsed time causes 40 days of estimation error when you discover the task (generally at the last moment).

Misunderstanding Your People

Extensive research by Jones (1994), Boehm (1989), and others has shown conclusively that the skills and experience of your team and your stakeholders are among the biggest factors in productivity and estimates of productivity. When making your initial estimates, you've assumed that you will have a skilled business analyst with at least two years' experience in the business area that your project is focused on. Instead, you are allocated a new recruit straight out of college. Your estimates are now seriously wrong.

In effect, as shown in Figure 14.3, these factors can be seen as a series of filters that clean up your estimates as they are applied. In effect, as you are undertaking the RAP process described in this book, you're improving your estimates as a by-product.

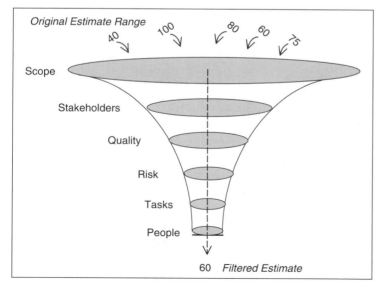

Figure 14.3
The funnel of increasing accuracy

Estimation Overview and Principles

Before we examine the estimation process, we need to do some linguistic house-cleaning.

Getting Our Language Right

Whenever the term *estimate*[2] is used in business and IT projects, we are using it to represent one of three completely different concepts, as described next.

Guess   A *guess* is an uninformed prediction. For example, ask 20 people "How many jelly beans are in the world now?" The answers will vary dramatically because people don't know—they are guessing. Statisticians will tell you that when guessing is happening, the more people you ask, the more *random* the answers become! When you ask your team "How long will Task A take?" and the answers are 10 days, 12 weeks, and one year, your team is guessing.

Guesstimate   A *guesstimate* is an informed and expert prediction based on informal or undocumented experience. This is the most common form of estimation in IT and business projects. It is also called *expert judgment*. Although purists dismiss guesstimation as a poor alternative, our experience is that guesstimation is more accurate than the standard estimation techniques (provided the issues covered in this chapter are addressed). The technique of wide-band Delphi covered in this chapter is a powerful guesstimation technique suitable for all business and IT projects. With relevant experts, when you ask, "How long will Task A take?" and the answers are 10 days, 12 days, and 20 days, your team is guesstimating.

Estimate   An *estimate* is an informed and expert prediction based on formal or documented experience, measures, or metrics. For engineering, IT, and construction projects there are a number of estimating techniques based on either static (simple variables and total effort results) or dynamic (complex variables and effort/duration results) calculations. In IT, the widely adopted function point technique (and its variations) is an example of a static technique. Barry Boehm's COCOMO 1 and 2 is an example of a dynamic technique. The problems with these estimation techniques are that they require organization-specific metrics and they are not suitable for business and infrastructure projects. In addition, these techniques are more suited for conventional software projects, not e-projects. Most important, they address only the technology-specific components of the business project.

---

2. Other alternatives to the word *estimate* include "gut feel," "wild ass guess," "wet finger in the air," "making it up," and so on.

Project Estimation Points

The estimation process is an incremental one. In all industries it is understood that the accuracy of estimates improves as the project progresses. As shown in Figure 14.2, the accuracy of IT and business estimates can be dramatically improved during the initial project development phases. It should be noted that, whereas in other industries such as building and construction the accuracy of estimates at the concept/feasibility study phase can be on the order of plus or minus 50%,[3] extensive research by experts such as Barry Boehm (1989) has shown that larger estimate variances are experienced in IT projects.

It is important to recognize that the estimates you make early in the system development life cycle are probably incorrect and, by using sensitivity analysis (discussed later), project sponsors, and steering committee members should gain some idea of the potential range of estimation accuracy.

Estimation Principles _____

You should remember the following principles when undertaking project estimates. These principles have been shown to improve estimation with any formal techniques that are being applied.

Avoid Single-Person Estimation

The estimates for a project should be undertaken by more than one person and preferably in a team-based estimation process as described in this chapter. An estimate from one person includes biases and does not benefit from the approach of the project from various viewpoints and expertise. If you estimate for another person you are making two estimation errors. The first is that you are making an estimate based on how much effort you would need (generally flawed); second, you are estimating how different the other person is from you (seriously flawed).

Always Complete a Risk Assessment Prior to Estimation

As we discussed in Chapter 12, there are at least 70 factors that have been shown to affect project cost, quality, and duration. Any estimate undertaken without a formal risk assessment as described earlier is incorrect. At a minimum, you should never

---

3. It should also be noted that for high-risk building projects such as the Sydney Opera House and the New Australian Parliament House, the building industry experiences estimation errors of +500% and greater.

estimate without a good understanding of what we call the "Top 10" factors[4] (see Figure 14.4). These 10 factors have been shown by Jones (1994) to be the biggest influence on a project's productivity, cost, and effort.

Where Possible, Use Relevant Experts

You should determine whether there have been similar projects in your organization or other organizations and whether there are experts such as vendors or consultants who could give you advice about project estimates.

Always Carefully Document Estimating Assumptions

You will always be making a number of assumptions when undertaking estimates. The Risk Assessment process covers many of the assumptions, but you should follow a careful process of documenting assumptions such as your access to key people, the relevant skill levels of your project team members, and so on.

The Top 10 Project Factors

1. Team skills and experience
2. Level and quality of executive sponsorship
3. Level and quality of stakeholder buy-in
4. System or product size
5. System or product complexity
6. Required product quality
7. Development tools and environment
8. Level of innovation
9. Product requirement stability
10. Schedule constraint

Figure 14.4
The Top 10 project factors

---

4.   These factors are also useful as the basis of a quick and dirty risk assessment.

Review the Work Breakdown Structures

As we discussed earlier, one of the most common causes of poor estimation is the missing of major tasks such as education, documentation, and so on. As we discussed in Chapter 13, you should always check and re-check your project task list.

Always Undertake Sensitivity Analysis

Your initial estimates for a project should be stated as a range from best case (i.e., everything going better than expected) to worst case (i.e., the project experiences major difficulty). The use of single-figure estimation and fixed price quotes should be avoided at Estimation Points 1 and 2 at a minimum. This is a major concern as most business and IT project managers have been taught to estimate in single figures. Other professionals involved in estimating such as accountants, economists, and quantity surveyors estimate in ranges. The use of sensitivity analysis is widely adopted in the construction, economics, and statistical areas and is well suited to IT and business projects.

JUST SAY NO

In many cases, the best estimate is no estimate. As we cover later, it is very common (too common, in fact) for business and IT project managers to be expected to give "ballpark" estimates before they have had a chance to really understand the business requirements. This practice is a game that has been played by both business and IT management for years. The "ballpark" becomes the expectation and you have been made a sucker.

The Detailed Estimation Process

The recommended estimation process for business and IT projects is outlined in Figure 14.5. It involves slightly different steps for software developments and business and infrastructure projects such as PC installation, mainframe upgrades, LAN installation, wide area network (WAN) installation, and so on.

As we noted earlier, whereas there has been extensive research into techniques such as function points for estimating software development, there has been little research into formal estimation techniques for business and infrastructure projects.

As for all our planning techniques, the process of estimation is team-based and participative. This is very important even if you are using an estimation technique such as function points. If you do not have a team formed when the estimates are required, at a minimum, you must involve key stakeholders, peer project managers,

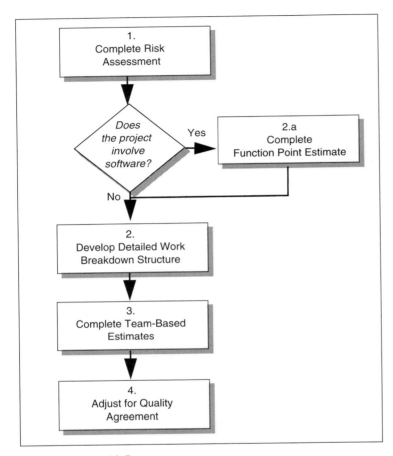

Figure 14.5
The generic estimation process

and relevant IT and other technical support people. Again, the RAP process handles this perfectly.

When the team is created, the initial estimates must be revisited to enable team members to provide their input.

Saying No Revisited

The process of estimation can be negated by the need for senior management and other people to obtain quick answers to the question "How long will Project X take?" The process of project estimation must be taken seriously and professionally. In many cases, a "quick" estimate commits organizations to project investments, which, had a more professional approach to the estimation been undertaken, the organization would never have undertaken.

Terms such as "gut feel," "ballpark," and "professional judgment" are often excuses for poor estimation made under pressure. Project sponsors should take responsibility for ensuring that the estimates for their projects are produced in a professional manner.

Producing a reasonable project estimate requires time, effort, and commitment from the project sponsor, project manager, team members, and relevant stakeholders. The time and cost of professional estimation will be paid back many times in the improvement of decision making on project investments.

The quick "ballpark" quickly becomes a slow nightmare.

A Review of Risk Assessment

As we covered in detail in Chapter 12, risk assessment is the formalization of an "intuitive" process that has always been undertaken by project managers when planning a project.

Risk is critical in understanding the dynamics of projects and improving estimating accuracy. Project risk has an impact on four key project management concerns.

In general, the higher the risk of a project, the lower the expected quality, the higher the estimates and costs, and the longer the schedule. Conversely, the higher the required quality for the project's deliverables, the higher the risk; the shorter the schedules for the project, the higher the risk; the more severe the cost constraints, the higher the risk and; the higher the skills profile of the team, the lower the project risk should be.

The process of risk assessment is critical to ensuring that as many factors as possible are considered before you begin the estimation of effort and cost. The evidence is clear that high-risk projects have higher levels of incorrect estimation and lower probabilities of success. A complete risk model ensures that the project owner and steering committee are fully aware of the dynamic of the project that they are about to approve and the likely inaccuracy of the estimates.

Having completed the project risk assessment, you and your team can undertake the next step in estimation. If the project involves software development, the team would undertake a function point analysis and estimate. However, for all projects, the development of a project task list or work breakdown structure is required for the team-based estimation process.

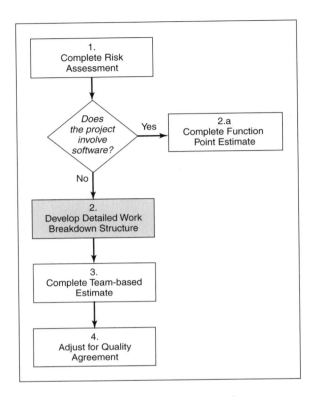

The use of two or more estimating techniques enables a multipoint correlation. For example, if the estimates from function points are in the same "ballpark" as those derived from wide-band Delphi, then you should have a higher degree of confidence in your team's estimates.

Develop a Work Breakdown Structure

The development of a task list or work breakdown structure for the project is a relatively simple yet important step. Within a typical system or product development model, phases are broken into tasks and tasks are broken into subtasks (remember Chapter 13).

The process of work breakdown or task listing is essential for estimation, as it ensures that the team understands what work has to be done. One of the most common causes of poor estimation is simple failure to list all tasks required. In the team-based project estimation session, the use of experts and full participation by the team and stakeholders usually results in an accurate task list.

Having developed the work breakdown structure for the project, the project manager and the team can begin to develop the detailed estimates for each task.

Complete a Function Point Estimate

If the project involves software, it is useful to see if you can apply a function point estimate. Jones (1994) and many others have written comprehensive books on function point estimation so, if you need more detail, check out their material. Of course, there are other software estimation techniques (e.g., COCOMO), and you might want to explore these as well.

However, the following quick and dirty approach is a great start.[5]

1. Count the number of logical data files and user views, not physical database files.
2. Multiply by 10 (average weight for file complexity).
3. Multiply by 5 (files are on average 20%–25% of total function point).
4. Adjust by –30% for low risk, 0% for medium risk, and +30% for high risk projects.

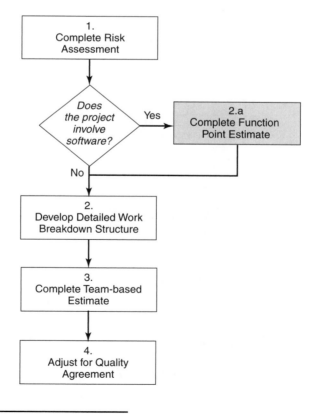

5. *Capers Jones Applied Software Measurement,* New York, McGraw-Hill, 1996. *Worldwide Software Develop-ment Benchmark,* International Software Benchmarking Standards Group. Thanks to Peter Hill.

This will give you a very rough guide to the size of the software component. You can then use the following productivity factors to derive a "first cut" estimate in hours of effort:

- Visual development environments (e.g., Visual Basic, Microsoft Access, Power-builder, etc.): 2 to 4 hours per function point.

- Hybrid development environments (C++, third generation language [3rd GL], and visual front-end, Natural, etc.): 6 to 8 hours per function point.

- 3rd GL development environment (COBOL, PL/1, etc.): 14 to 18 hours per function point.

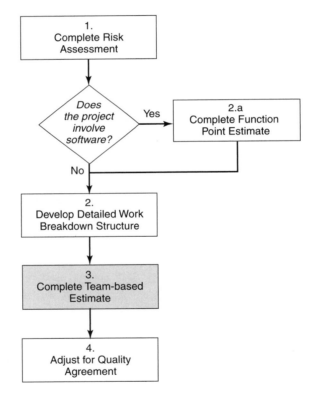

Complete Team-Based Estimates

In the absence of any formal estimating history, estimation in many projects would be better termed guesstimating.

ZIP YOUR LIPS AGAIN

The team will be conscious of your reaction when they are estimating. Be careful that you don't get into behaviors that influence the estimation process. So, avoid "Whhhat!!!" or "Holy Fang" exclamations when the team comes up with really big numbers.

The following technique for guesstimating based on the Delphi technique developed by Herman Kahn of the Hudson Institute has been shown to be very effective in many projects. It is a team-based technique that is easily embedded in the RAP process.

At least three people (preferably relevant experts) need to be involved in the estimation process for the technique to be fully effective. It involves nine simple steps:

1. **Information sharing**: If the team has not been involved in the RAP process, you must provide team members and stakeholders with the relevant information regarding the project (i.e., the business case, quality requirements, etc.).
2. **Review project risk**: If it has not already been done, you should conduct a formal risk assessment with all participants.
3. **Review the work breakdown structure**: Review and refine the work breakdown structure for your project or the phase or release you are going to be estimating.
4. **Individual estimation**: Each person individually estimates each task or activity using sensitivity analysis to provide a best case, likely case, and worst case estimate.
5. **Review "first-cut" estimates**: All estimates are written on to a whiteboard or some public area and grouped in the three ranges.
6. **Undertake Delphi analysis**: Each person discusses the various assumptions and issues they considered when developing their estimates.
7. **Adjust estimates**: Where required, the various estimates are adjusted based on the team discussion.
8. **Discard outriders**: Each range is averaged with outriders discarded.
9. **Final reality check**: The final results are reviewed and discussed again before the estimates are published.

This process results in a highly discussed ranged set of estimates, as shown in Figure 14.6.

extreme tool

This variation on the Delphi technique will work very well, provided a free-ranging discussion about assumptions made by each participant while deriving their estimates (Step 6) is allowed and that the

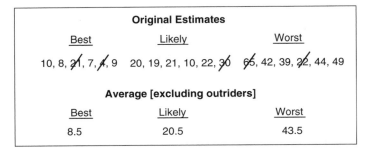

Figure 14.6
Wide-band Delphi estimates

original estimates from Step 5 are adjusted to reflect the discussions. In Figure 14.6, the outriders in each range have been deleted after discussion and before averaging the remaining estimates.

Again, it is the discussion incorporated in the wide-band Delphi technique that is important. Your team and stakeholders learn more about their various assumptions during the estimation process.

When conducting the wide-band Delphi process, it is critical that the process not be dominated by the project manager. The key to the success of wide-band Delphi is the sharing of different views—risk, tasks, and estimates—and the development of a common understanding of what is required to undertake each task.

In our experience, the process of wide-band Delphi works more efficiently and ac-curately than other estimation techniques because it involves a detailed discussion of assumptions from various viewpoints. It is also powerful for all types of projects.

Not Another Note on Sensitivity Analysis!

It is essential to state estimates as a range rather than a single figure, especially dur-ing the early phases of the project development cycle. The use of sensitivity analysis techniques is highly recommended. This technique involves making estimates that are ranged into three figures:

- Optimistic or best case,
- Realistic or likely, and
- Pessimistic or worst case.

The optimistic estimate would be based on everything going better than ex-pected, the realistic estimate would reflect the likely situation, and the pessimistic estimate would be based on the worst case scenario.

Then, based on risk assessment, you should select one of these figures as a base for scheduling. For low-risk projects, the optimistic or the realistic estimates would be the estimates used for scheduling. The higher the risk of the project, the more the realistic or pessimistic range would be used. However, all three sets of figures would be included in the project estimates.

In many cases, the realistic estimate would be the most useful estimate for scheduling. However, certain tasks may entail a higher risk than others and these may require the pessimistic estimate. In other words, using an informal risk assessment of each task, the low-risk tasks would be scheduled using the optimistic estimate, medium-risk tasks would use realistic estimate, and high-risk tasks would be scheduled on the pessimistic estimate.

An alternative method borrowed from the engineering area (PERT) is to input all three estimates into the following equation:

$$\text{Expected} = (\text{Optimistic} + 4*\text{Realistic} + \text{Pessimistic})/6$$

This gives a single estimate (Expected) that reflects the range and distribution of all three initial estimates, as shown in Figure 14.7.

The use of sensitivity analysis is vital in ensuring that all contingencies are evaluated at the early stages of the project. As discussed earlier and shown in Figure 14.2, the variances between the best case and the worst case will become smaller as the project progresses through development.

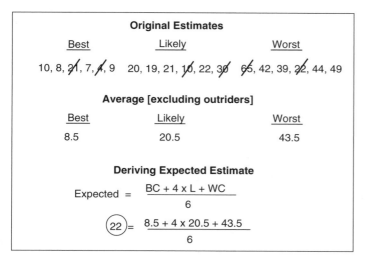

Figure 14.7
Wide-band Delphi estimates and sensitivity analysis

Adjust for Quality Agreement

Quality is generally perceived as a technical issue. However, as we covered in Chapter 9, it has a significant impact on project management. It is the nature of projects that they consist of a series of tasks that add value by processing the project's product through a series of dependent tasks. For example, the outputs from the requirements analysis phase are passed into the system design phase.

The Defect Ripple Effect   The dependent nature of project tasks means that any defect (human or machine-induced error) in one task is passed on to the next task, where it may be detected, adding unscheduled and unplanned time and effort to remove the defect.

In other words, Task A passes input to Task B. Task B was scheduled, for example, as four days of work effort and eight elapsed days' duration. However, some of the defects from Task A are detected during Task B and these defects require another day of effort. Task B now has five days of work effort to allocate but still only eight days of duration. In other words, the person undertaking Task B appears to have misestimated the actual effort for Task B. In some cases, if Person B is not prepared to work harder, the elapsed duration for B will expand to 10 days. Of course, this

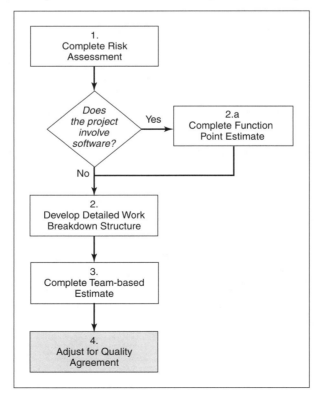

process continues in a more significant way for Task C, which has to account for defects from Task A and B (see Figure 14.8).

The impact of this in a project of more than 80 tasks is clearly massive and the traditional phase-end reviews will not be able to detect all the accumulated defects.

This defect ripple effect has been recorded by Jones (1994) and others as accounting for up to 40% of the total effort of a project over its development cycle. In other words, without an effective quality assurance process, a major cause of the difference between estimated effort and actual effort is the defect ripple effect.

Poor quality assurance is one of the biggest causes of poor estimation and project slippage, as it is obvious that by the middle of a project the actual effort required to remove embedded defects passed on from all the previous tasks can exceed the estimated effort required to perform the task currently being completed.

All experts on quality agree that the most effective way of detecting and removing defects is to assure quality and review each task's output before it is passed to the next dependent task. As a rough rule of thumb, each task should be expanded by 10% to allow for the quality assurance process to occur before the commencement of the next task.

It is also essential that the project tracking documents (time recording) have a recording category for defect repair and removal (see Chapter 7). Do not despair if the amount of time recorded for defect repair is high, as it is better to find them than to hide them.

Quality Requirements and Estimates   Another important aspect of quality in relation to project management is the definition of quality with respect to requirements and the impact of quality on estimates. As we introduced in Chapter 10, quality can be defined as a series of attributes.

Revising the approach introduced in Chapter 10, you should attempt to gain a consensus on what quality attributes are required for the project's deliverables and negotiate a formal quality agreement before planning and estimating the project.

In a landmark experiment with a number of computing teams in the late 1960s, Freedman and Weinberg (1977) showed that given the same data and functional

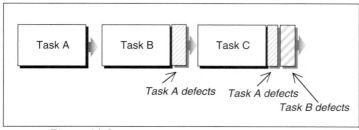

Figure 14.8
The defect ripple

requirements but differing quality requirements (e.g., one team was asked to produce the most readable output and another team was asked to minimize the use of the CPU), each team, although meeting its quality requirement, required a very different effort to achieve this. The productivity variance was 7:1!

Simply, different quality attributes have a different impact on the project estimates. Whereas some attributes such as maintainability and flexibility have relatively low impact (i.e., a requirement to make a system maintainable would not add a significant cost to the project), others have a major impact. In particular, high requirements for job impact, efficiency, usability, and portability require significant effort to achieve.

The extreme project manager and team must clearly understand the requisite quality requirements before they finalize the project estimates.

Whew! This was a big chapter, but we hope that the relatively simple and pragmatic approach to estimation covered will help you. Alternatively, you can just follow Indiana Jones and make it up as you go. It seems to work for him!

THE P FILES EPISODE 11: THE FLOATING BRAIN

Fans of *The Simpsons* will remember the episode in which Homer runs into Ned Flanders in the mall. Ned starts talking and Homer's brain says "That's it. I'm out of here!" and leaves Homer's head, floating off. Homer just collapses and Ned keeps talking. We love *The Simpsons*. We saw an identical incident in a major project in Hong Kong. It was an extremely high-profile project that was running more than a year behind schedule. As we were interviewing the project people, the project manager described how, at the beginning of the project, she had been called (with no warning) to meet with the CEO. She walked into the room and the CEO was at one end of a large conference table. All the executive team was also around the table. The CEO gave her a five-minute overview of the project and then asked, "Well, Betty, how long do you think the project will take?" He then leaned back in his very large CEO-type chair. She told us, "I was so scared. I heard my voice say 500 days."

The P Files Team Comment

This is a classic case of the estimation ambush. All of you have been caught in this trap. Some big cheese comes to your desk and, after a very brief overview of some requirements, says, "So, ballpark, how long do you think this will take?" We cover this and many other estimation games in an article on our Web site (www.Thomsett.com.au) called "Estimation Games." However, the way out here is to get out as fast as possible without saying anything except "Right now, I don't know. Give me some time and I'll get back to you." By the way, when we finally resolved the Hong Kong project, the task of writing the software, which Betty managed, took 500 days! She hadn't had time to realize that the project also required a complete upgrade of the communications network, experimental hardware, and a massive corporate restructuring.

CASE STUDY—ESTIMATES

Joan and Kim sit with you and another Web developer from No Object and derive various estimates. After much discussion (wide-band Delphi), you all agree on the following estimates (in raw effort hours):

Task	Best Case	Likely Case	Worst Case
Analyze data requirements	8	16	40
Develop basic data design	4	8	16
Design database (client and accomodation)	16	24	40
Analyze Web content	8	16	40
Design Web content	8	16	40
Prototype screen design (look and feel)	16	32	40
Design basic Smuthe training requirements	2	4	8
Determine hardware requirements	2	4	8
Analyze site performance requirements	1	2	4
Build HTML	16	40	80
Test Web site	4	8	12
Design new work processes for consultants	16	24	40
Buid database	24	32	80
Train City 1 Smuthe consultants	4	8	16
Total	129	234	464

Given that the project risk has been assessed as medium, you agree to commit to the likely case range:

Initial estimate: **234** hours (Release 1 only)

You review and discuss the high-level tasks required for Releases 2 and 3. The major tasks in these releases involve training the Smuthe consultants in the other cities and capturing accommodation details in those cities. The more significant tasks are the marketing to and training of clients in Big Bucks. These are out-of-scope (we love the Kepner–Tregoe tool!).

You agree that the additional costs for Releases 1 and 2 are Smuthe costs.

Revised estimate: **234** hours (Releases 1, 2, and 3).

Develop Schedule

"If you build it, he will come." ■

The Voice[1]

The next step in developing your business case is to develop a project schedule using Microsoft Project or similar project scheduling tools (see Figure 15.1). In this chapter we also look at another step in developing the business case, which involves allocating the actual team members and clearly documenting your assumptions regarding team members and skills.

Most project management texts spend a considerable amount of time on the issue of project schedules, so we cover only the key concepts.

To be honest, the concept of task scheduling is so easy that, for example, if five-year-old children hadn't grasped the concepts of tasks and dependencies they would be having a shower with their clothes on and going to bed before they got up (with apologies to Monty Python).

For novice readers, software packages such as Microsoft Project (which is an industry standard) have very easy tutorials that we strongly recommend as a guide.[2]

[1.] *Field of Dreams*, Phil Alden Robinson, Director; W.P. Kinsella (book), Phil Alden Robinson, Writer, 1989.

[2.] It is amazing to us how many "project management" books are really Microsoft tutorials in disguise.

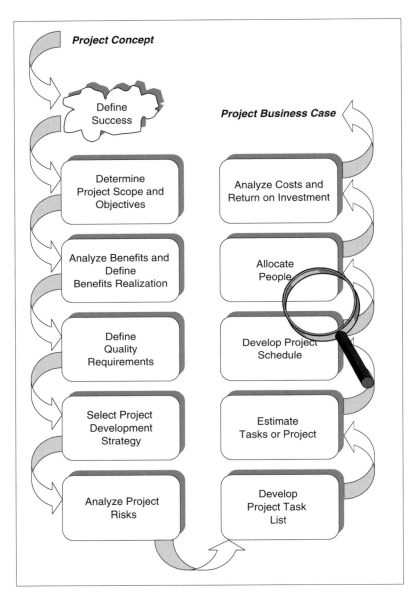

Figure 15.1
Developing a project execution plan and project staffing

In many extreme projects, the rate of change is so high that using lower tech tools such as Post-it notes as tasks placed on a board is perfect.

The second process we cover in this chapter is more complex. It involves the allocation of actual people to the tasks or, even more interestingly, the abstract allocation of "resources" unknown to the project manager at the time of planning. It is in this process that many eXtreme project managers are confronted with the nature of eXtreme projects. In our client base, it is more common that the people undertaking the initial project planning are not the actual team that will be undertaking the project.

Develop Project Execution Plan

As shown in Figure 15.2, the development of a project schedule involves five steps. The development of a schedule for a project is best completed on an electronic whiteboard so that all participants in the RAP session can be involved. Also, the process is iterative and you'll generally need to loop through the five steps a number of times to get an appropriate schedule.

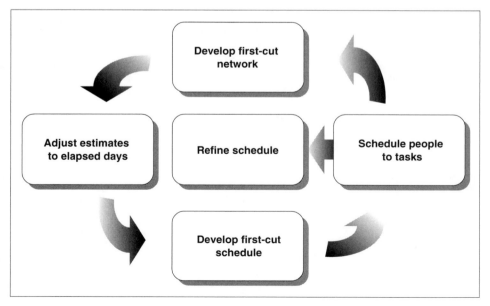

Figure 15.2
Developing a schedule

The key in scheduling is to understand that there is never one schedule. There will be many alternatives for scheduling a project and the optimum schedule depends on deadlines, the skill levels of the team members, and availability of people. Again, the advantage of team-based planning is that you'll have lots of people to help you work out the alternative schedules and to select the optimum one for your project, team, and stakeholders.

As we discuss later, the process of developing a project schedule (or project execution plan) involves further refining of your initial estimates and, in many cases, this process also leads to major estimation errors.

Step 1: Develop a First-Cut Network

This step requires the team to examine the tasks identified during the planning session and determining the relationship in terms of inputs and outputs.

There are two questions that need to be asked when developing the network:

- Which tasks are dependent on other tasks' outputs for their input?
- Can other tasks that are not dependent on the task currently being scheduled be commenced concurrently?

All PC-based scheduling tools will enable the diagram shown in Figure 15.3 to be created. The use of alternative relationships such as start-to-start becomes more important in later steps. The typical relationship in dependency is a *deliverable dependency*. For example, until the initial interviews with the business stakeholders are

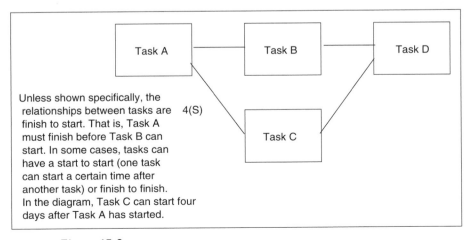

Figure 15.3
Developing a first-cut network

A Dangerous Myth

A number of people believe that out of an eight-hour day, they can be productive for six hours (often stated as the 70% effort "rule"). The origins of this myth are lost in time but, based on our surveys, the amount of lost time in nonproject activities such as nonproject meetings, teaching newbies the ropes, fixing general things, answering useless e-mails and general switch time is around 50% of the day for many people. Measure it yourself just to be sure (see Chapter 17).

complete and an interview summary is produced, the initial analysis cannot start, as it needs the interview summary for input. You can also have a *resource dependency;* that is, until one person finishes a task, another task cannot start, as he or she is going to do it.

The key to the first step is brainstorming as many variations to the network as possible for optimizing in later steps.

Step 2: Adjust Estimates to Elapsed Days

The next step is to enter or load the network with the raw effort estimates developed during the RAP session. As discussed earlier, the estimated effort needs to be adjusted to include nonproject activities. In most scheduling tools, there are calendars for each person who is to be scheduled. The default setting in most tools is eight hours per day. Most organizations will have some guideline on productive time (e.g., five hours per day), so the calendars need to be modified to reflect five-hour, not eight-hour days.

You need to be very careful here. As we state in the sidebar, there are a number of nonproject activities that most people seem to seriously underestimate when converting the effort to elapsed days.

Step 3: Develop First-Cut Schedule

By entering the adjusted effort into the task entry screens in the scheduling tool, a first-cut schedule can be viewed. This step simply provides a schedule that assumes that only one person is completing the project. Figure 15.4 shows a loaded network and the first-cut schedule.

The most important steps are the final two, in which the actual resources, their costs, and other factors such as resource dependencies where a person is undertaking two concurrent tasks or where a task depends on a person completing another task so that person can commence another because of his or her skills are factored into your plan.

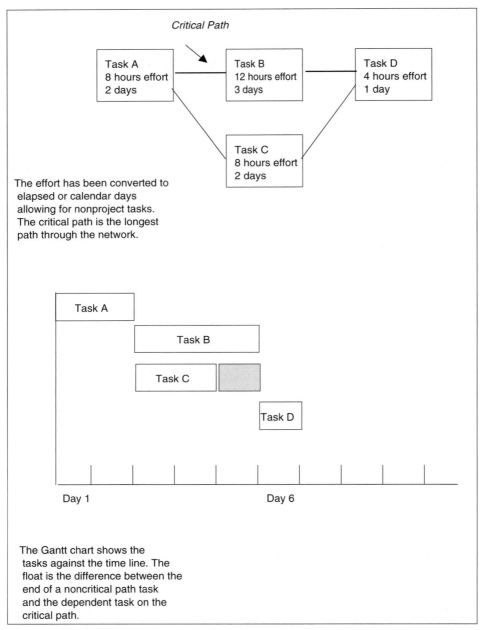

Figure 15.4
Developing a first-cut schedule

RADICAL SCHEDULING

Steven Eppinger "The Speed of Information," *Harvard Business Review*, January (2001, pp. 149–158) makes the point that traditional scheduling concepts such as PERT and critical path method (CPM) ignore feedback and other chaotic loops that are part of eXtreme projects. He developed a tool called the design structure matrix that addresses these and other failures of task dependencies. We strongly recommend his article and his approach.

As we cover later, this is where you start making assumptions about your team members and their skills and, of course, this is another cause of estimating error.

In addition, as discussed in the sidebar (Mythical Man-Month), you have to be careful when adding more than one person to a task, as the default in scheduling tools is that each person adds an equal amount of effort. That is, a two-day task for one person would be automatically scheduled for one day with two people. You'll have to adjust the person calendar option in the software.

BROOKS'S MYTHICAL MAN-MONTH

In his famous book, *The Mythical Man-Month*, Fred Brooks (1975) showed that the process of adding new people to a task actually leads to expansion of elapsed time and effort rather than shortening the elapsed time. This is often known as Brooks's Law, which states "Adding manpower to a late software project makes it later" (p. 25). In effect, adding people leads to lost effort through training, communication, administration, and other overhead. A rough rule is that for every person you add to a project subtract 10% accumulative from that person's effort. Adding a new person thus results in 90% additional effort and adding a second person results in that person adding only 80% effort, and so on.

Step 4: Schedule Actual Resources

This step involves the allocation of the actual people to the tasks identified in the schedule (see Figure 15.5). This step can be quite complex, as factors such as skill levels, costs, time lost through communication, and the specific nonproject activities of each person (as distinct from the organization norm) need to be calculated and reviewed. For example, Bill is a key analyst in the project but he is working on production support activities as well as supervising some new programmers. As a result, Bill may have only two hours per day to spend on the project, rather than the five hours assumed. The sidebar provides you with the typical guideline that we recommend when adding more than one person to a task.

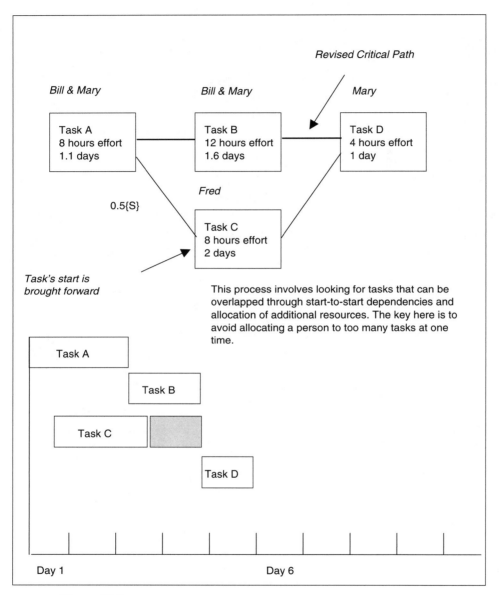

Figure 15.5
Scheduling actual resources

In addition, there are many tasks (e.g., conducting interviews) that make adding people to the task increase the total effort (and cost) rather than shortening the duration.

These final two steps need input from the actual people, as the calculations and various combinations can be quite complex.

Step 5: Adjust the Schedule as Required

The final step involves optimizing the schedule to use the project people most efficiently and minimize the development duration.

The use of alternative dependencies (start-to-start, finish-to-finish, and start-to-finish) and the more effective allocation of people to the same task are the type of activities that will be required (see Figure 15.6). Most scheduling tools will provide reports on overallocation of resources, resource conflicts, and similar information that can assist with this step.

It should be noted that PC-based scheduling tools are becoming more feature-laden and that the learning curve can be quite considerable. Most Windows-based tools are more than capable of handling business and IT projects and the use of the real-time planning approach means that the complexity of tasks is limited. However, formal training courses are available for most tools and a professional project manager should complete these courses to ensure competency with some of the advanced features of the tools.

A Really Clever Tool

If we had any influence over Microsoft and the other companies that develop project scheduling tools, we would ask them to build an intelligent software agent into their tools. You see, many of these tools allow you to schedule your project into the Year 2020 and beyond and to manage thousands of tasks. Clearly, the developers of these tools live in another world than that of our projects and our clients. A really clever scheduling tool would check to see if you are developing detailed plans beyond three months into the future and a little dialog box (or talking Java Applet) would pop up and say "You must be joking! Do you think this is going to happen? Have you seen the latest organization restructure? Do a reality check, dude!"

Scenario Planning Revisited

As we discussed in the earlier chapters of this book, the turbulence of the business environment, the need for compressed development cycles, the number of alternative development scenarios, and the regaining of power by business people over

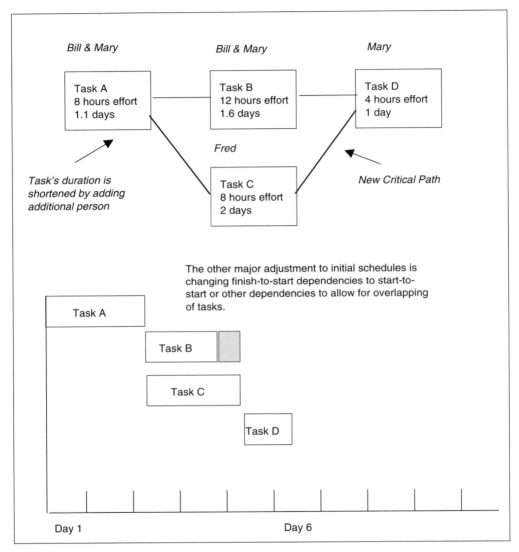

Figure 15.6
Adjusting the schedule

their IT and other expert-based projects means that detailed project schedules should not be longer than three to six months in total.

As shown in Figure 15.7, for longer projects, you should identify scenarios and the major events in each scenario for your project over the estimated project development period. However, only the schedule to achieve the next deliverable is taken to any level of detail (i.e., an execution plan).

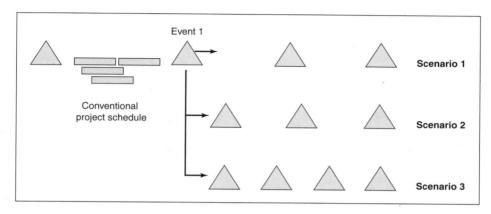

Figure 15.7
Scenario planning revisited

Develop Project Staffing Agreements

During both the estimation process and the scheduling process, you could be making some major assumptions and, as a result, some major estimation errors.

As we discussed earlier, the people you will have on your team and the experts that you have from your critical stakeholder areas are the main determinant of your project's success.

Oops! Wrong Planet, Wrong Person

Every project manager has experienced the sinking feeling that the person you assumed you were going to have allocated to your project, either as a team member or a stakeholder representative, turns out to be unavailable and you get a substitute.

As shown in Figure 15.8, the work of Weinberg (1971), Jones (1994), Boehm (1989), and Putnam and Myers (1992) has shown that the variance between excellent and poor performers in the project environment is huge. If you assumed a fairly high-skilled person and end up with a person with below-average skills, your estimates for the tasks that person is going to undertake could be off by an order of magnitude!

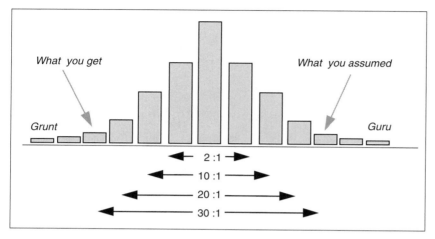

Figure 15.8
A really bad mistake: A common reality

PROJECTS AS ELEPHANT GRAVEYARDS

One of the great tales we all hear as children is the tale of the elephant graveyard where elephants go to die. In the project world, there is another variation on this tale. The process culture simply uses your project as a convenient "graveyard" for business people who have out-lived their usefulness in their own jobs. You need to be very aware of this behavior and part of the purpose of the project staffing agreements is to give you some room to negotiate if your project is becoming an elephant graveyard.

A Typical Skill Model

There are different types of skill models. In addition, some organizations are moving to the concept of competency analysis rather than just skills analysis. Competency analysis or modeling extends the analysis of an individual or a job to three areas:

- Knowledge: What does the person know?
- Skills: How is the knowledge converted to skills?
- Behavior: Is the person's attitude and application of the skills appropriate?

For example, a person may know the theory of systems analysis (e.g., data modeling, cost–benefit analysis, etc.) and he or she can develop reasonable analysis requirements. However, his or her attitude and behavior toward business people and ability to work with other people is not good.

However, for the purpose of project planning the model contained in Figure 15.9 would be sufficient for documenting your key assumptions about your project team and stakeholder experts.

extreme tool

If you already have your team members, then you should still use the skill level model in Figure 15.9 for each team member. Of course, you would do this participatively with each one. It may also be useful to get other team members to review each other's skill levels to avoid any bias.

Having determined the appropriate levels of skill that you have assumed when developing your estimates and adjusting your schedules, you should then take the extra step and develop a formal staffing agreement, as shown in Figure 15.10.

The project staffing agreement or contract simply documents your assumptions regarding team skills and assists in documenting any specific timing requirements regarding access to various experts, any costs or fees involved, and, most important, what person or what skills could be used as a "backup" if your requirements cannot be met. You'll recall our partnership agreements; this is just another variation on that concept.

Skill	Skill Level
Business Analysis *Process Modeling*	**1. Entry** Able to apply skills to simple activities without supervision **2. Basic** Able to apply skills to complex activities without supervision **3. Practitioner** Able to apply skills to complex activities with high standard and professionalism **4. Expert** Able to apply skills in very complex environments, undertakes basic research **5. Consultant** Highly advanced skills, undertakes innovative research, recognized in industry

Figure 15.9
Skills matrix

| Project: *Chicken Sexer* | Phase/Activity: *Analysis* |

| Skills Required: *Business Analyst* |

Skills Level:	1. Entry	☐
	2. Basic	☐
	3. Practitioner	☑
	4. Expert	☐
	5. Consultant	☐

| Dates/Timing:*On project by 1 September* |

| Costs/Fees: *$100 per hour* |

| Contingency Skills: *Systems Analyst Level 3* |

Figure 15.10
Project staffing agreement

Virtual Team Twist

With a virtual team, you may need to complete a staffing agreement with your virtual team members. This is a little bit of overkill, as the team member effort should be shown in your project's schedule. However, you are still more exposed to virtual team members than traditional team members, so use your common sense here.

THE P FILES EPISODE 12: THE FANTASY PLAN

We were involved in the initial planning of a major project involving the takeover and merger of two significant companies. A corporate project office had been created to report to the CEO and executive team on the status of the project. The merger team, in the company that had taken over the other company, was using the event concept that we developed for eXtreme project management. Until the two organizations signed off on the merger, there was almost no information available to the team about the structure, technology, systems, or products of the acquired company. We had planned all the tasks required prior to the takeover scheduled for about two months in the future. The corporate project office person (stricken with Newtonian neurosis) insisted on a one-year detailed task list. We explained that we couldn't identify the tasks until after the takeover and detailed examination of the real situation in the new company. Frustrated, he said, "Look, I know the plan you will give me for the CEO will be wrong, but at least it proves to him that you are working and thinking."

The P Files Team Comment

What can we say? The project was very successful, as the team adopted the *L.A. Law* model of planning that we discussed earlier. Each morning, for more than a year, all the project managers (more than 50 of them) met every morning in "the war room" to plan, replan, and to network. The original "plan" that proved we were thinking was never followed.

CASE STUDY—DEVELOP SCHEDULE

Working with Kim, Joan, Edwina, and the hardware guru from No Object, you develop the schedule shown here:

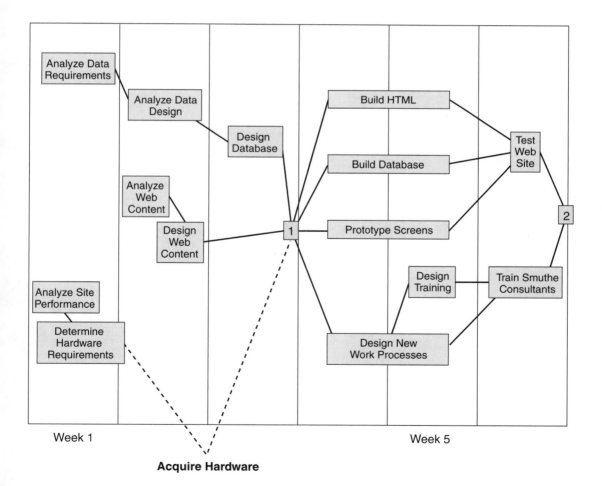

The major assumption is that Joan is full-time on the project as she has to work with Kim on tasks such as the Web content and quality assurance. What the scheduling process reveals is that you need a quality assurance person for Kim. No Object agrees to provide an external Web guru for 16 hours of quality assurance. The cost will be $1,600.

You and the team are confident that you can deliver Release 1 within six weeks. Remember that the schedule is based on likely case estimates. However, your project is dependent on the acquisition of hardware, which is shown as Event 1 in the schedule.

Develop Return on Investment

16

"Follow the money." ■

Deep Throat (Hal Holbrook)[1]

So you're nearly there. The final process in developing a complete, state-of-the-art business case is to finalize your project costings and to calculate the financial return on investment (ROI; see Figure 16.1).

You will probably do this after the RAP is complete, but, as for all our planning and project management processes, you'll have to completely involve your stakeholders.

In many cases, you will have to reconvene key participants of the initial RAP sessions to review the numbers, assumptions, and other key information required to complete an ROI analysis. In some projects, your stakeholders will need to consult, experiment, and gather information on current process costs, volumes, and so on, to validate cost and revenue models identified in the RAP session. As we discussed earlier, there will be a number of sessions required to complete this step.

In addition, most organizations have a project office that verifies the processes used in deriving the ROI.

---

[1]. *All The President's Men,* Alan J. Pakula, Director; Carl Bernstein (book), Bob Woodward, Writer, 1976.

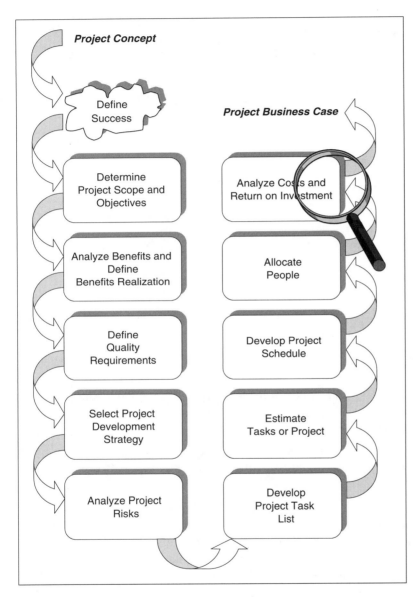

Figure 16.1
Develop cost and ROI scenarios

Develop Cost and ROI Scenarios _____

As you remember, we have calculated our benefits (financial, strategic impact, technological impact, and organizational impact) earlier in the planning process and, by now, you'll have your project schedule and your estimates of people costs.

As shown in Figure 16.2, the cost and return (benefit) estimates will be initial estimates that, as your project proceeds, will be refined as your estimate accuracy improves and you select your final development option or scenario and technology.

Again, as for benefits analysis, most organizations have specific guidelines for costing models, so we'll examine the basic framework for costing ROI in this chapter.

ROI Fundamentals

There are some fundamental issues that you should consider before you commence your ROI analysis.

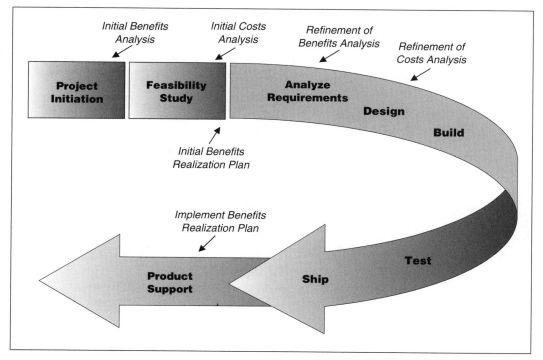

Figure 16.2
Cost–benefit and project lifecycle

ROI and Risk   The impact of project risk on ROI is simple but important. As in other investment decisions, the higher the risk of the investment, the higher the ROI the investor would expect.

Many organizations use different hurdle rates[2] or discount factors depending on the risk of the project. For example, if the project was assessed as low risk, a low-risk discount rate such as the 10-year government bond rate (around 6%–10%) would be used. If the project is assessed as a medium risk, a rate of 150% the low risk rate would be applied. For high-risk projects 200% of the low risk rate (16%–20%) would be applied to the present value calculations.

The risk weighting of discount rates is organization-dependent but, whether the organization has such guidelines or not, the project manager should ensure that the risk of the project is reflected in the ROI calculation.

Sensitivity Analysis and ROI   As we discussed in Chapter 13, it is impossible to produce an accurate single-point estimate for effort and costs. As a result, it is preferable to state estimates in three ranges:

- Optimistic or best case,

- Realistic or likely case, and

- Pessimistic or worst case.

The optimistic estimate would be based on everything going better than expected, the realistic estimate would reflect the likely situation, and the pessimistic estimate would be based on the worst case scenario.

At the beginning of a project, it is essential that the costs and benefits be presented using a similar model. As a result, you develop the following matrix for ROI:

- Best case benefits—Best case costs. This is the optimal result: The project meets the best case of costs (i.e., the lowest) and the best case of benefits (i.e., the highest).

- Best case benefits—Worst case costs. The project meets the worst case costs and the best case of benefits.

- Worst case benefits—Best case costs. The project delivers the worst case benefits, (i.e., lowest) and the best case (or lowest) of the costs.

- Worst case benefit—Worst case costs. This is the least satisfactory result.

---

2. A hurdle rate is generally a rate of return set as a minimum that all projects must return to be viable. It is set to some other investment benchmark such as investment in low risk shares, for example.

A high-risk project should be justified on worst case benefits and worst case costs, whereas a low-risk project would be justified on best case benefits and best case costs.

Benefit Curves and Calculation Periods   This is a complex and, generally, organization-specific issue. However, given the life-cycle model of project management advanced in this book and the need to estimate the ongoing support costs for full added-value analysis (see later), the need to determine an appropriate support and investment period and the impact of technology and rates of competitive change is very important.

In traditional accounting practice, payback periods were determined by considering factors such as taxation depreciation rules currently in force, the expected useful life of the equipment, and similar factors. In addition, consideration was often given to the financial situation of the company. For example, a company that had a policy of immediate payback to shareholders would often give priority to projects with shorter payback periods and as a result would set arbitrary limits such as "All projects must pay back in two years to be considered viable."

YOU ARE NOT AN ACCOUNTANT

The analysis of costs is highly specific to an organization. Always consult with your finance or accounting gurus in this step of planning. They are the experts; you are the integrator.

Some organizations have fixed rules such as "All projects must pay back in two years or less" and others vary the payback calculation period by the technology involved (e.g., PC projects are calculated over three years, minibased projects over five years, and mainframe projects over seven years). As shown in Figure 16.3, these simplistic models are not realistic and, in general, the project ROI calculation period should be contingent on the nature of the project, the proposed benefits and benefits curve, and, in some projects, the technology.

There are three basic benefits curves:

- Recurring: The benefit is permanent and grows over time. The most common example of this type of benefit is staff reduction, in which the salary and other cost savings are permanent.

- First-to-market: The benefit is essentially a one-off until competitors match the product.

- Strategic: The benefits are long-term and dependent on a long-term take up by clients.

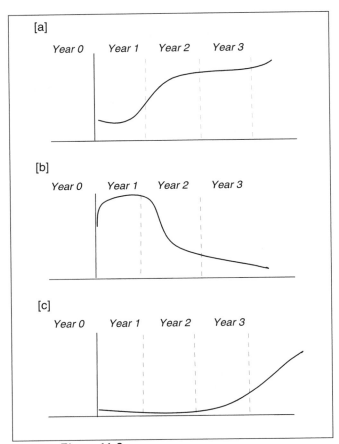

Figure 16.3
Alternative benefit curves

If, for example, a two-year ROI rule is in force, the projects with long-term bene-fits curves would not be viable, yet the organization could have a substantial pay-back of benefits in the third year.

The selection of ROI calculation period also has an impact on issues such as strategic planning. For example, a project with a strategic impact of five years out would probably not begin to pay back until after five years. The benefit curve would again be similar to that in Example (c) in Figure 16.3. If the organization had a two-year payback rule, many strategic projects would not be approved.

Support Costing   The estimation of support costs is extremely difficult but crit-ical for professional ROI analysis. The effort and cost of support work is highly de-pendent on the delivered quality of the system or product.

The first issue in accurately estimating and tracking support costs is to clearly distinguish among support, development, and enhancement work.

Any activity that alters (adds or subtracts) the system's data, function, technical infrastructure, or documentation is treated as a project or, as it is more commonly known, an enhancement project. The maintenance of the system at the status quo is production support and includes the following categories of work:

- Defect repair: The correction of errors in the delivered process, data, function, or documentation.

- Performance tuning: The alteration of process, code, or data structures to improve response times, execution efficiency, and data communications use.

- Perfective maintenance: The engineering or restructuring of existing process, code, data, and documentation to make it easier to maintain.

- Adaptive maintenance: The expansion of data size, alteration of calculation variables (that were correct but need to change), "cosmetic" alteration of screen, and input and output layouts that do not require new data.

- System education or consulting: The provision of help and advice on how to use the production system.

Many organizations simply track support work as a single category (with some tracking of system education and consultation via a help desk). In fact many organizations include small enhancements as support work. In both cases, the real cost of support and the delivered cost of quality cannot be determined, as all the categories of postimplementation work are mixed together. Later in this book, we revisit the support issue.

Based on metrics kept by some of our clients, if the real support work is recorded and separated from enhancements, the following costs are a reasonable rule of thumb for systems that are of average quality:

- Development costs: 30%

- Enhancement costs: 40%

- System supports: 30%

Of course, these percentages are indicative and the relative effort or cost across the categories depends on many factors. However, to develop a first-cut ROI that includes support costs, you could assume that the estimated ongoing support costs should be equal to the estimated development costs.

For example, if a system is estimated to cost $1,000,000 in development and it is estimated that the system will be in production for five years, then the estimated ongoing support costs would be $1,000,000, or $200,000 per year. Of course, detailed tracking of actual support costs would quickly confirm these initial estimates.

All enhancements to the production system should be treated as new projects and be subject to ROI and project value analysis as a stand-alone project.

Analyzing Project Costs

It should be noted that for all cost calculations, categories, and other related issues, project managers should consult with the finance or accounting experts in their own organization.

In projects, there are typically two types of costs:

- Recurrent, ongoing: These costs recur over a number of years. Salaries, rents, and lease payments are examples of this type of cost.

- Capital, one-off: These costs are incurred once typically for a finished product or service. Purchase of physical plant, computers, and software are examples of these costs.

The calculations of recurrent costs that would normally be the number of people (business and IT) involved in the project is dependent on the estimates produced in the planning session. Capital costs would also be identified during the planning session. In some organizations all costs are based on actual salaries rather than using costs such as accommodation, use of office supplies, superannuation, or pensions and bonuses, which are often treated as sunk costs. However, in some organizations, on costs can be 100% salary and higher. Use of computer time may also be treated as a sunk cost unless a specific piece of hardware or software is required for the project.

Let's assume that your project planning process has determined that two programmers will be required for two months to develop a system that will meet your client's requirements. Let's also assume that a new PC must be purchased for a manager to enable him or her to access some data.

The recurrent cost of development (assuming the programmers are paid $50,000 per year) is $15,152. The capital cost for the dedicated PC is $8,000. The development cost is $23,152 and total cost, including support over five years, is $46,304.

Future and Present Values

Before the costs and benefits can be compared, the financial estimates have to be converted using discount cash flow analysis or present value calculation. In effect, a dollar today is worth more than a dollar in two years. This technique converts all future dollar values to a common baseline—present value. In effect, $1 today is not worth the same as $1 in 2 years. So the $1 (future value) has to be discounted to reflect inflation, interest rates, or some other discounting factor back to a present-day value.

In most organizations, all benefits and cost figures for a project are projected forward for at least three years; therefore the use of present value calculations is essential.

In addition, you'll need to determine the discounting factor for your organization. Typically, the discounting factor or discount rate is based on the weighted average cost of capital (WCCC). This represents the relative cost of borrowing or raising money for the organization. However, other organizations may use other rates (e.g., the treasury bond yield), so, as previously stated, the project should consult the organization's accounting experts to obtain the prevailing discounting factor.

The technique for converting future values to present values is:

$$\text{Present value} = \text{Future value} / (1 + DF)^n$$

$$\text{Future value} = \text{estimated value}$$

$$DF = \text{discounting factor}$$

$$n = \text{future year}$$

For example, let's assume that we gain a benefit of $10,000 in two years and that the discounting factor is 9%. The present value of that return is:

$$\$ 8{,}403 = \$10{,}000/(1 + 0.09)^2$$

Of course, you do this for both benefits and costs.

Developing Your ROI

There are three common ways to analyze ROI:

- Net present value: Derived by subtracting the total of the costs (converted to present values using the discount rate) from the total present value of the benefits.

- Pay-back period: The period required for the total costs (development and support) to be met or paid back by the accumulated benefits.

- Internal rate of return: Derived using an exponential equation that calculates the interest rate required to make the total future value of the benefits equal to the total future value of the costs (Microsoft Excel can calculate this as a function).

Cost-Effectiveness

As we covered in Chapter 9, if your project is simply upgrading equipment such as computers and there is functional replacement only, it is acceptable to ignore benefits and use cost-effectiveness as an alternative to ROI. This technique assumes that the new technology has the same implicit benefits as the technology that is being replaced.

THE P FILES EPISODE 13: THE RETURN OF THE CONSULTANTS FROM HELL

We were consulting at an executive level to a major government organization. We had worked with the team during project initiation and feasibility to work up figures for the ROI calculation. We left to work with another client and the organization hired some experts on cost–benefit from another well-known consulting organization. The sponsor of the project sent us by e-mail the ROI undertaken by the consultants prior to it being sent to the premier of the state (a governor in U.S. terms). It took us no more than 10 minutes to realize that the ROI had been based on the best case estimates for both costs and benefits. Our team had also developed worst case scenarios for costs and benefits (which were right under the best case scenarios in the document given to consultants). On the best case scenario, the project returned 100%. On the worst case scenario, the project returned –50%. It was a high-risk project. It was canned before it started.

The P Files Team Comment

It is really too easy to knock consulting companies. We'll leave that to Lewis Pinault (2000), a former Boston Consulting and Cap Gemini consultant, whose book *Consulting Demons: Inside The Unscrupulous World of Global Corporate Consulting* does a complete exposé of the tricks of these companies. However, this deliberate fiddling with the project financials to get a project approved is still far too common.

CASE STUDY—DEVELOP ROI

Benefits Summary

Working with Edwina you analyze the expected volumes, fees, and charges. These figures are based on Big Bucks clients only.

- Expected number of Premium clients (per year):
    200 (best case), 120 (likely case), 100 (worst case)
    Additional fee per premium client: $1,000

- Number of revisits caused by poor client preference information (per year):
  20 (best case), 18 (likely case), 12 (worst case)
  Cost per revisit (to Smuthe): $200
- Number of Big Bucks clients who seek other services:
  30 (best case), 15 (likely case), 10 (worst case)
  Fee normal client: $1,000
- Estimated retention:
  25 (best case), 10 (likely case), 5 (worst case)

Remember that the outputs all lead to the same outcome so as long as we calculate the outcome benefits stream, we can add the output benefits as a bonus.

Objective	Output	Outcome
To capture extended client personal details	More information about the client's family, lifestyle, and accommodation preference for Smuthe consultants	More appropriate placement for clients
	Improve service (to Smuthe clients and Smuthe consultants)	Increased revenue (increase in fees for premium service)
	Avoid costs (less research required for consultants, fewer accommodation showings)	Best case $100,000 p.a. Likely case $60,000 p.a.
	Best case $4,000 p.a. Likely case $4,000 p.a. Worst case $4,000 p.a.	Worst case $50,000 p.a. Notional avoided cost (reduced level of potential clients loss) Best case $25,000 p.a. Likely case $10,000 p.a. Worst case $5,000 p.a.

Edwina is "on a winner" here.

Costs Summary

Based on the likely case estimates of 234 hours (which include Joan Jette's effort), plus 10% for project management and 10% for internal quality assurance (don't forget the $1,600 for external quality assurance), you derive a cost estimate of 300 hours (rounded) at $100 per hour.

- Basic Costs
    Development: $30,000
    Support (for 3 years): $30,000

ROI Analysis

You calculate the ROI using just the likely case costs (you are pretty confident) and over three years. Just for illustration, we'll use the likely case benefits estimates. Of course, you'd derive a complete set of ROI calculations based on best case benefits, best case costs, best case benefits, likely costs, and so on.

The discount rate you agree on with Edwina is 8% and you assume no yearly increase in clients' usage.

	Year 0	Year 1	Year 2	Year 3
Returns (F.V.)		$74,000	$74,000	$74,000
Returns (P.V.)		$68,517	$63,440	$58,741
Costs (F.V.)	$30,000	$10,000	$10,000	$10,000
Costs (P.V.)	$30,000	$9,259	$8,573	$7,938

FV = future value; PV = present value.

This gives you the following ROI

- Net present value
    $190,698–$55,770 = $134,928
- Payback period
    0.8 years

Clearly, this is a viable project for Edwina (remembering that it scored high on the added value drivers as well). In addition, there is the expected growth into Watchout Insurance at a later stage.

Project Tracking and Reporting

17

> "We can dispense with the pleasantries, Commander. I am here to get you back on schedule." ■

> *Darth Vader (David Prowse)*[1]

As Homer J. Simpson loves to say, "Woo hoo!" Now you have your plan, your stakeholders are excited, and your team is ready to go. Once the business case has been approved by your project sponsor, your project can proceed. The next processes in project management are the tracking and reporting of project progress.

Project Tracking

Project tracking (see Figure 17.1) has one major objective: to determine whether the project is in control (i.e., meeting the agreed business case) or out of control. To achieve this objective, project tracking typically involves tracking five variables:

- Time: The estimated effort and duration versus the actual effort and duration.

- Costs: The estimated costs versus the actual costs.

---

[1]. *The Return of the Jedi,* George Lucas, Director; George Lucas and Lawrence Kasdan, Writers, 1983.

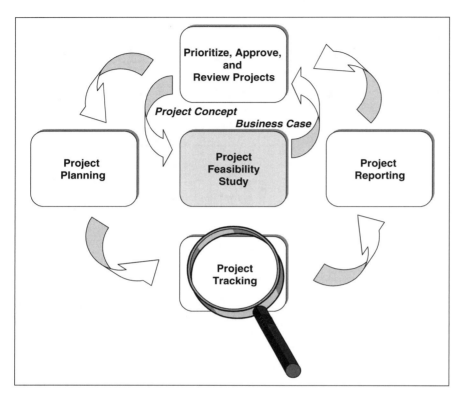

Figure 17.1
Project tracking

- People utilization: The effectiveness of the effort versus the duration.
- Quality: How well are the deliverables being completed?
- Deliverables: What products or components have been delivered?

Information on the first three variables can be easily gathered by the use of the information already implemented in the PC-based scheduling tool, and the fourth and fifth are by-products of the normal quality assurance process.

The Tracking Mechanism

Like all our project management processes, project tracking should follow the participative process that is used for planning. Regular team-based tracking meetings are the most useful mechanism, as these sessions can gather subjective information as well as the more quantitative data such as actual effort and costs. Subjective information such as warning signs, rumors, informal communication, and other "soft" data can often provide early warnings of potential project problems.

Time Tracking Versus Project Tracking   As we discussed in previous chapters, one of the most common problems in project organizations is the distortion of project tracking data through confusing the tracking of projects with time sheets. This occurs when management uses project tracking forms for attendance recording.

Never confuse tracking projects with tracking people.

The fact that a person spent eight hours in the office has no significance in tracking projects.

Project tracking simply tracks tasks—their costs and effort—not the person or persons who are undertaking the task. The fact that only one hour in an eight-hour day has been spent by Bill could mean that Bill had a large number of nonproject activities and work on other projects. It could also mean that Bill is having trouble getting motivated and is not working efficiently. It is clear that if the second reason is the case, a time sheet or tracking report will not show this, as Bill would distort the reports to hide the situation. Poor motivation and inefficient work will generally not be found by reports, but instead by the project manager and team leaders being able to spend time with their people. Time sheets may be required for administrative purposes but project tracking should be kept separate and, preferably, anonymous.

TRUST

It is vital that you do not put yourself into the position of always asking, "How is it going?" You must learn to trust your people. As we covered in earlier chapters, if one of your team members needs four weeks to do a task, you give them four weeks. The agreement you must have is that they tell you as soon as they realize that they can't meet the deadline. This frees you up to build relationships with your sponsor and stakeholders.

The tracking form can record certain activities such as production support work, training, and other specific nonproject activities, but the key is that the tracking form does not have to equal eight hours or whatever the normal hours of work are for the organization.

Many organizations further complicate the process of project tracking by imposing global rules such as making 95% of all project work billable to a client. This accounting and consulting company model is highly problematic in normal IT groups. As discussed in Chapter 15, studies have shown that 50% of the day can be lost in nonproject work such as nonproject meetings, mentoring, and so on.

The billing of these categories of work is at least unethical and at worst illegal. Clients should only be billed for project work done for them. However, you should examine the need to track this "lost" time, as we covered earlier.

The Role of Quality Assurance in Tracking   The role of quality assurance is vital in both ensuring the client's requirements and in triggering the tracking of tasks.

All project tracking should be based on reports from the quality assurance processes such as walkthroughs, technical reviews, and inspections (covered in Chapter 10) that the deliverable from the task has been reviewed.

The fact that a task is finished does not mean that it is right.

At a minimum, no task should be recorded as complete until at least one other person, apart from the person who undertook the task, has reviewed the deliverable for quality.

The Use of Automated Project Management Tools

Project tracking is based on team members tracking their work on each task allocated to them. PC-based scheduling tools should be the vehicle for capturing the actual effort and, as a result, produce a series of reports that form the basis of tracking.

As shown in Figure 17.2, the two critical reports are the individual Gantt chart and the task forms for each task that the individual has been scheduled for. These reports can be produced at the end of the planning session.

Various Tracking Concepts

There are four basic tracking approaches. Most scheduling tools will support them however, each tool uses a default technique and you should refer to the manuals of whatever tool you are using. The tracking approaches are:

- Linear progress: The portion of the actually expended work is calculated as a percentage of the total work. For example, if the task was scheduled for 20

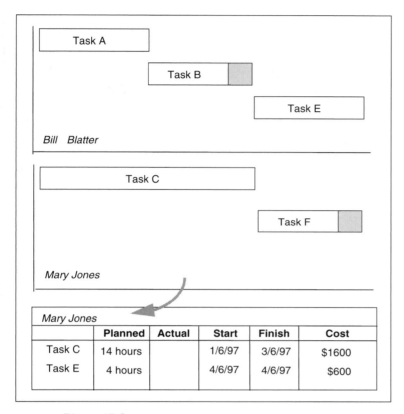

Figure 17.2
Essential tracking reports

hours and 5 hours are expended, the task is recorded as 25% complete (this is the default of Microsoft Project for Windows and other PC-based tools).

- One hundred–zero: The task is either not started or it is complete. That is, as soon as the task is commenced it is considered 100% complete.

- Fifty–fifty: As soon as the task is started it is considered 50% complete and is not 100% complete until it is finished.

- Subjective progress: This involves the person doing the task making a subjective evaluation of actual progress. For example, after 5 hours (25%) of a 20-hour task, the people report it is only 10% complete.

Clearly, there are problems with each of these approaches. The linear progress method assumes that work effort and output are linked to sequential and even progress. (We talk more about this later.) That is, if Mary has done 10 hours of work on a 20-hour task, it is assumed it is 50% complete. Computing work rarely takes this form and, for example, after 10 hours Mary may have done the easy components of the task and might still have 80% of the work to complete. However, the subjective progress method could be incorrect because it is subjective. If the work is being completed on a fee basis, then either of these techniques may need to be used, as the person providing the service may require progressive payment for work undertaken.

A more complex variation on project tracking is earned value. This technique involves a series of calculations based on actual versus estimated or budgeted costs and is rarely used in IT organizations.

We Aren't Painting Walls: We Are Building Dreams

The real problem with traditional project tracking is that it uses linear tracking concepts borrowed from the construction industry. For example, if a painter requires 10 days to paint a wall or a mason needs 10 days to pour concrete, then at the close of the fifth day, it is reasonable to expect about 50% of the painting or concrete pouring to be completed.

However, creative work such as business or systems analysis has a completely different completion dynamic. As shown in Figure 17.3, there are three basic completion curves in creative work:

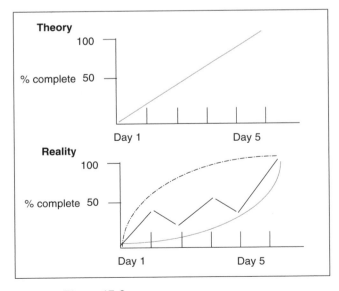

Figure 17.3
The nature of creative work

- The 10/90: The problem requires considerable interviews, research, and work-out until, in the last 10%, all the background work "gels."

- The 90/10: After the first few interviews almost all the requirements are clear and the remaining 90% of the effort is in tidying-up.

- The sawtooth: The initial work is found to be flawed so considerable rework is required.

The inevitable conclusion is that the 0/100% model is the only valid model for eXtreme projects.

Tracking Mechanism

The tracking mechanism is simple. Your team members should enter the actual effort spent on each of their allocated tasks on a daily basis (let's not have the Frantic Friday Finagle[2] here). This is essential for accurate tracking and the building of a project metric database. At an agreed time (weekly or biweekly), the individual task forms can be aggregated during a team-based tracking session to determine the overall progress of the project.

Tracking Summaries

Assuming that team members have honestly recorded their efforts into the task forms, the types of reports that can be produced from the scheduling tools include the following:

- Start and finish dates: Which tasks did not start and finish as planned?

- Effort: What is the actual effort versus the estimated effort, task, or total project?

- Duration: Which tasks took longer or shorter than expected?

- Costs: Which tasks cost more or less than expected?

Most scheduling tools can produce these reports for individuals, the team, and the total project, and can produce other reports such as earned value. However, these four basic reports provide a simple yet powerful progress and tracking summary.

It should be reemphasized that simply relying on reports is not sufficient for tracking progress in a project. Because of the complexity and creativity of project

---

2. This is where you go into detective mode to determine where all the hours you worked in the week disappeared to.

work and the nonlinear nature of creative work (i.e., 50% of the effort being spent does not mean that 50% of the work has been completed), the project manager, team members, and stakeholders must always supplement formal tracking with informal and subjective tracking information gathered during meetings.

Building a Project Metric Database

As a by-product of project tracking, you and your team can begin building a project metric database. This database can be invaluable in enabling you and other project managers to learn from the project and to assist in both macro and micro estimation in future projects. Typical information would include the following:

- Description: This would be contained in the business case.
- Project development strategy: If fast track or RAD strategies were used, these could affect the productivity measures.
- Phase and task lists: These could be used to develop phase percentage models.
- Risk assessment: This captures more than 80 factors that influence productivity and quality.
- Estimates: This measures both effort and duration.
- Actuals: This measure both effort and duration.
- Rework effort: The amount of effort spent on defect repair throughout the life cycle.

All of this information is simply collated from the work already undertaken during the RAP session and the project tracking process. The key here is that the major deliverables required for developing a project metric database have already been developed during the planning process.

Project Reporting

The final step in the project management model is the reporting of the status of the project at a summary level to the project sponsor, project steering committee, and stakeholders (see Figure 17.4).

The proactive nature of the project sponsor and project steering committee was introduced in early parts of this book. Rather than the rubber stamping and passive behavior that many steering committees were relegated to in traditional project management, eXtreme project management actively involves these executives in:

- The selection and initiation of projects;
- The monitoring and review of projects;

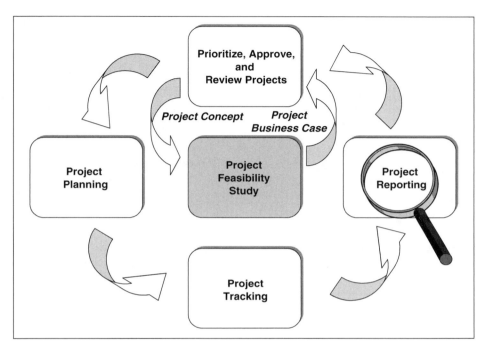

Figure 17.4
Project reporting

- Providing assistance to projects when required; and
- Active resolution of project conflicts.

The selection and initiation of projects was covered in Chapter 5 of this book. In this chapter, we explore the other key functions of steering committees and project sponsors.

As also discussed in earlier chapters, it is important that the senior management take responsibility and accountability for the projects they are sponsoring. Your role, as a project manager, is critical in assisting senior management (who are generally from the process culture and are generally not sure of their role in projects) in both gaining access to the right information regarding their project and the right decisions to make.

Project Management and Technical Deliverable Reviews

As discussed in Chapters 3 and 5, projects involve the interrelationship between the managerial aspects (business case) and the technical aspects (system or product development deliverables). Review of the quality of the various technical deliverables such as system data, function requirements, designs, and so on, is best achieved through quality assurance processes such as walkthroughs and inspections, covered earlier.

The same distinction between technical reviews and project management reviews applies to the role of steering committees and project sponsors. The project sponsor and steering committee reporting and reviewing roles are to focus on the business case and whether there is any variation in the agreed-on business case.

Should the project manager wish to use either the project sponsor or members of his or her steering committee to provide technical input or to review detailed technical issues, this should be done outside the normal sponsor and steering committee reviews. It is common for project sponsors and members of the steering committee to be experts in areas of knowledge relevant to the project. For example, the general manager of marketing might be one of the most experienced people in the marketing issues relevant to a new retail banking system. This person is also on the project steering committee. As a result, you should separate the two roles that the general manager of marketing has on his or her project.

HIGH RISK, HIGH FEEDBACK

There is a very simple principle here. The higher the project risk, the higher the level and frequency of executive feedback and governance.

The governance of the business case is a steering committee role and the detailed technical input role regarding marketing issues is a technical review role and should be handled as part of the system development process. In our example, if the project manager wishes to alter the scope and objectives of the project based on new information gathered during the system development process, this is a decision that must be made by the steering committee. If there are some detailed issues on the impact of the new system design on marketing strategy, this is a technical issue and would be resolved as part of a quality assurance review or systems analysis.

The Project Reporting and Review Process

The format and timing of project reporting will vary in each organization and will also depend on the size and risk of the project.

No Surprises

You should always prebrief your sponsor and steering committee members before the meeting. You need decisions, not surprises in a steering committee meeting.

For small projects, there is normally only a project sponsor and because small projects are generally less than three months in duration, a project review with the sponsor should occur either weekly or biweekly. For medium projects, there would normally be a steering committee and meetings would normally be monthly. For larger projects, there may be a project steering committee and an IT steering committee, so meetings might be monthly or quarterly. High-risk and extreme projects are subject to more change and turbulence and, as a result, the project reporting and review process may be more frequent and demand driven. In large, high-risk projects, it would be normal for the steering committee to delegate the demand-driven reporting role to the project sponsor or a subcommittee, as it often is too difficult to convene the steering committee on short notice.

As discussed earlier, the following information is the core of the project reporting and review process:

- The state of the project; that is, is it still proceeding to plan or not?
- If not, what is the revised situation and what are the causes for the variation?
- What actions have been taken by the team to solve any problems?
- What alternative scenarios are available?
- What actions can be taken by senior management?
- What is the revised or updated business case for review and approval?

Figure 17.5 provides a sample form that can be used for smaller projects, highlighting the essential information required by project sponsors and steering committees.

extreme tool

In addition, project reporting would typically involve a summary of the project tracking information such as costs, effort and schedule progress, and variations.

As detailed in the sidebar, there should be adequate information and time for the project sponsor and steering committee to understand the issues and be able to make informed decisions.

Project Report	Project :

Overall Status

    ◯ Green: Project is meeting business case

    ◯ Amber: Project is meeting business case but has some issues

    ◯ Red: Project is not meeting business case and has major issues

Key Issues

Revised business case attached   ◯ Yes   ◯ No

Actions Required by Steering Committee

Actions Taken by Project Manager

Other Information

Report read by Team/Stakeholders   ◯ Yes   ◯ No

Figure 17.5
Project report

Really Radical Reports

An extremely radical model implemented by one of our clients based the project reporting process on the success sliders introduced in Chapter 7. This approach is shown in Figure 17.6.

This approach recognizes that senior management are only interested in those success criteria that really matter to them. For example, if quality really mattered ("on") and budget was "off," why would you report on budget?

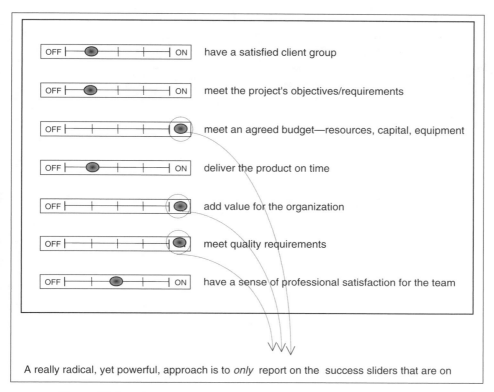

Figure 17.6
A really radical report

Assistance to Projects

As detailed in earlier chapters and later in Chapter 20, the key role of the project sponsor and steering committee is to "add value" to the project and to the project management process. This requires the members of these groups to focus on proactive problem resolution of changes before they are implemented rather than the traditional reactive approval of changes after they have happened.

Resolution of Project Conflicts   Also, as discussed in Chapter 5, a common form of assistance that the project sponsor and steering committee members will be required to provide is in the area of stakeholder management.

PROCESS CULTURES AGAIN!

The concept of regular steering committee meetings is a reflection of the "mechanical" model of the process culture. You need to be able to quickly get to your sponsor whenever serious issues arise in your project. Unfortunately, these do not happen on a regular (e.g., monthly-to-monthly) basis. Make sure that you can arrange to see your sponsor on a demand basis, if possible.

Given the number of different stakeholders in most projects, you will inevitably experience conflict between yourself and key stakeholders (and their managers) and conflict between stakeholders themselves.

For example, a project manager may find a stakeholder, who is organizationally more senior than the project manager, not prepared to release a key person to assist in the project. Alternatively, a project manager may find two key stakeholders not agreeing on scope, objectives, or quality. In these and similar cases, it is legitimate for the project manager to raise the problems with either the project sponsor or project steering committee for assistance and resolution.

Project Steering Committee Meeting Structure   The structure and agenda of project steering committee/sponsor meetings will vary, but all project steering committee/sponsor meetings should focus on the following topics or agenda items:

- The status of the project—has the business case altered since the last meeting?
- If so, what changes are there to:
  - the scope of the project?
  - objectives?
  - the priority of the objectives?
  - the project development strategy?
  - risks?
  - benefits or returns?
  - costs?
  - project plans or schedules?
  - quality agreement?
  - staffing agreements?
- What actions has the project manager or team taken to resolve the issues?

- Who can assist in resolving the issues?
- Who is responsible for follow-up?
- What caused the changes?
- Are there any future or expected issues?
- Other items as required.

Reporting to Stakeholders

It is essential that the same processes and information be both gathered from and distributed to the project's stakeholders.

MEETING THE ENEMY

While any attempt by the business groups to change the business case in your project will be relatively easy to determine and manage, you should watch your back. In our experience, the most common form of change is internal—from your team.

For critical stakeholders, the project reports should be actively reviewed via stakeholder meetings or one-on-one sessions. For nonkey stakeholders, it would be adequate for them to receive copies of all project tracking summaries and project reports.

Ideally, an executive from each of the key stakeholder areas would be on the project steering committee as well.

The Project Change Control Process

Contemporary projects are subject to many changes throughout the development process. It is almost inevitable that the need for change will occur some time before implementation. First- and second-wave project management handled changes via a reactive process of "freezing" system requirements and not allowing for changes after the client had signed off.

A rigorous process of project change control must be designed and approved by the project sponsor, project manager, and stakeholders during the initial RAP sessions. Project changes can be internal or external:

- Internal changes are those that originate from within the project team.
- External changes are those that arise from stakeholders outside the project manager's team.

Control of changes involves three steps:

- Request for change: All requests for change must be documented, whether they are internal or external. The documentation should include the originator's name, date of request, description of the problem addressed, description of the change, and justification for it.

- Evaluation: You, the project manager, liaising as necessary with other people such as project team members and stakeholders, should evaluate the change. This may require the convening of another RAP session. Evaluation should cover such points as the following:

  - Is the change really justified?
  - If justified, is it essential that it be made at this time or could it or another feature be deferred until after the postimplementation review phase at the end of the project?
  - Does the change alter the business case of the project?
  - What tasks, whether completed, in progress, or to be commenced, would be affected?
  - Can you estimate the duration and work effort required to implement change?
  - Will it require rescheduling of the project or extend the completion date of the project?
  - Will it require additional resources to carry out?
  - Does the change impact across related projects or systems?
  - Does the change require an alteration of the project development strategy?
  - Does it alter the complexity and risk of the project?
  - What stakeholders are impacted by the change?
  - What risks are involved whether the change is implemented or implemented?

- Decision: Assuming the project manager has no doubt that the change should be made at this time, and provided it will not require additional resources, alter the complexity, alter the business case, or extend the completion date of the project, it can be accepted. However, if one or more of these conditions are not met, a meeting of the steering committee should be called to enable their review and approval.

The results of the evaluation and impact analysis should then be added to the memorandum requesting the change.

Maintaining the Project Management File

All the information discussed throughout this book should be integrated and stored as a managed document—the project management file. All changes to this information should be recorded and, where appropriate, approved by the project sponsor and steering committee:

- Initial business case,
- Detailed project schedules,
- Stakeholder agreements,
- Stakeholder reports,
- Project tracking reports and summaries,
- Project reports,
- Project metrics,
- Quality assurance summaries,
- Any changes to the business case (approved by the project sponsor and steering committee), and
- Other project management reports.

The Business Case Is the Focus of Everything

Too many traditional project management models further complicate an already complex process by adding additional concepts such as issues logs, change request logs, and risk logs.

If your project has not changed, be afraid, very afraid.

These models reflect the old-fashioned idea that change is bad and that it can be managed by a "separate" technique from project management. In eXtreme projects, these change logs quickly become unmanageable.[3]

---

3. In one project being managed by a well-known consulting group, the change log and risk issues log had more than 60,000 entries. The consulting group then proposed another project (which they would run, of course) to automate the change logs. As we pointed out to the client, who would manage the changes on the project to automate changes?

In eXtreme project management, all changes are *immediately* reflected in the business case. In other words, the business case is a living and changing document (see Figure 17.7).

Of course, as we have been emphasizing throughout this book, all changes to the business case are approved by the sponsor and critical stakeholders before they are accepted.

The file should be maintained so that the current business case is the first document in the file when it is opened. It would also contain a revision log as is normal for controlled documents. The business case is a public document and all team members should be able to access it.

If you maintain your business case, you'll maintain your sanity.

THE P FILES EPISODE 14: THE ABUSIVE PARENT CATCH-22

We were working in a major bank with a team when, a very senior manager stormed into another team's area. "You, #$@@8**, you lousy %%$@!!!. I'll get you all. ###$$@#&," and so on. We were amazed, as we had not seen such a display since political correctness

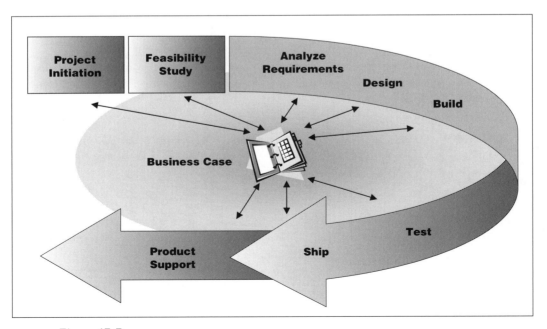

Figure 17.7
The living business case

became part of normal corporate life. We asked the team that had been blasted what was going on. "Oh, he's our sponsor and one of his peers has just told him that his project is way behind schedule," we were told. "Why didn't you guys tell him yourselves?" we asked, "Why did he have to find out from one of his colleagues?" Another team member answered, "Well we knew if we told him, he would just yell at us." Another team member spoke up, "Yea. And you just saw him do it."

The P Files Team Comment

This is a wonderful example of the self-fulfilling prophecy. Again and again, we have seen examples of sponsors being placed in the position of finding out too late about the status of their projects to do anything else but "kick a few heads." Great project managers ask for help quickly. We'll talk more about this in Chapter 20.

CASE STUDY—CHANGES, CHANGES

You assemble all the information you have gathered in your RAP session and smaller stakeholder sessions, produce a business case, and review it with Edwina, Uri, Joan, Kim, and the people at Smuthe.

Well done! Woo hoo!

The project starts and Edwina decides to include Watchout Insurance as a client group. If you hadn't read this book, you'd deal with the change on the run.

Not eXtreme project managers, though!

You assemble the stakeholders and re-RAP the project and the business case.

What emerges is that there are some small changes to Release 1 but the bigger impact is on Release 3 (which you haven't scheduled yet). The benefits of scenario planning are revealed. The big impacts are as follows:

- Increased hardware capacity,
- Increased costs of data capture,
- More training effort,
- A broader marketing campaign, and
- Increased security requirements.

Interestingly, almost all these impacts are on Smuthe rather than your project. Edwina agrees to "ease off" further on the timeframe to allow for acquisition of new hardware and to allocate additional support for Joan in the training area.

In effect, there is no need to change your business case.

Postimplementation Reviews

"What do you want, a happy ending?" ■

"Painless" Peter Potter (Bob Hope)[1]

Congratulations! You, your team, and your stakeholders have finished your project and your new system and associated products are in production. After your project has successfully delivered its required outcomes, there are three remaining project management activities that must be completed:

- The postimplementation review,
- The development and implementation of the benefits realization plan, and
- The design of system support reviews.

The Postimplementation Review

The postimplementation review is a team-driven process that reviews the key project deliverables and the development process, and assesses how well the business case was delivered.

---

1. *The Paleface,* Norman McLeod, Director; Edmund Hartman, Frank Tashlin, and Jack Rose, Writers, 1948.

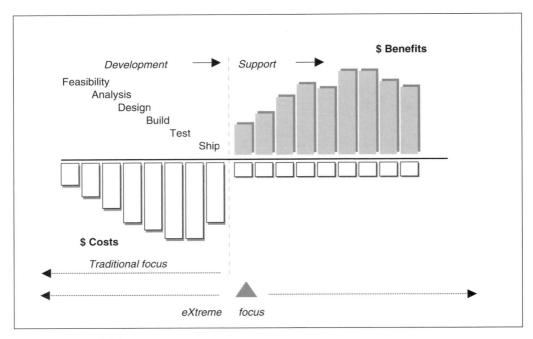

Figure 18.1
Postimplementation review

Again, eXtreme project management has a different approach to these reviews than traditional project management, as shown in Figure 18.1.

The postimplementation review is a vital component in eXtreme project management, as it is the basis of measuring success, updating and reviewing the project metric database, and providing you and your team with a vital feedback mechanism for personal and organizational satisfaction. As discussed in Chapter 9, the postimplementation review also marks the beginning of benefits realization and value analysis.

The Postimplementation Review Focus

Many experienced project managers have experienced traditional postimplementation reviews, in which the focus seemed to be who was to blame. These "witch hunts" are one of the most political and cynical of all organization practices and generally result in the victims (the project manager and the team) being blamed by the senior management, who are the most common cause of project failure (remember Chapter 2). No wonder few organizations have found the postimplementation review process to be an effective activity.

Postimplementation Review

PROJECT :

P.I.R. Team Leader Date: ---/---/---

Was the project a success as determined by Success Sliders?

Yes ☐ No ☐

Quality was	☐ as agreed	☐ below expectations	
Budget was	☐ as agreed	☐ under	☐ over
Time frame was	☐ as agreed	☐ under	☐ over

What factors were significant in the project?

What was done well?

What was done poorly?

What recommendations are there for other projects?

Figure 18.2
Classic postimplementation review form

In eXtreme project management, the postimplementation review looks forward as well as backward: forward into the support process and benefits realization process and backward to the development process. It is critical that the postimplementation review be seen as a positive process designed to determine the following information:

- Did the project meet the agreed-on business case?
- What were the successful features of the project?
- What things could have been undertaken better?

- What are the key things learned from the project that can be applied to future projects?
- What do we have to do now to manage the support process?
- When do we start the benefits realization plan?

Figure 18.2 shows a typical postimplementation review form that captures the essential information.

Don't Forget Your Sliders

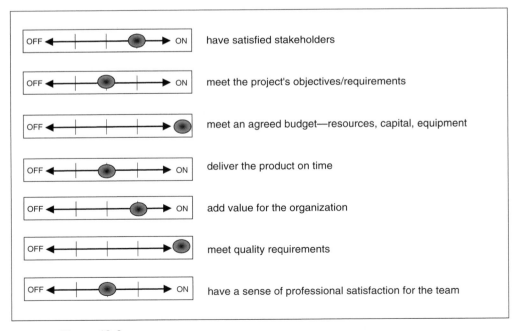

As we discussed in Chapter 7, you must define project success using our slider tool before you start detailed planning (see Figure 18.3).

As the project changes throughout the development process, you will be maintaining the business case and, by default, the success sliders. Clearly, the final negotiated version of your sliders is the eXtreme project manager's measure of success during the postimplementation review.

The critical "on" criteria are the ones that must be focused on during the postimplementation review and, although all criteria are measured, only the "on" criteria are the true measure of success.

OFF ⬅——⟋——➡ ON   have satisfied stakeholders

OFF ⬅——⟋——➡ ON   meet the project's objectives/requirements

OFF ⬅——————➡ ON   meet an agreed budget—resources, capital, equipment

OFF ⬅——⟋——➡ ON   deliver the product on time

OFF ⬅——⟋——➡ ON   add value for the organization

OFF ⬅——————➡ ON   meet quality requirements

OFF ⬅——⟋——➡ ON   have a sense of professional satisfaction for the team

Figure 18.3
eXtreme success measurement

The Timing of Postimplementation Reviews

Traditional project management approaches included simplistic rules for the timing of postimplementation reviews, such as the postimplementation review will be undertaken after one month of production or 10 production runs of the system.

Our new approach to project management recognizes that the timing of postimplementation reviews is dependent on a complex relationship between the development strategies of the system or product and the production support activities during the initial operation of the system.

As we discussed earlier, once a system or product has been placed into production, the following production support activities would normally be required:

- Defect repair: The correction of errors in function, data, process, components, and documentation introduced during the development or support process.

- Performance tuning: The restructuring of data, functions, processes, or components to improve response times, execution efficiency, and so on.

- Consulting and education: The provision of advice, information, help, and consultancy to clients on use of the new system.

- Adaptive maintenance: The expansion of variable lengths, adjustment of mathematical values, cosmetic changes to reports, and screen layouts not requiring new data. In other words, the adjustment of existing components rather than the addition of new components.

There are other production support activities that are covered in the next chapter.

As shown in Figure 18.4, experience has shown that in the immediate postimplementation phase, defect repair, consulting/education and performance tuning would rise and then fall over a period of time depending upon the size and quality of the delivered system. As the system stabilizes, adaptive maintenance would normally be the most common support activity with an on-going but predictable level of the other categories of support work.

Clearly, any postimplementation review conducted at the peak of the postimplementation stabilization activities would result in distorted feedback as business users would still be having trouble with the system. In addition, a key set of data that should be input to the review is the quality of the delivered system or product. This won't be known clearly until the system has stabilized.

In other words, the timing of the postimplementation review is driven by the quality of the system, not the clock.

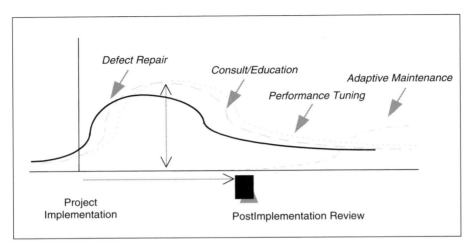

Figure 18.4
Postimplementation profile

TRY TO KEEP YOUR TEAM TOGETHER

There will be pressure to let your team members move onto new projects as soon as you ship. At least try to keep the key members of your team together through the stabilization phase. If they leave, they will be called back consistently to assist anyway. Worse, they don't get to be involved in the learning loop and other feedback processes.

This means that it is critical that you and your team remain involved with the project and the system until the stabilization point shown in Figure 18.4. It also means that you must ensure that tracking of the occurrence and cost of the four categories of support work is rigorously undertaken (this will require team members, the data center, and any help desk function to be coordinated).

Particularly important is the recording of the numerous phone calls that the team will receive from clients and other stakeholders. Although production defects will normally be recorded by data center people, the recording of phone calls is vital (our research has shown that client phone calls can consume 50% of the postproduction support effort). The form shown in Figure 18.5 should be copied and available on the desk of all team members involved in supporting the new system.

This requires significant discipline and it is the responsibility of all team members to complete this form every time they receive a query regarding the system.

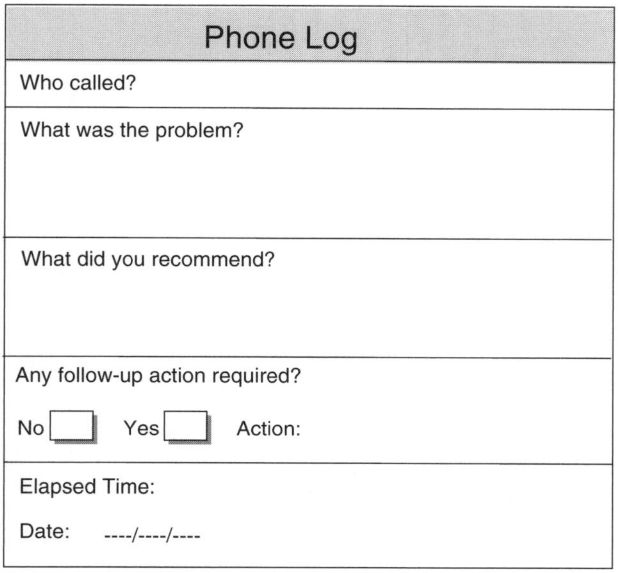

Phone Log
Who called?
What was the problem?
What did you recommend?
Any follow-up action required? No ☐   Yes ☐   Action:
Elapsed Time: Date: ----/----/----

Figure 18.5
Phone log (the missing link)

During the postimplementation review, you would also update and finalize the project metric database that you should have been monitoring during the development process.

The Learning Loop Concept[2] _____

One of the most interesting behaviors that we have observed in organizations is the apparent inability of organizations to learn from their mistakes. This is particularly true in the case of projects. Probably through a combination of poor postimplementation review practice and the "victim" mentality, very few organizations have a formal mechanism for sharing lessons—both good and bad—among projects and project managers.

The use of groupware technology can be very powerful in enabling project managers to share and access learning. The postimplementation review forms shown in Figures 18.5 and 18.6 should provide a good building block for establishing a postimplementation review knowledge base and a *learning loop* among projects.

---

2. This is one of the many brilliant ideas from my partner Camille Thomsett.

Client Satisfaction	
PROJECT :	
P.I.R. Team Leader	Date: ___/___/---

Improve Service Survey

difficult to use	☐☐☐☐☐☐	easy to use
provides poor service	☐☐☐☐☐☐	provides easy service
costs me time	☐☐☐☐☐☐	saves me time
worse than before	☐☐☐☐☐☐	better than before
disrupts workflow	☐☐☐☐☐☐	improves workflow

Which of these factors is more important to you?

Can you estimate the time saved by the system [if any]?

Are there other questions we should ask?

Other comments?

Figure 18.6
Client survey (improve service) form

The postimplementation review is a valuable process for learning about how to manage projects better and for formalizing the learning process so that other project managers, stakeholders, sponsors, and members of steering committees can benefit for future projects.

Typically, the postimplementation review will be too early in the support cycle to determine whether any financial benefits have been accrued. The postimplementation review will initiate the benefits realization plan that is discussed later in this chapter and will generally involve initial client satisfaction surveys.

Client Satisfaction Surveys

As outlined in Chapter 9, many projects will have improve service categories of benefits and these need to be measured, as well as the financial and tangible benefits of increased revenue and avoided costs.

You can learn more about a project from outside it rather than inside it.

Figure 18.6 shows a typical client satisfaction form that can be used for determining whether the system has improved service to the various clients. Wherever possible, specific stakeholder meetings in which the system service impact can be openly discussed should be conducted with the forms as a supplement.

Of course, if you had been applying the various eXtreme project management models and tools that we have covered in this wonderful book, then you should have already been gathering anecdotal evidence from your stakeholders about how well the project has been going and how wonderful this book is. (This paragraph has been deliberately inserted to see if you read it—hopefully you will have found the book wonderful. You can always contact us at our Web site.)

The Postimplementation Review Team

The postimplementation review team is the group that undertakes the process and should include the following people at a minimum:

- Project manager,
- Key team members,
- Critical stakeholder group representatives,
- External groups (including internal auditors), and
- Project sponsor or delegate.

Again, this differs from the traditional approach in which postimplementation reviews were often conducted by purely external (to the team, that is) people. The noninvolvement of you, the project manager, and your team reduces the opportunities for learning and reflects a nontrusting attitude toward the team. Any chance of the postimplementation review being distorted by the project manager will be offset by the involvement of key stakeholders and external people.

The postimplementation review report is sent to the project sponsor and members of the steering committee and copies should be forwarded to all stakeholders and related project managers. The learning loop information should be shared with as many people as possible.

The System Support Review

When the postimplementation review has been successfully completed, you and your team would normally be available for undertaking new projects such as enhancements to the product or system or new products. However, the project manager should complete or be involved in two more activities before the project is considered complete.

You should negotiate the system support review process with the project sponsor and the team that is going to support the new system or enhancement.

In our approach to project management, it is essential that the total life of the system be managed as distinct from just the development process. As we have discussed earlier, studies and research by our group have indicated that the original development of the system accounts for only 20% to 30% of the total investment the organization will undertake. The remaining 70% to 80% will be spent after the initial implementation. We'll discuss the system support review process in the next chapter.

The next and final process is one of the most interesting, satisfying, frustrating, and political project management processes you can be involved with: the *realization* of benefits.

Benefits Realization Planning

As we have discussed throughout this book, one of the major distinctions between traditional project management and our group's approach is the issue of benefits analysis and realization.

As discussed earlier, the traditional approach to cost–benefit analysis (and project management, in general) did not involve business clients in any meaningful manner. The "arm's length" model of IT as a service provider left the business people alone to determine and garnish benefits. As a result, through lack of education and lack of effective cost–benefit analysis models and accountability, many business people have sponsored projects that eventually did not provide the benefits expected. A typical example of this is where a project is justified based on the elimination of five staff positions, but no one is made accountable for the redeployment of the five people currently in those positions.

The process of benefits realization planning is critical to eXtreme project management and involves a partnership among the project team, service providers, clients, and, in many cases, external stakeholders.

Benefits realization planning has become a critical issue in our project management approaches. It involves a complex examination of both the projected estimated benefits and costs of the project during the initial RAP sessions which, as shown in Figure 18.7, are conducted during the project initiation, feasibility, and requirements analysis processes.

As we discussed in Chapter 9, the conduct of the added value analysis would normally occur interactively with the definition of the project's scope, objectives, related projects, and stakeholders. This is critical, as many of the project's stakeholders and related projects would have a role to play in the benefit realization planning.

Again, it should be emphasized that the involvement of key stakeholders and project managers of related projects in the benefits realization planning process is vital. Not only are the stakeholders expected to commit to both the garnishing of the benefits and the time frame for the garnishing, but they will assist the project manager in both identifying and estimating benefits and in establishing the validity of the added value chain.

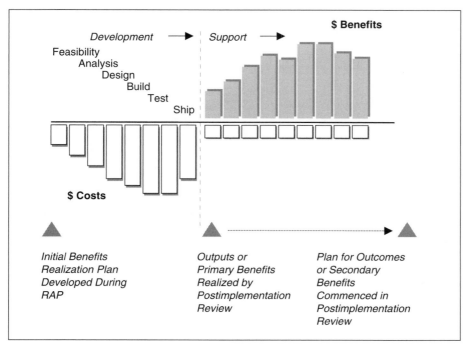

Figure 18.7
Benefits realization events

Of course, the analysis shown in Figure 18.8 should have occurred in the initial RAP sessions for your project.

UNTANGLING THE SPAGHETTI

Don't wait until the project has gone live to begin realizing the benefits. If you haven't got the benefits realization plan agreed to in the initial RAP, you must have it agreed to before implementation. After you ship, there will be too many factors and excuses available to the stakeholders for nonrealization of the benefits. For example, your product may generate new business but this benefit can be "poached" by other project managers unless you have the added value chain established.

Using the techniques and approaches introduced in Chapter 9, the project manager, team members, and stakeholders together would undertake the following steps:

- Review the project's scope and objectives.
- Obtain the organization's strategic plan, technical architecture, and other relevant documents to review the organization's objectives.

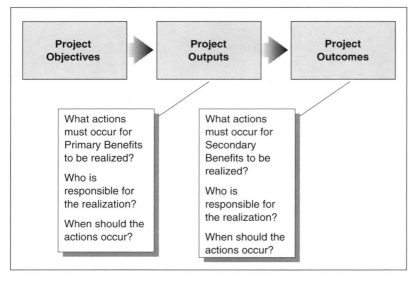

Figure 18.8
Benefits realization planning analysis

- Analyze each project objective using the IRACIS model and the Polaroid test to determine the primary benefit (output) and benefit class.

- For any improved service objectives, analyze the value chain and determine the secondary objective and secondary benefit (outcome) class.

- Gather and analyze any data, costs, and so on to estimate the potential increase in revenue or savings (notional or actual).

- Determine which person (project team or stakeholder) is responsible for the proposed benefits.

- Estimate the likely benefits curve and likely timing of each benefit.

- Obtain a formal agreement from the relevant stakeholders as to their "buy-in" for realizing the benefits.

CAPTAIN KIRK, BEAM DOWN!

If you experience any concerns in the stakeholder group and/or any reluctance from stakeholders to commit to the benefits realization plan, you should raise them immediately with the project sponsor/steering committee for resolution. Should a benefit not be guaranteed for realization, then it should not be included in the benefits realization plan and business case.

The Benefits Realization Plan

Figure 18.9 shows a sample benefits realization planning document for completion for each objective.

This agreement would be completed and signed for each project objective during Step 2 of the RAP process and the completed benefits realization planning forms would be assembled into the benefits realization plan and submitted as part of the business case to the project sponsor and steering committee at the end of the project initiation phase.

extreme tool

As discussed earlier, during the initial RAP sessions, the data required to develop a full project added value analysis may not be available and there may be a requirement for the business analysis phase to include sample measurement, interviewing, and other data gathering techniques.

Benefits Realization Agreement

Project:

Objective

Objective Class

Increase Revenue ☐   Avoid Costs ☐   Improve Service ☐

Objective Justification

Stakeholder Responsible

Estimated Benefits

Period 1	Period 2	Period 3	Period 4	Period 5

Required Action/s

Period 1 _____ Est. Date Complete _ / _ / _

Period 2 _____ Est. Date Complete _ / _ / _

Period 3 _____ Est. Date Complete _ / _ / _

Period 4 _____ Est. Date Complete _ / _ / _

Period 5 _____ Est. Date Complete _ / _ / _

Agreement

_____ _ / _ / _

Figure 18.9
Benefits realization agreement

During the project, as for other key project management information, you, your team, and your critical stakeholders must monitor the project value analysis figures as more detailed costing and estimates become available. Of course, any data that alters the project value analysis should be immediately reviewed and the new project value analysis submitted to the project sponsor for review and action.

The Project Sponsor's Role

The role of the project sponsor is vital in contemporary project management. In benefits realization, the project sponsor has a particularly important role. As discussed earlier, it is the nature of the added value chain that the project manager and team are responsible for achieving and realizing primary or direct benefits (outputs). The project sponsor and project stakeholders are responsible for achieving and realizing secondary or indirect benefits (outcomes).

For example, in the office automation project, the team is accountable for developing and installing the appropriate OA technology and software. The people using the OA technology (i.e., the stakeholders) are accountable for using the OA technology and the avoid cost benefits.

In the process of benefits realization planning, the project sponsor is responsible and accountable for all benefits (primary and secondary). As a result, the sponsor must ensure that all stakeholders are involved and committed to the benefits realization and must undertake whatever action is required to ensure that stakeholders have "bought in" and are held accountable for their role in realization.

Benefits Reviews

As shown in Figure 18.7, during the postimplementation review stage of the system development process, the actual implementation of the benefits realization plan is commenced. Using the benefits realization agreements completed in the project planning sessions (Figure 18.9), the project sponsor, project manager, and key stakeholders develop various timetables for the realization of the benefits.

To ensure that this happens, the project sponsor must also assemble a benefits realization steering committee (or similar management group) that represents all major stakeholder groups.

Depending on the nature of the project and the specific benefits curve, there should be a series of benefit review points determined at which the progress of the realization process can be monitored and evaluated. At a minimum, these reviews should occur quarterly.

THE P FILES EPISODE 15: THE RETURN OF THE CONSULTANTS FROM HELL. WHAAAT AGAIN!

Gosh, we love these guys. We came across a consultant from another well-known global consulting company. When he introduced himself he gave us a business card. His title was Exploitation Journey Manager. Huh? It turned out that a company had recently used his consulting company to implement a massive Enterprise Resource Planning package. The project had failed and the clients had actually turned off the new software so they could use the old system, which apparently was better. Not content with this disaster, the company had hired the consultant's company (the very consulting group that had screwed up the project) again to encourage the business people to "exploit" the new system. We can learn so much from these consultants!

The P Files Team Comment

Getting yourself a really big title that confuses people is the lesson here. How about instead of project manager, you call yourself "Dream Enabler" or "Change Journey Guide." Let us know if you do!

Support

In a series of surveys conducted by our group with a number of business people who had many years of experience with IT, one important issue emerged: The support and management of products, services, and information systems is the clearest indicator of the professionalism of a project development group.

WHEN THE @$$% HITS THE FAN!

If you are a reservation clerk at an airline, for example, and the reservation system crashes, how would it feel to listen to some recorded music from the help desk while customers abuse you?

After all, if you are a business person who depends on existing production systems to provide services to your external clients, the quality of product and system

---

[1]. *The A Team*, Rob Holcomb, Director; Frank Lupo and Steve Cannell, Writers, 1987.

support is paramount: "I'm sorry that we can't process your application, the computer system is down. If you can ring later…after all we pride ourselves in our customer service."

The Support Problem

Whereas many organizations are beginning to address the serious issues associated with the project management, quality management, and project development techniques associated with new products, systems, and infrastructures, the management and control issues of production systems support have been generally ignored (with the exception of help desks).

In many organizations, the support of production systems is seen as "second-class" work and is often undertaken by new graduates or by developers on a part-time basis. As discussed by many experts (see Cougar & Colter, 1985; Parikh, 1979; and our *P File* for this chapter), this has resulted in the premature degradation of production systems and poor cost tracking and reporting.

At best, many organizations only track the level of production crashes and phone calls (through the help desk). At worst, organizations have a category of work called support (it might as well be called "stuff") that is used to capture time and effort following system development. This loose categorization of work that is not perceived as project work enables computer people to include enhancements, lost time, support, and all sorts of meetings as support. As a result, few organizations really understand what is happening to their vital production systems.

The Production Portfolio Concept

In effect, organizations invest time, money, and resources in five major categories and one minor category of project-related work. This investment should be viewed as a series of investment portfolios, each having an ROI for the company. The first three portfolios are, by nature, project work and should be managed using project management approaches.

 Managing product support is as important as managing a project.

New Products, Systems, Services, and Infrastructure   This includes the development of new business processes, products, or services; information systems (data, function, or business process); and technology infrastructures (hardware, communications, tools, etc.) and information system services (standards, consultancy, etc.). This work alters the organization's status quo in terms of capability for the business groups.

Enhancement or Continuing Development of Existing Products, Systems, Services, and Infrastructure

This includes the continuing development or enhancement of new business processes, products, or services; information systems (data, function, or business process); and technology infrastructures (hardware, communications, tools, etc.) and information system services (standards, consultancy, etc.). This work also alters the organization's status quo in terms of capability for the business groups.

Strategic Planning and Research and Development

This includes the analysis and determining of directions and opportunities for information systems (data, function, or business process), technology infrastructures (hardware, communications, tools, etc.), and information system services (consultancy, etc.). This work alters the organization's status quo in terms of awareness for the business groups.

The following two major portfolios for IT and business work are different in that they maintain the status quo of business capability and, as such, require different management approaches and skills.

Consultancy

This is the provision of expert and general (as distinct from system-specific) advice on technology application and opportunities, standards, practice, and techniques to both IT and business groups.

Production Support

This is the maintenance and support of existing products, services, production systems, infrastructure, and services at the status quo. This portfolio involves a number of subcategories of work (see later).

Termination of Production Systems

This minor portfolio is the complete removal of existing products, information systems (data, function), infrastructure, and services. Although this work is relatively minor and often occurs in conjunction with the redevelopment of a system, there are cases where an existing information system or product is no longer required.

Portfolio Investment Effort

Although the relative effort and investment in each of the preceding portfolios varies to some degree in each company, research by our group, Jones (1994), Rubin (1996) and others confirms the following average figures:

- New products or systems: 30–40%
- Enhancement: 40–50%
- Production support: 30–50%
- Others: < 5%

However, as discussed, few organizations effectively monitor their investment in production support and some don't even manage the enhancement investment to the same degree of rigor as new systems work.

The Production Support Portfolio

Organizations insist on the development of a set of business- and management-related information for new systems such as the following:

- Scope and objectives,
- ROI (costs and benefits),
- Project risks,
- Stakeholders, and
- Project quality management approach.

In other words, for the business case model that we have been exploring throughout this book, a set of management-related information should be gathered for each production system and technology infrastructure using the system efficiency review.

This information provides management with a snapshot of their investment in each system and technology and provides the basis for management tracking and decision making.

The System Efficiency Review

The purpose of the product or system efficiency review is to ensure that the system continues to provide both service and the expected quality over its life cycle.

Whereas the process of benefits realization will monitor benefits, the product or system efficiency reviews provide a vehicle for monitoring both the costs of supporting the system and ensuring that it is still "healthy" and meeting clients' requirements.

The product or system efficiency review would aggregate all work undertaken (including effort undertaken by business clients) on the production product or system and would contain the following information at a minimum:

- Name and description: A brief overview of the business functions supported by the product or system.

- Product or system age: The age of the product or system including the date of first production and the dates of major enhancements.

- Size and profile: The size of the production product or system. For IT systems, this is measured in function points, lines of code, number of nodes, or other relevant factors. Also, a brief overview of the programming languages used in the system.

- Annual product or system growth: A summary or average of the number of new functions or data added each year. Alternatively, for software, a graph showing increase or decrease in size annually using a sizing metric such as function points or lines of code.

- Number of active business clients: How many business people depend on the product or system and the nature of their relationship with the system. For example, how many people depend on the system to perform essential activities.

- Strategic impact: The relationship between the product or system and the current strategic direction of the organization. This is generally measured from low to high.

- Interfaced systems: The other systems with which the system has interfaces.

- Product or system quality: An assessment of the internal quality of the product or system. Using models such as the one in Chapter 10, an assessment including structuredness of code, internal design structure, data quality, and so on would be made (also expressed from low to high).

- Product or system risk: This assessment is a summary of the quality, client impact, and team skills, but includes additional factors. The measure is from low to high and provides a clear indication of potential system failure.

- Estimated replacement value: The replacement value can be easily derived from the production product or system size using well-established industry benchmarks for development such as $800–$1,000 per function point (equivalent to 100 lines of code in COBOL). For example, a system of 100,000 COBOL lines of code would have a replacement value of between $800,000 and $1,000,000.

- Team/skills: A summary of who is maintaining the support system and their skills.

- Monthly support costs: A monthly update and summary of the support activities undertaken on the product or system and a graphical representation of the total support costs or system. This also should include any production running costs (e.g., disc storage, transaction costs, operating system, and/or CPU costs).

This information should be gathered on each production system and presented to the executives of your organization and reviewed with them at least every three months.

Production System Activities and Support Costs

As we have mentioned a number of times (after all, support is that important), the following subcategories of support work occur to differing degrees in production system support work. It is important to understand that the following categories of work are, in effect, "transparent" to business clients if performed correctly:

- Defect repair: The correction of errors in the delivered process, data, function, or documentation.

- Performance tuning: The alteration of process, code, or data structures to improve response times, execution efficiency, and data communications use.

- Perfective maintenance: The engineering or restructuring of existing process, code, data, and documentation to make it easier to maintain.

- Adaptive maintenance: The expansion of data size, alteration of calculation variables (that were correct but need to change), "cosmetic" alteration of screen, and input and output layouts that do not require new data.

- System education or consulting: The provision of help and advice on how to use the production system.

- Operating support: The support of systems in computer operations (e.g., the effort and cost in executing systems).

- Environment monitoring: The monitoring of the operating and technical environment. Monitoring network usage, DASD, and CPU usage are typical of this work. The alteration of the environment as a result of this monitoring is treated as performance tuning.

A monthly summary including the effort, cost, and rate of all the production support work completed and in the backlog for each production system should be attached to the production portfolio and forwarded to senior management.

It is of note that in a number of the client companies of our group, adaptive maintenance and system help or consulting comprise more than 50% of the total production support effort.

Passages: The Life Cycle of Production Systems_____

It is a common belief that as people get older they start behaving like children again. This phenomenon is also found in buildings, most classes of products, roads, computer hardware, and systems. In fact, by careful monitoring of the production system costs, a very clear pattern of "life stages" emerges for the majority of production systems.

1. New Product or System: Childhood

As we discussed in Chapter 18, all new products or systems exhibit the same patterns of work effort. On implementation, there is a peak of three categories of support work:

- Defect repair,
- System help or consulting, and
- Performance tuning.

The duration of this peak depends on a complex relationship between product or system size and quality.

2. Mature Product or System: Adulthood

After the product or system has stabilized, the most common form of support activity will be adaptive maintenance.

Depending on the life of the product or system, there may be a requirement for an additional activity, upgrade and conversion.

In addition, there will be ongoing, lower, and generally predictable levels of the following activities:

- Defect repair,
- System help or consulting, and
- Performance tuning.

During the mature stage, the product or system will be subjected to enhancements, which lead to increased complexity and size of the production product. This continuous expansion also results in periods of new system behavior as new components are stabilized.

3. Old Product or System: Geriatric[2]

Most interestingly, after a period of "healthy" adulthood, production systems begin to show signs of aging. Because of the lack of maintenance of product or system documentation; the departure of developers, experts, or programmers who developed

---

2. A particularly interesting euphemism for these systems is *legacy*.

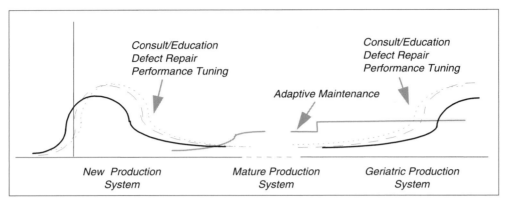

Figure 19.1
Passages of product or system life cycle

the original system; the inexperience of the support people or maintenance programmers; and the increasing complexity of the system caused by numerous enhancements and turnover of business clients, the support of the product or system begins to suffer.

Defect repair effectiveness (i.e., the number of defects introduced by the correction of existing defects) begins to fall and the system begins to "age" more quickly (see Figure 19.1).

Conclusion

Major crises such as the so-called millennium bug[3] have the effect of raising the profile of the problem of supporting old systems. However, most organizations ignore the issue of their investment in production systems.

Apart from raising the profile of support work, the production system portfolio model is vital in enabling life-cycle management of information systems. Without clear tracking and reporting of information system support costs, there is no way for effective cost–benefit approaches to be implemented.

For example, a new system estimated at $100,000 for development and $100,000 for support with $300,000 of benefits looks like a reasonable investment, until it is revealed that the actual ongoing support costs are heading toward $200,000, not the $100,000 originally estimated.

---

3. Purists argue that the millennium bug is not a bug, but rather an adaptive maintenance issue. We agree with them.

In addition, without accurate production system support data, many organizations are not effectively maintaining their development investment and, in many cases, are placing systems (i.e., their investment) at risk of early degradation.

THE P FILES EPISODE 16: THE BOTTOM FEEDER LIVES

One of our favorite *The X Files* episodes is the one in which a sailor is turned into a really ugly worm-type creature. I like this episode because it reminds me of the start of my IT career. I did my basic IT training in 1969 and I had a wonderful year with lots of parties (and lots of the demon weed—after all, I am not running for public office). My payback was that I failed the training course (with all my friends). While the rest of the group were sent to development to play with new machines and languages, my bunch were punished for failing. We were sent to production support to maintain old systems. The exquisite paradox was that the systems I maintained were written in a language called FORTRAN and I had failed the FORTRAN exam. Oh, I was treated by my IT colleagues as a bottom-feeding, ugly worm-type creature. A lower life form began its struggle toward the light.

The P Files Team Comment

The real kicker here is that in those days, there were no help desks or call centers. If a system crashed, the business people came straight to see us (another part of the punishment). Of course, I learned very quickly that IT was not about slick technology but people, the impact on them of poorly designed systems and about building good and open relationships with business people. Of course, we are not suggesting that you fail your training, are we?

Additional Resources

Getting the Sponsor You Deserve

"You'll excuse me, gentlemen. Your business is politics. Mine is running a saloon." ∎

Rick Blaine (Humphrey Bogart)[1]

If there is one common theme shared by virtually all 20,000 people who have participated in our project management workshops, it is their relationship, or lack of, with their project sponsor.[2]

The role of the project sponsor is critical in ensuring the success of both IT and business projects. Our research and experience has shown that the effectiveness of the project sponsor role is the *single best predictor* of project success or failure. Simply put, a project without the appropriate degree of executive sponsorship will fail.

As a result, for you—a project manager—the relationship that you build with your sponsor is the most critical relationship in your project.

Over the past 25 years of project management consulting and education, we have discovered a series of patterns and rules for developing and managing your relationship with the person undertaking the project sponsor role. We have confirmed

---

1. *Casablanca*, Michael Curtiz, Director; Julius J. and Phillip Epstein, Writers, 1942.
2. Although this chapter concentrates on the sponsor role, all the rules and situations covered apply equally to project steering committees.

the validity of these rules with many executives who have undertaken project sponsor roles. They work!

Rule 1: The Bag of Money and the Baseball Bat _____

This rule is the most important of all the rules we are covering in this chapter.

The management of contemporary business and IT projects involves many stakeholders and service providers. For the project manager, the need for a sponsor who can assist in the resolution of the inevitable conflicts that arise throughout the project is critical.

A simple example comes from the area of project scope and objectives. We have seen this issue on literally every project that our group has been involved with. As shown in Figure 20.1, it is likely that each of the represented stakeholder groups will

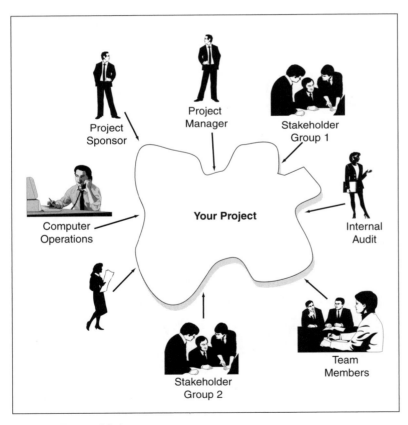

Figure 20.1
The stakeholder environment

see the scope and objectives of the project differently. The project team members supported by the members of Stakeholder Groups 1 and 2 agree that process and system documentation can be added after implementation and is therefore out of scope. However, internal audit and the system support groups strongly disagree with this position. Clearly, it is part of the project manager's role to negotiate between these stakeholders and attempt to find some resolution through compromise. However, should this fail, the project manager must be able to escalate or "push back" the problem to a person who can make a unilateral decision as to whether project documentation is in or out of scope.

Here the "bag of money and the baseball bat" test becomes relevant.

The bag of money refers to the level of authorization of spending available to the project sponsor. Simply, the larger the authorization level for spending available to the sponsor, the more corporate power the sponsor has to wield. If the person appointed as the project sponsor is, in fact, paying for the project from his or her budget, he or she would typically have the authority and authorization to decide unilaterally[3] whether project documentation was required or not.

However, should the person who has been allocated the sponsor role not have the appropriate level of financial authority and authorization, then he or she would most likely "pass the buck" either back to the project manager or upward to the person with the authority. Either action results in delays in problem resolution and delays to the project.

The baseball bat refers to the level of organizational and political power available to the project sponsor. The bag of money and the baseball bat are often linked together, but in many cases, there is a more complex relationship. For example, although the project sponsor may not have the financial authority, he or she may have the organizational authority.

Although organizational authority typically is associated with the level of organizational position, the project sponsor may have additional organizational power through his or her use of allies, powerful mentors, personal charisma, and so on. A "bright star" may have more organizational power than other people at the same organizational level. What is important here is your project sponsor's ability to use his or her organizational power (i.e., their baseball bat) to assist you in resolving project conflicts.

As shown in Figure 20.2, the simple rule here is that the best sponsor is the one with the biggest bat and bag of money. Project X crosses organizational boundaries between

---

3. The concept of unilateral decision making in a project environment is complex. A sponsor can make decisions by him or herself, but that decision will impact many other people, including people outside the sponsor's legitimate scope of control. Therefore, although the decision may be unilateral, the results may not be.

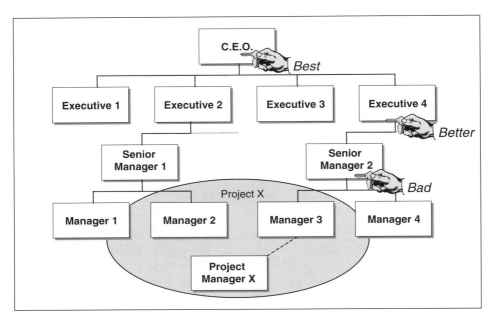

Figure 20.2
The hierarchy of bats

Executive 2 and Executive 3. If Senior Manager 2 was delegated the project sponsor role, then, it would be unlikely for that person to have either the right level of "bat" or "bag of money" to resolve conflicts between stakeholders in Executive 2 and 3 areas.

This inappropriate level of delegation would inevitably result in one of two results: At best, it would result in project delays, as the sponsor would need to pass decisions upward to the person with the right level of authority and power. At worst, it would result in the problem being left for the project manager to solve. As many experienced project managers have found, attempts to solve boundary disputes without an effective power base typically result in the project becoming mired in a series of political battles between different stakeholder groups.

One thing we have learned about senior executives is that they love using their baseball bats. All you have to do is to show them where to swing it.

Rule 2: The Passive Conduit

This rule is really a corollary of Rule 1. One of the most common and serious mistakes that you can make as a project manager is to compensate for an inadequate sponsor role by making major project decisions such as scope, objectives, risk management, quality expectations, benefits realization plans, and so on by yourself.

As a project manager, your job is to take the sponsor's concept for his or her project and, through participative project management processes, to define, refine, plan, and manage the development of the initial concept through to successful implementation and support.

The key is that although it is your responsibility to manage the realization of the concept, it is not your concept; it is your sponsor's.

Simply put, you are the "passive" conduit through which the dreams of the sponsor flow.

What we mean by passive in this context refers to the ownership of the sponsor's concept. In other words, the project management process is far from passive and it is your responsibility to proactively negotiate, communicate, plan, enable, facilitate, and manage the project team, stakeholder involvement, and so on. However, should you come across differences of opinions between stakeholders about the scope and objectives, quality requirements, and so on, of the project, it is your job to attempt to resolve the conflict using whatever organizational authority or personal power is available to you.

Should this fail, it is your responsibility to "push back" the conflict to your sponsor, explaining what you have done to resolve it and what decisions your sponsor needs to make to get his or her project back on track.

At this stage, you may find that your sponsor attempts to redelegate the problem to you by saying, "Oh! Thanks for letting me know. However, I am a bit busy at the moment. Why don't you handle it?"[4]

You are now facing the most critical decision you will face in the project. If you accept this behavior, you will be in violation of Rule 1 with all its associated consequences. Alternatively, you must firmly and politely resist the redelegation.

Try to explain again what you have already done to resolve the conflict and the impact of nonresolution of the problem on the project. Other tricks include using the "royal we" as in, "Thanks for the vote of confidence, boss, but unless we resolve this together, our project will…"

Should this fail, read Rules 7 and 8 and do your best to survive.

One of the most experienced and competent project managers we have ever met—Chris Wooley at A.M.P.—has a wonderful comment he shares with new project managers. When asked for his opinion on major issues of scope and objectives,

---

4. More likely, they'll say, "Why am I being bothered with this? Aren't you paid to manage the project?"

for example, for a project he is managing, he replies, "I have no opinion. I am just the project manager."

Rule 3: You Generally Get the Sponsor You Deserve ___

It is often said that people get the government they deserve. While acting as project management consultants on a large reengineering project, our group observed a similar situation with respect to project sponsors. The CEO of the organization had decided to fully empower a group of nine senior project managers. These project managers were managing a group of related projects involved in over $1 billion worth of organization redesign projects. The CEO made it clear that the project managers had the authority to decide what and how many meetings and committees they had to be involved in during their projects. This included whether they wanted to have project steering committees as well.

Initially, all the project managers decided on using project steering committees comprised of very senior executives. After three months, we reviewed the steering committee situation. Five of the project managers were adamant that their own steering committee added value to their projects and, as a result, they wanted the steering committee process to remain. The other four project managers felt that their steering committees were a waste of time and wanted to disband them.

The problem that our group had with this result was that all nine project managers had steering committees comprised of the *same* executives! Clearly, the issue here, given that all project managers had the same people on the steering committees was: (a) the members of the steering committees acted differently for different projects or, (b) the individual project managers acted differently toward their steering committees, resulting in different behavior.

After some research, we established that the behavior of the project managers was indeed the issue. Those who wanted their steering committee to remain had communicated openly with and proactively involved their steering committee members in decision making. Those project managers who wanted to abolish their steering committees had communicated poorly with and generally placed the members of their committees in reactive decision-making roles.

As we explain in Rules 4, 5, and 6, by communicating honestly, clearly, nontechnically, and in a timely fashion, you can influence the behavior of your senior executives in a positive manner. By delaying your communication and by using, in effect, blackmail tactics such as, "The project is in trouble and unless you…then it'll fail," you could also influence the behavior of your senior executives in a negative manner.

We have since observed and confirmed this situation on many projects.

Rule 4: In the Absence of Information, Executives Still Make Decisions

Since the 1970s, experts in executive decision making such as Henry Mintzberg (1973) have proven that executives prefer "informal"modes of communication such as face-to-face discussions and meetings to "formal" modes of communication such as reports, metrics, and statistics.

With the increasing pressures of competition, deregulation, takeovers, mergers, and economic rationalism, most executives that we work with are under substantially more pressures than those studied in the 1970s by Mintzberg. As a result, their reliance on informal and fast communication has increased.

For you as a project manager, this is an important understanding. Your executives will make decisions based on either good information or bad data. You decide what they get!

It has been our experience that the typical executives in project sponsor roles operate in an information vacuum.

One example of this rule occurs in the approval of new projects. Many of the organizations with which we are familiar have established "filters" for executive information. For example, the senior executive committees are only given information on the really large projects. One company we have worked with had a guideline that senior executives only approved and reviewed projects over $5 million. As a result of this guideline, the executive steering committee had information on only 12 projects. There were more than 200 other projects underway in that IT organization that were not reported on at all. These "smaller" projects were consuming over 50% of the IT resources. It is completely understandable, given the information vacuum that this executive committee worked in, that they would continuously approve new IT projects when there were no IT resources to allocate to the project. After all, they were only seeing a fraction of the picture.

Another example of this rule is shown in the area of project reporting. In discussions with a number of executives, we have determined that most of them do *not* read the complex project status reports that are sent to them on a monthly basis (see Figure 20.3). Worse, many of these executives report to us that even when they do read them, they either don't understand them or don't believe them! After all, do you?

As a project manager, you must learn to communicate to your project sponsor in short, information-rich messages. In general, most project sponsors want to know two things: The first is, "Is the project OK or not OK?" (what is meant by "OK" would be determined by the specific agreed-on business case or project charter developed at the beginning of the project). The second piece of information is, "If it is not OK, what must the sponsor do to assist the project manager in fixing it up?"

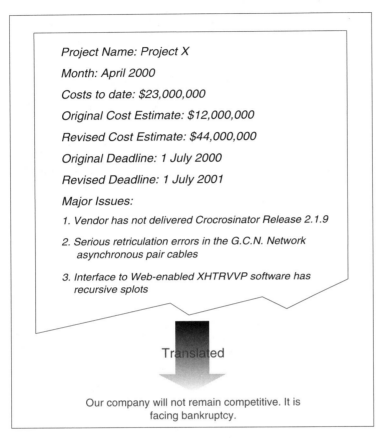

Project Name: Project X

Month: April 2000

Costs to date: $23,000,000

Original Cost Estimate: $12,000,000

Revised Cost Estimate: $44,000,000

Original Deadline: 1 July 2000

Revised Deadline: 1 July 2001

Major Issues:

1. Vendor has not delivered Crocrosinator Release 2.1.9

2. Serious retriculation errors in the G.C.N. Network asynchronous pair cables

3. Interface to Web-enabled XHTRVVP software has recursive splots

Translated

Our company will not remain competitive. It is facing bankruptcy.

Figure 20.3
Data not information

This rule also applies to issues of business alignment, cost–benefit analysis, project risk management, estimation, and other critical project management information. For example, if the project risk analysis, benefits analysis, and estimation have been done poorly, it is rare that a senior business executive would have either the time, information available, or expertise to discover the errors (see Rules 5 and 6).

In effect, faced with poorly developed and presented information, the executive will simply operate on "gut feel," informal information, and organizational political concerns to make the project decision.

Rule 5: Educate as Well as Inform

During the more than 25 years we have been involved in project management education and consulting, we are constantly amazed by the lack of project management education and support offered to senior business executives. However, on many occasions, we have been asked to present seminars and tutorials to very senior business people. In conducting these senior executive seminars, we have learned a powerful insight: **The majority of senior business executives do not understand projects or project management!**

As discussed in Chapter 4, there are two distinct categories of work in all organizations.

The first is *process* work. This work is "business as usual" and has the following attributes:

- It repeats.
- It has a short time frame (usually measured in minutes).
- It is standardized, noncreative, and structured.
- It is documented.
- It is easily measured.
- It minimizes variation between people undertaking the work.
- It operates within the status quo.

This type of work is found in factories, offices, restaurants, airlines, construction, hospitals, banks, and so on. We estimate that between 70% and 80% of all work belongs in this category.

The second category of work is *project* work, which is the exact opposite of process work. It is designed to change "business as usual" and has the following attributes:

- It is unique.
- It has a long time frame (usually measured in months).
- It is nonstandardized, creative, and generally unstructured.
- It is difficult to document.
- It is not easily measured.
- It maximizes variation between people undertaking the work.
- It changes the status quo.

This work is found in all organizations but, in most organizations, it is clustered in groups such as marketing, IT, research, policy, and other specialized groups. We estimate that, for most typical organizations, this work is around 20% to 30% of all effort.

It would be typical for your sponsor to have worked for many years in process work, not project work cultures. As a result, he or she is simply poorly informed on the dynamics of projects. More important, your sponsor is also not sure of his or her roles and responsibilities as a sponsor.

This insight explains much of the frustration that project managers experience with their sponsors.

For example, in a process culture, it is an accepted belief that great leaders empower and delegate. Indeed, it is the nature of process work that it operates in a machine-like and predictable fashion so the executive can generally leave the day-to-day operations to his or her people and focus on strategic issues. Given this, it would seem natural and normal for the same executives to also delegate many of the critical decisions for their projects to their project managers.

As a result, the behaviors described in Rules 1 and 2 are not the result of stupidity or simple-mindedness, but rather, the result of poor executive education and support.

Therefore, as a project manager, one of your key roles is that of educating your business stakeholders and sponsor on the nature of project work.

For example, you are planning to present a complex project risk assessment report to your sponsor that shows that the sponsor's project is facing potential failure (remember Rule 2). As we'll discuss later, you might make the assumption that the sponsor understands project risk assessment. However, it is a useful strategy to spend some time with your sponsor explaining the difference between business risk (which he or she should be aware of) and project risk before you show him or her the project risk assessment. If you can't get time with your sponsor send him or her a small summary of project risk assessment.

Rule 6: The Level of Help You Get Is Inversely Proportional to Your Delay in Asking _____

In our discussions with senior business executives, we found one project manager behavior that annoyed them more than any other. This was the tendency for project managers and other intermediate managers to avoid or slow down the escalation of bad news. This typically results in the executive sponsor being placed in a reactive position of fixing up the mess rather than a proactive position of taking action to avoid the mess in the first place.

With one of our clients, we were reviewing a high-profile and very expensive project being undertaken in an outsourced relationship. Our client, the consulting company developing the software, had a project manager who had run into a personal problem with the business project manager of the company for which the project was being developed. Although the consultant project manager had documented the situation it had not been "flagged" as a critical issue. When we became involved, the breakdown of effective communication between the consulting project manager and the internal project manager had remained unresolved for five months! The consulting project manager was determined to resolve the problem by himself. In fact, our conclusion was that the personality conflict was unresolvable. Worse, the project's deadlines had become compromised and the contract was for a fixed price and fixed deadline.

We escalated the situation to the CEO of the consulting company. He met with the CEO of the client organization and on the following day, a more experienced and reasonable person replaced the business project manager. More than five months had been lost in the project before the executives became involved.

Remember, great project managers ask for help and ask for it as soon as possible.

This is extremely important for those of you in larger and more bureaucratic organizations. You will probably find that there are built-in delays in any information (good or bad) getting to the top. Worse, the more levels that your report passes through, the higher the probability of filtering and distortion. You all have had a laugh at the classic office joke where a message from the front-line people that an executive idea is "shit" gets altered by each level until the CEO is told that the company should invest in a fertilizer factory.

Should your project get into trouble, you should do everything possible to get the message to the relevant executive as quickly as possible. Given the issues discussed throughout this book, you may need to be creative in breaking through the organizational barriers that prevent you from getting to the "real sponsor."

In one project, we couldn't get an appointment with the true project sponsor for six weeks. However, we found out from his assistant that he started work at 7:00 each morning so that he could get some quiet time before the chaos of the day started. We simply "ambushed" him in the company parking area at 6:45 one morning. He was initially annoyed with our behavior, but as soon as he was briefed quickly on the status of his project and the decision he had to make regarding the solution, he made the decision and was in his office, as normal, at 7:00 a.m. The project was saved and we had no trouble getting access to him from that point on.

Rule 7: Show Them the Money

Another great rule for getting great sponsors is to watch your language. Too many project managers and project reporting systems overcommunicate with executives and, worse, overcommunicate in the wrong language.

We observed a perfect example of this problem when we were advising a client regarding a project that was in serious trouble. The project involved upgrading operating systems on the corporate PCs. The client company was an early adopter of a new operating system release and the project was more than six months behind schedule. A significant factor in the delays was the operating system vendor's inability to solve technical problems without shifting the blame to other impacted vendors, such as the network supplier.

HOT BUTTONS

Although we have focused on cost–benefit in this book, there may be other issues or "hot buttons" that you can use. For example, in your company, the executive hot button may be customer service, so the trick is to convert the problem you are facing in your project into how it impacts customer service. The use of the relevant hot button is a powerful communication tool to draw your sponsor's attention to the impact of his or her decision making in terms that he or she can relate to. You can usually uncover your organization's hot buttons from your company's mission or vision statements.

By the time we became involved, the project was considered such an issue that the CEO requested a briefing for himself and the entire executive team. This sent the team into a panic and, fearing a Spanish Inquisition, they assembled a complete record of all the technical problems, how the vendor had responded, and so on. They then spent hours preparing full briefing documents (in full color) and actually rehearsed the presentation.

We were invited to attend the CEO briefing and watched as the project manager began to present a very complex and technical presentation along these lines: "Now if you'll turn to page 26 you will see that we raised the problem of the recursive articulator bug with Vendor A who then replied that it wasn't a recursive articulator bug but in fact a circular articulator bug caused by Vendor B's network concrosinator!"

The CEO, who happened to be one of the highest paid people in Australia, became increasingly restless as he flicked through the report in front of him. He raised his hand, which stopped the project manager in midsentence, and said gently, "Look, tell me how the organization will be better off when the project is over."

The project manager and the team members were simply lost for words. They (and the project) were saved by another executive whose group had been a test site for the new operating system. This executive explained that her people had found the new operating system more stable and this led to significant productivity gains. The CEO was satisfied and simply said to the project manager, "Continue the project."

The meeting was over and we saw no executive either read or take the complex report that so many hours had been spent on.

The rule here is simple but powerful. As the wonderful scene from the movie *Jerry McGuire* put it, "Show me the money." In the case of your sponsor, show him or her the money. You should avoid technical jargon and you should put everything not in English, but in money terms.

For example, you might have some trouble getting your information to the executive who needs to make the decision (see Rule 3). You have a team of five people at an average cost of $1,200 per day. So instead of saying, "The situation is that each day we lose means that we could miss the deadline," try this: "Each day there is a delay in this decision being made means we are losing $6,000." Better still, try this: "Each day there is a delay means that we are losing $6,000 and placing at risk the benefits realization of $2 million." That should get some action!

The key point of this rule is to keep your communication short and focused on the business and financial impact. In effect, this is a variation on a standard risk management concept known as consequence-based reporting. This technique focuses on the consequence of not acting rather than simply reporting the action required.

Also, there are a couple of associated subrules that deal with the broader issue of why people change. The first is that people won't change unless there is either an advantage to them for changing or a disadvantage for them if they don't change. The use of these rules and, in particular, this rule should help you here. The second is that people are often unaware of how their behavior affects other people. By simply explaining (in a factual and nonemotional manner) how their action (or lack of) affects the project, you'll often find the person simply saying, "Oh! I didn't know that was the situation. I'll deal with it straight away."

Rule 8: "Beam Us Up, Scotty"

This rule is so important and is poorly understood in most organizations that we have worked with. It really deals with risk management.

However, just as Rules 1 and 2 stated, many executives operate in an information vacuum. In 1998, studies by Accenture revealed that two thirds of business executives did not understand the issues of risk management in IT projects. Worse, of the one third that did understand the risk management issues with IT projects, 50% said that they were not satisfied with the risk management processes that they had in place!

It constantly amazes us that many organizations would use "best practice" due diligence and corporate governance procedures when faced with a low-risk acquisition of a company for $50,000,000 and yet approve a high-risk IT project of $50,000,000 with no formal business or project risk assessment. More interesting, the same organization appoints an inexperienced project sponsor who has multiple projects to oversee as well as managing a functional business unit.

This situation that is familiar to many project managers (it is mentioned by people at every project management workshop our group conducts) provides the framework for a powerful rule.

You should never undertake a project (especially a high-risk one) without a formal, written, and public contingency plan agreed to by your project sponsor. This is your "Beam me up, Scotty" position.

If you have a formal business or IT project risk management process, this will already be part of the process. However, for those of you who don't have access to such a process, it involves two key considerations: What are the situations that could arise in your project that would place your project at risk of total failure? Should these situations arise and your attempts to solve the situation directly and by asking for assistance fail, what are you entitled to do as a fallback?

Clearly, the best time to negotiate your fallback position is at the beginning of the project (when you have full control over all your faculties). You need to have agreed on a "Beam us up, Scotty" position with your sponsor. For example, you have been asked to undertake a project and you are already aware that the project sponsor is too busy and is going to delegate responsibility to one of his or her minions (see previous rules). You should have already figured out that Rules 1 and 2 are likely to be in play as a result.

Simply document, as a result of the decisions being made by the real sponsor, the impact on the project and the consequences of those impacts, as discussed in Rule 7. However, you should also document clearly that if no action is taken or the actions taken fail to resolve the impact of the risk, then there is a point in the project plan where a fallback strategy will be put into place.

Rule 9: No Sponsor, No Start

Hell on Earth is to be a project manager without the bat, bag of money, and other executive support offered by an effective project sponsor.

This rule raises some very significant questions regarding professional behavior. The most significant is this: If the evidence is that a project without effective sponsorship will fail, why would a professional project manager start a project without effective sponsorship?

Typical answers to this question include:

- When the project gets into trouble, the sponsor will emerge to sort it out.
- This is not a big project so it doesn't matter.
- The project manager can act as a project sponsor by default.
- Our sponsors are always useless anyway.

These responses reflect the difficulty many organizations and project managers face in attempting to build effective sponsorship roles.

It is our group's belief that professional project managers—like you—must take some responsibility for changing this situation. Strategies include giving copies of this book to your senior managers, using this book as support, talking with your peers, consulting your internal audit or risk management group (if you have one), and educating and educating again.

Most likely, the organization that is placing you in this situation will already have a history of projects that failed because of poor project sponsorship. This should give you additional ammunition in this battle.

 Your sponsor is your most important stakeholder.

Hopefully, these rules will assist you in avoiding having to decide whether you are masochistic or not.

Getting the Stakeholders You Deserve

> "Remember, no matter where you are—there you are." ∎
>
> *Pig Killer (Robert Grubb)*[1]

This resource is a tutorial on various considerations that an effective project manager must understand to be able to obtain real commitment from his or her stakeholders. They all deal with organization politics and relationships between people.

It is one of the great paradoxes of organizations that they assign project managers to manage $10,000,000 projects and give them almost no power or authority. We have reviewed many projects in which the limit of the project manager's financial authority was less than $500.

As a result, advanced project managers must learn to use what limited power and authority they have, coupled with any other tricks available, to ensure that they get the level of support they need from other people.

Rob's Corporate Mathematics

Many years ago, I was in the public service and we all had different classifications based on a numeric grade. For example, most people started out in the public service as a Class 1 and, if they were really well behaved, could rise to a Class 11.

---

1. *Mad Max: Beyond Thunderdome*, George Miller and George Ogilvie, Directors; Terry Hayes, Writer, 1985.

Whenever I needed someone to help me I would do a quick math exercise before I went to speak to the person. For example, when I was a Class 4 and the person I needed to help me was a Class 8, I simply subtracted our Classes.

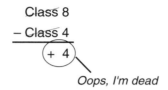

Oops, I'm dead

If the result was a positive number, it meant that I was in trouble; the bigger the number, the bigger the trouble I was in and the less likely that the person would help me (or needed to).

Although many contemporary management consultants would be appalled at this simplistic model, it worked for me and, even more important, it is the fundamental rule of hierarchies.

As a project manager, you will often be going to people whose "numbers" are much larger than yours and you need to be able to call in all the help you can to deal with this situation.

Why You Need Your Stakeholders

Simply put, you need your stakeholders for their numbers. We have discussed stakeholders throughout this book, but there is another definition of stakeholder. These people have large stakes (two meters long and sharp at both ends), and if you don't look after these stakeholders, they'll take their stakes and put them somewhere where it hurts.

However, if you can get your stakeholders on your side, they will use their stakes to assist you.

For example, you have managed to convince a key stakeholder to attend your RAP session and another stakeholder you need to attend is "too busy." You can use the supportive stakeholder to put pressure on the busy stakeholder as you apply some pressure.

Clearly, going back to Rob's Corporate Mathematics, two stakeholders at Class 8 can bring some considerable positives (sic) to bear on another stakeholder who is a Class 9. We'll come back to this concept later in this chapter.

How to Win Stakeholders Over_____

There are many good books on how to influence other people. Two of our favorites are *Influence: Science and Practice* by Dr. Robert Cialdini (1988) and *The Anatomy of Power* by Kenneth Gailbraith (1983). Like most experts on the use of power and techniques for influencing people, Cialdini and Gailbraith make the distinction between sources of power and techniques used for influencing people.

In effect, as shown in Figure 21.1, the sources of power are like a battery that you can use to charge your ability to influence. Influence styles are how you use your power source.

As a project manager, you will generally have these sources of power available to you:

- Organizational: Clearly, the higher your level in the organization, the greater your source of power.

- Expertise and reputation: If you are perceived as an expert project manager by the members of your organization, you can use this as a source of power.

- Precedent: If other project managers have done a similar thing before and it has worked, you can often use this precedent as a source of power.

- Referent: You can use the power, reputation, and position of another person as a source of power. For example, you could say "Rob and Camille Thomsett say that RAP sessions are powerful and they are world experts and authors (ahem)." Alternatively, you can use the project sponsor and other stakeholders as a source of referent power (see later).

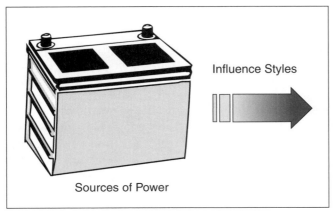

Figure 21.1
Power and influence

- Reciprocity: In other terms, one good turn deserves another. This is a very effective source of power. Make it clear that if the stakeholder attends your planning session, you will be obliged to assist him or her at some later date.

- Information: Most people know how to use this source of power. You can use the fact that participants in the RAP session will know more about the project and have a greater chance of influencing it by attending the session.

As we've discussed throughout this book, the role of the project sponsor and how you can use this person's power and influence to assist you is critical in contemporary project management.

Using whatever sources of power you have, there are different techniques for using that power to influence people. The model we like makes the distinction between *push* and *pull* styles of influence. Push styles attempt to push people toward where you want them to go. Pull styles attempt to bring the people to your position.

Push influence styles include the following:

- Logical persuasion: This style of influencing uses logical reasoning supported by facts and figures to attempt to persuade someone to do something. For example, "If you can attend the RAP session, you will be able to ensure that the requirements you have are completely understood by the team. Also, the RAP process saves over 50% of the time required for planning."

- Goals and reinforcement: The use of both positive rewards and negative punishments to ensure compliance: "As you know, we are ISO 9000 compliant and we must ensure that all requirements are fully documented. In addition, the use of RAP sessions is now an organizational standard and we don't want the standards police to notice that you weren't at the session, do we?"

Pull influence styles include the following:

- Participation and trust: This is a very powerful influence style. By admitting mistakes, uncertainty, and asking for others' assistance, you can often get people to change their position: "Look, I'm very nervous about undertaking this project without your expert input. I am sure that the project will go better if you could help me by attending the RAP session."

- Common vision: Most experts agree that this is the most powerful of all influence styles. By invoking a common goal or by emphasizing the positives, you can really get people to change their views: "We all want this project to succeed. We'll all have a much more secure future if this project produces the killer product ahead of schedule. By joining us all in the RAP session, you'll become part of the A team and help us win."

The key to power and influence is to "mix and match" your approach. Most people tend to use the same sources of power and the same influence styles all the time. As a project manager, you must learn to be more flexible and become comfortable using all sources of power and all influence styles.

Remember They Have Other Jobs as Well

If you remember back to Chapter 4, you will be aware that many of your most important stakeholders are important because they are real experts. As a result, they will also be under a lot of pressure from the following areas:

- Other project managers who need them as stakeholders as well,
- Their day-to-day process work, and
- Downsizing and demands for increased productivity.

THE POWER OF COMMON VISION

If you watched a video of Martin Luther King's famous "I Have a Dream" speech or those of Churchill, Malcolm X, J.F. Kennedy, and other great communicators, you understand the power of common vision as an influence style. Perhaps a less dramatic but more relevant example is the pirate flag that flew over Apple headquarters as they were developing the Macintosh. Steve Jobs understood how the common vision of corporate brigands and bureaucracy busters unified the Mac team.

When these people look a little less than excited about you asking them to attend your RAP session, take a moment to understand their position. Indeed, in most organizations, the amount of time that business experts spend attending project sessions is not taken into account in the measurement and appraisal of their "normal" work.

For example, you need an expert in insurance client relationships to attend a planning session. These people are measured and rewarded by the number of insurance policies they sell per week. Every hour that he or she spends in your RAP session will reduce his or her selling rate as compared to colleagues. The use of formal stakeholder agreements can solve this problem, but you must be aware of the other pressures on your key stakeholders and see if there is anything you can do to make participating in your RAP session easier for these people. **Remember, you have your project. Your stakeholders have their jobs as well as your project.**

How to Get the Project You All Want_____

One of the most common activities we do is negotiate. Every parent trying to get their children to bed must become an expert negotiator to remain sane.

Negotiation is one of the key activities of a project manager. You must negotiate every aspect of the project that you are managing—its scope, objectives, risk management, staffing requirements, and so on. In addition, getting buy-in from your stakeholders will also require negotiation.

Again, there are many excellent books on negotiation and reading any of them will give you some valuable tips and techniques for negotiating with your team members, stakeholders, and management. However, one book that helped us a lot in developing some of the techniques in this book is *Getting to Yes* by Robert Fisher and William Ury (1983). We also like Fisher's and Ertel's *Getting Ready to Negotiate* (1995), as it has a number of great tools to help you get ready for the negotiation.

These excellent little books contain powerful frameworks for negotiation and the following are some of their key models.

As shown in Figure 21.2, when most people commence a negotiation, they state what is termed their most preferred position (MPP). However, they also have a least preferred position (LPP).

You go to your boss to state clearly that you need a holiday, a raise, and a bigger office (your MPP) and instead you leave the meeting being made the project manager of the project from hell (LPP).

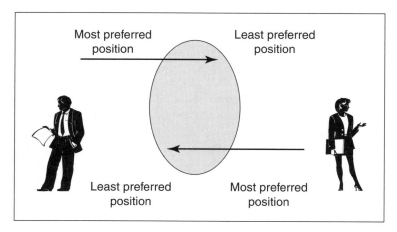

Figure 21.2
Negotiating positions

Typically, when two people are negotiating, their MPPs are far apart, but hopefully there is some overlap between each person's LPP. If there is no overlap, there will be no change for a win–win outcome, as one person will have to use his or her LPP (win–lose) or, alternatively, both parties will not be prepared to shift their LPP and both will walk away (lose–lose).

One of the keys to successful negotiations is to understand clearly both your own and the other person's MPP and LPP. To do this, you must be open in stating both your MPP and LPP during negotiation in an effort to gain an understanding of the other person's MPP and LPP.

For example, you are having a meeting with a key stakeholder whose clear MPP is to attend your RAP session for one hour only as he or she is busy. This person's LPP is to attend the RAP session for the two days that you have requested. Your MPP is that the stakeholder attends for two days and your LPP is that this person doesn't turn up at all. There is thus some room here for you to negotiate.

Fisher and Ury (1983) provided a number of great principles for negotiation but the three that we use all the time are as follows:

- Facts, not emotions,
- Invent options for mutual gain, and
- Separate the person from the problem.

These principles can help you in the preceding situation. First, try to use facts and hard data to support your negotiation. If, for example, a sponsor is holding firm on a deadline, you could show him or her the results of your RAP session. In the RAP, six critical stakeholders agree that the project needs another six months. Faced with the fact that six other people agree with you, the sponsor must negotiate. Next, separate the person from the problem. Your stakeholder is busy and the work pressure is the problem, not the stakeholder. You could ask if there is something you could do to relieve the work pressure on your stakeholder to free up his or her time. For example, you could ask your project sponsor to talk with the stakeholder's boss to see if schedules could be rearranged to free up time. Finally, invent options for mutual gain. Perhaps you could break up the RAP session into a series of one- or two-hour sessions over a couple of weeks. This would allow your stakeholder to be away from his or her work for smaller periods each day.

Remember, by showing them that you understand the pressures that they are under, you build a better relationship with your clients.

Your stakeholders are your best friends or your worst enemies . . . you decide.

A Question of Ethics

"Ethics! Ethics! Who's got ethics? Am I a gentleman or ain't I?" ■

Jimmy Corrigan (James Cagney)[1]

Before we start examining the complex and difficult area of ethics and project management, or ethical behavior and project management, we'll examine a few typical situations found in most project groups.

Situation 1

Fred has been recently appointed as the project manager for a new, high-profile information system. After undertaking an initial estimation, Fred recognizes that the project will cost four times the costs being talked about by the project's business sponsor. Fred realizes that when informed of the revised estimates, the project sponsor will not approve the project. Fred also knows that if the project is not approved, his job and the jobs of a number of system professionals will be at risk. After some

---

1. *Jimmy the Gent*, Michael Curtiz, Director; Bertram Millhauser, Writer, 1934.

consideration, Fred deliberately underestimates the cost of the project, taking a relatively low risk that by delaying notification of the true costs until the project is well underway, the project sponsor will be reluctant to stop the project.

Situation 2

Mary is a project manager specializing in PC-based applications. She is evaluating a new mission-critical system request and is considering alternative development platforms. Although she is sure that the system can be developed in Clipper, a development platform in which she and her team have considerable experience, she is interested in Smalltalk and its associated object-oriented approach. Although the Smalltalk platform will raise the inherent risk of the project and would require a much longer development time frame, she decides that Smalltalk will be more personally interesting and challenging and recommends it as the development platform.

Situation 3

John is an applications programmer working on a project that is in serious trouble. The development technology being used in the project is "leading edge" and appears unable to successfully provide a platform for implementing the system within the agreed time frame. For a number of reasons, the senior business area management who are funding the project and are depending on the deliverables for a strategic advantage are not aware of the technical problems. However, they are concerned about the lack of progress and request a demonstration of the system's progress. John is directed by the senior project manager to write a program to "simulate" the success of the technology. John writes a program to display a series of predetermined results to set actions that will be entered by the business managers. Impressed by the "live" system, the business area management continue the funding of the project and extend the deadlines. Some months later, the project is canceled as it becomes obvious to the business people that the technology cannot deliver the required functionality.

Situation 4

Lee is a project leader working in a system group that has implemented a metrics program. As part of this program, she has been given a predetermined productivity factor measured in function points per month per team member that she is expected to achieve. Due to a number of external and internal factors, Lee's team does not meet the desired productivity for a month. Recognizing that this will mean a reprimand from her managers and that her remuneration package may be affected, she adjusts the figures to meet the required productivity.

Situation 5

Angela is working on contract for a large consulting group. During her contract, she notices that the organization's accounts people do not appear to worry about the accuracy of her contract invoices and they do not require a detailed timesheet for her work. She also learns from informal discussions with employees of the organization that their travel and shift allowances are often overpaid and no one seems to care. Finally, when she sees that the organization has spent thousands of dollars on PC-based software that is not being used, she begins to bill the company for work that she has not undertaken.

Best Practice and Best Behavior

Although each of these scenarios, which are based on real occurrences in Australian companies in the past three months, might appear to be an isolated example, they are in fact common everyday facts of life for many information system people.

In 1996 we did a road show for the Australian Computer Society on computer ethics and we discussed these and similar scenarios with more than 1,000 Australian, Hong Kong, U.S., and New Zealand business and system people. A significant majority of these people agreed that these types of situations are common events and they felt that such behavior is justified in most cases.

These situations are not just examples of poor management practices, but a clear indication of a deeper problem—a lack of ethical standards.

Most project groups are undertaking serious reviews of the current levels of service, practice, productivity, and costs associated with information system development and support. Many of these reviews are being undertaken by external consultants at significant expense and effort. The typical outcome of these reviews includes recommendations on the following:

- Best practice in project development and support,
- Investment in development tools and technology,
- Outsourcing of system development and operations,

- Establishing of strategic partnerships with global consulting groups, and

- Highly mechanistic productivity, cost tracking, and quality measurement.

What these reviews generally fail to understand is that there is a long-established and undocumented set of values and attitudes (in essence, a culture) within the computing groups that can and do undermine attempts to improve computing group productivity and service. As discussed in Chapter 1, these values and attitudes have evolved throughout the 30 years of commercial computing. They are passed on by senior computer people to new entrants through a combination of actions and other specific but undocumented practices. For example, most junior programmers have been taught an almost mythical rule of estimation: Derive your estimate, double it, and then add 30% for contingency. This informal culture is further enforced through a lack of effective project and quality management procedures, management training, cost measurement, and accountability that is widespread in computing groups.

These values and attitudes, which experts such as Maddux and Maddux (1989) and Henderson (1992) agree define a code of ethics, have produced an environment in which the situations described earlier can happen without any examination or concern. Indeed, as described by Bhide and Stephenson (1990) and many others, the high incidence of major corporate fraud and unethical behavior during the 1980s and 1990s has led to a corporate environment in which any professional, business or computer, must be cynical about the whole issue of ethical behavior. In simple terms, when you see business behaving unethically, it's easy to justify your own unethical behavior.

This situation is particularly deplorable when so many of the computing concepts and approaches are drawn from other professions that all have well-established codes of ethics and associated disciplinary procedures for breaches of ethical behavior. For example, the term *software engineer* reveals computing wishes to adopt the technical practices and disciplines of engineering without adopting the formal codes of ethics associated with the engineering professions. In another example, project management is another computing term that has been adopted from a professional management body (i.e., the Australian Institute of Project Management) with a published code of ethics and disciplinary procedures. It is true that the Australian and British Computer Societies and other professional IT bodies[2] have a published code of ethics, but the majority of computer people are not members of a professional body. For business project people, there is no support at all.

---

2. Porfirio Barroso Asenjo wrote in "Key Ethical Concepts for the Internet and for Ethical Codes of Computer Professionals," *Australian Computer Journal,* Vol. 29, No. 1, February 1997, pp. 2–5, that he received 15 different codes of ethics as the result of an international survey.

In a tremendous summary of these issues, *The Responsible Software Engineer*, editors Colin Myers, Tracy Hall, and Dave Pitt (1997) assembled a number of papers that address many aspects of ethics, project management, and project work in business.

Simply put, professionalism is not merely the adoption of best practice, but also the adoption of a meaningful code of ethics.

Organizational and Individual Impact

The lack of a prescribed set of ethical behaviors within most project groups has major impacts on the organizations using these groups as internal service providers.

In the examples earlier, three of the organizations involved invested substantial money, resources, and technology on projects that should not have been approved (in one case, many millions of dollars were involved). The remaining organizations' investment in external and internal consultancy, productivity measurement software, and performance appraisal processes were compromised by widespread "cooking of the books."

The implications, however, go far beyond simple investment or measurement issues. The existence and acceptance of such behavior challenges the control of the information system effort.

In eXtreme project management, the adoption of a partnership or fully independent service relationship between computing groups and business clients must be based on a code of ethics that recognizes the fundamental right of clients to control their own businesses.

eXtreme project management is ethical management.

A second and perhaps less dramatic impact of the lack of prescribed ethical codes is the personal impact on individual project people. In discussions with thousands of project people, it has become clear that many do understand that, in some cases, their behavior is unprofessional and unethical. However, the individual team leader or project manager must face these dilemmas and conflicts of interest by using their own values as a guide as their managers and often their organizations provide no formal ethical framework. As reported by Dwyer (1993), only 42% of Australian companies have a formal code of ethics and the majority of these are oriented toward being compliant with the Australian Securities Commission duties of directors.

For the vast majority of project people, there has been no formal opportunity to discuss the issues of ethics. As a result, they either use precedent behavior that they have observed in their peers and managers or attempt to draw some guidelines for their behavior from their organization's general practices. Unfortunately, as the excesses of the 1980s continue to be revealed, there are many examples of questionable corporate ethics that provide little support for an individual looking to his or her organization for guidelines on ethical behavior.

Drawing the Line—An Extreme Project Management Responsibility

In the situations previously described, the behavior could be seen as simply the behavior of individuals who lack guidelines on ethics. However, in all cases, the behavior was either directly or indirectly condoned by the project managers of those individuals.

Just as it is expected that management must prescribe and support standards for best practice, it has always been expected that managers and project managers also prescribe and support ethical standards. As discussed by Berenbeim (1992), corporate ethics are one of the concerns of CEOs and they see the question of ethics as being integral to (a) the corporate mission, (b) constituency (client, employees, suppliers, etc.) relations, and (c) policies and practices.

In project groups it is critical that senior managers begin to address the question of ethical behavior. As suggested by Berenbeim (1992), they must ensure that the project group mission, constituency relations, best practices, and policies associated with system development and support, as well as human resource development, incorporate a clearly understood set of professional ethics.

This is even more important in general business and IT as, unlike medicine, actuarial studies and accounting, the basic tertiary and entry-level training offered by academic schools rarely provides entrants into the area with an opportunity to discuss the question of ethics. In other words, in general business it is the employer's responsibility to define the code of ethics, unlike in medicine, where the profession defines the ethical code and the teaching schools disseminate it to new members.

The development of an internal code of ethics for eXtreme project groups is essential as these groups move to form new relationships with their business clients. The code of ethics provides the foundation for establishing professional service relationships with clients; the adoption of consistent and repeatable best practice in the critical areas of project management, cost management, and strategic planning; and the measurement of productivity, service levels, and quality.

More important, the development of an organizational code of ethics draws a clear line for individuals to understand and use as a basis for their own behavior. It is true that the existence of a clear line of ethical behavior has not prevented people in other professions from crossing it, but at least the individuals knew that they were crossing it.

For many project people, the line simply does not exist.

A Draft Code of Ethical Behavior for eXtreme Project People

I will provide full disclosure regarding my projects and work to my managers, clients, team members, and service providers.

I will never give estimates or other commitments to my clients, other professionals, and managers that I cannot honestly support and achieve.

I will not estimate for or make other commitments for other professionals without prior and full consultation with them.

I will not agree to requirements, deadlines, and so on without explaining the risks and other issues involved, and without documenting those concerns for the client, managers, and other professionals.

I respect the right of others to renegotiate requirements, deadlines, and other service expectations.

My clients, managers, and other professionals must respect my right to renegotiate costs, schedules, resources, and quality on their changing of requirements.

I have a professional right to say "no" with full explanations and without recriminations.

I will never place my personal or professional interests above those of my client or organization.

I will record my work and relevant measures honestly.

I will endeavor to treat others as professionals even if they don't treat me the same way.

I will not disclose any information regarding my clients' business gained through working with them without their prior permission.

I will endeavor to provide an ethical role model for new members of my team and to discuss openly with them the issues of ethical behavior.

I will confront any breach of this code of ethics by other professionals.

The Success Sliders Redux

Of all the eXtreme project management tools, our favorite and our clients' favorite is the success sliders.

We developed this tool in the early 1990s as a simple and quick method to understand and model expectations.

When we mention the word *expectations* to most project managers and business analysts, we are met with groans, wise nodding, and responses such as, "Ah, expectations is such a fuzzy word. If we can give them their requirements, then shouldn't their expectations be met?"

Despite years of research and development into techniques and tools for modeling the requirements of business clients, it is still too common to hear the plaintive cry from frustrated project professionals, "But our clients don't know what they want!!"

There are many reasons why it has been hard to analyze and model the requirements for information systems. The first is that many of the analysis techniques that

---

1. *Apocalypse Now* Francis Ford Coppola, Director; John Milius and Francis Ford Coppola, Writers, 1979.

are suitable for modeling information system behavior are complex and confusing for business and other clients. Put simply, very few administrative people in a branch office of a bank think in terms of objects, types, normalized relationships, and scripts. Second, many business people are too busy to spend the time required by systems analysts for detailed system specification. Third, many systems analysts are too solution focused and lack the appropriate interpersonal and communication skills required to build an open relationship with the key business people.

Most important, as I argue in this chapter, we have been asking the wrong question with the wrong attitude.

Requirements Are Not the Same as Expectations _____

For many years, computing people have searched for techniques and tools to assist in the analysis and modeling of requirements. Techniques such as use case, data flow diagrams, data models, and even (shock! horror!) flow charts are useful in determining the system functionality, data, and events, but they offer little assistance in modeling the "softer" requirements that are a key part of the business client's expectations.

"What are your requirements?" is the wrong question. The right question is, "What is your world?" Once we have begun to understand our client's organizational culture, their pressures, their concerns, and their way of working, we can begin to get a clearer idea of them and then it becomes much easier to understand their requirements.

To understand their systems, we need to understand their organizational culture, their dreams, and their expectations.

So, What Are Expectations? _____

The word *expectations* has probably been abused and misunderstood more than any other word in the computing culture. To many project managers and systems analysts, expectations are simply those elements of the "requirements" that were not specified by the client. To others, expectations are the difference between what the client wants and what they really need. For the battle-hardened project manager, expectations are a wish list that begins a series of hard negotiations to reduce the expectations to minimum requirements. Finally, expectations are a hopelessly vague set of fuzzy requirements that defy documentation.

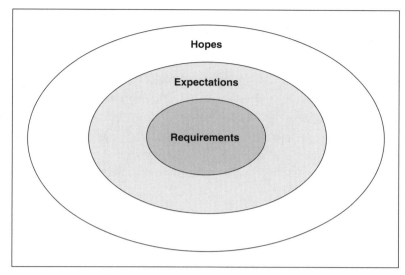

Figure 23.1
Expectations

However, it is our experience that expectations are a related set of specific requirements that can be analyzed and modeled. It's just that data flow and data model and other system-oriented techniques do not capture all the requirements for a business system.

When business experts or clients talk about their expectations, they are talking about three related concepts:

- Hope: The largest concept; for example, I hope the world lives in peace.

- Expectation: A subset of hope that is more achievable. I hope that my country lives in peace.

- Requirements: A subset of expectations that is achievable. I want my family to live in peace.

As shown in Figure 23.1, these can be seen as subsets.

The Swiss Army Knife

As explained in Chapter 7, the slider tool not only provides a tool for modeling expectations but also has three other powerful uses:

- As a quick snapshot of a project,

- As a health check,

- As a quick and dirty risk model.

Let's assume that we are undertaking a project to implement a new recruiting process for our company. We convene a RAP session and, after a briefing from our sponsor, we complete the slider tool. The result is shown in Figure 23.2.

To summarize, it is agreed that the key drivers for our project are that the team, quality, and added value are critical success factors, together with the degree of satisfaction of the stakeholders (many of whom will be impacted by the new recruitment process).

Our project is happily underway when our company decides to bring forward some management initiatives including cost constraints. As a result, the budget and time frame for our project become more important to our sponsor.

We conduct another RAP and the resulting sliders are shown in Figure 23.3.

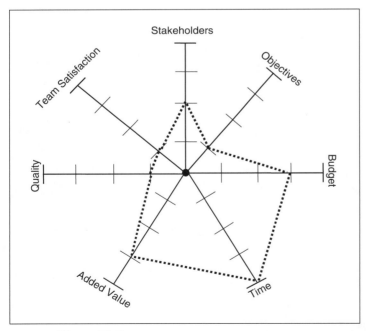

Figure 23.2
Project recruit initial sliders

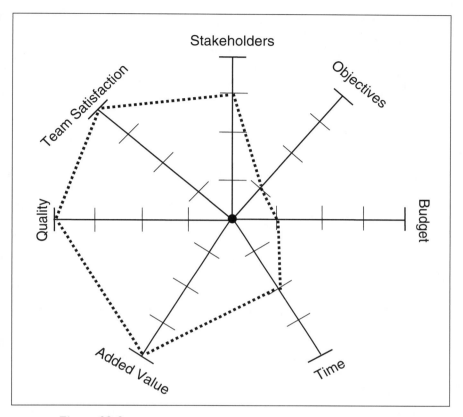

Figure 23.3
Project recruit revised sliders

Compare our two different sliders for the same project and answer this question: Is it the same project?

Clearly, our scope and objectives have not changed, but we are now facing a completely different project dynamic, risk, and success criteria.

With just one diagram and tool you can quickly take a snapshot of your project. We love the sliders!

Also, you can see how the same diagram can be used to review the status of the project: Have the sliders changed? Finally, the more sliders that are "on" for your project, the higher the risk of your project.

Other Tips for Understanding Expectations _____

Given our expanded concept of requirements as expectations, the following tips help in ensuring that your clients' expectations have been fully understood.

Become a Culture Vulture

You must understand the business culture of your clients. Spend time talking with various people from the client's business area and people from other business areas who work with the client's area. Check out factors such as these:

- What is their mission statement?
- How do they recruit new people?
- How do they train their people?
- How do they measure performance and what are their performance indicators?
- How do they celebrate success?
- How do they deal with mistakes?
- What formal organization structures exist—hierarchical, team-based?

Check out the Scenery

The physical working environment and cultural space in which the client's people work can often give you major clues about their culture and attitudes. Look at things such as these:

- Can people personalize their work spaces?
- What types of posters, cartoons, and photos are there?
- Do they have a place where their people can gather for informal meetings?
- Do they have a formal dress code?
- Do they socialize together? How? When?
- What are their common interests besides work, if any?

Learn Their Language

Listen to how your business client speaks and the jargon used when talking about work and private issues. The key issue here is to always ensure that you understand what their terms and jargon mean. Get used to saying something like "I want to get a better understanding of what you just said. Could you please go over it again for me?" Focus on the following:

- What are the key terms that are used regularly?
- How much jargon is used?
- How aggressive, hard, or soft is their language?

- Is their language based on optimism and hope, or on cynicism, pessimism, and negative attitudes?

- What metaphors and images are used commonly?

Say It Once, Hear It Many Times

Finally, never interview a client about expectations by yourself. Most people get overloaded during these types of sessions and either misunderstand or simply don't hear certain parts of the interview. At a minimum, have two people discuss requirements. One can ask the questions and focus on the interview process and the other team member can document the interview and follow up on certain issues. Always summarize your understanding of what was said in the interview and send it back to your client for confirmation. Use of tape recorders and so on would depend on the client's culture.

The best option is RAP sessions, which involve the client, other stakeholders, and the project team determining the scope, objectives (functional requirements), quality requirements, constraints, and added value for a project through intensive team-based techniques.

You must meet your client's expectations rather than just their requirements. Doing this requires you to get to know your clients as people first and as clients second:

Understand your client and you'll understand their expectations.

In Case of Emergencies

24

"Use the force, Luke." ■

Obi-Wan Kenobi (Sir Alec Guinness)[1]

So, you have applied all the terrific techniques that we have introduced to you throughout this book. The project is on target to deliver in six weeks. Your project sponsor has told you that she is really happy with the way that you are looking after her project. Your team and your critical stakeholders have just sent you a birthday cake. You are sitting pretty.

Then your phone rings. One of your team members has come across some additional requirements that were missed in the original RAP session. It is your team's fault that these requirements weren't documented. In addition, you and the team have apparently made a serious estimation error regarding testing. Your project plan looks like the mess in Figure 24.1. This means you will need another 12 weeks of work. The deadline is toast and unless you do something quick, you're the ham on the toast.

Well, you have two paths to choose. You could join the dark side of the force, hang out a bit with Darth Vader and the Emperor, and implement a series of "sneaky" and irrational options for surviving the project. Alternatively, you could move to the good side of the force with Luke, Han, Princess Leia, Obi-Wan, and Yoda.

---

[1]. *Star Wars*, George Lucas, Director and Writer, 1977.

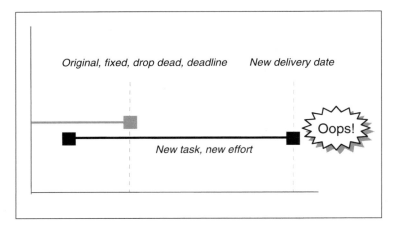

Figure 24.1
The anatomy of a disaster

The Dark Side

There are a number of dark side options. All of these will mean, at least, that you don't get blamed for the project being late. However, they are irrational in the sense that they won't solve the problem.

Dark Side 1: Don't Tell Anyone

This sounds silly but it can be very effective. Faced with the fact that you will be at least six weeks late, you and your team hunker down. You continue to report to your sponsor and stakeholders that everything is fine and begin to drop little hints that there are some small problems that you and the team are currently working on correcting. With luck, this will buy you enough time to put some of the other Dark Side strategies into action. With a lot of luck, one of your team members may leave (so you can blame his or her departure for the delay) or your sponsor will be promoted or moved to a more urgent project before anyone finds out the real situation.

Dark Side 2: Hope It Will Get Better

This is also known as entering the valley of unjustified optimism and it is typically used in conjunction with Option 1. Faced with the deadline blowout, you begin hoping that things will get better: Maybe tomorrow your company will be taken over or there will be a really big requirement change from your key stakeholder that will enable you to hide the 12-week error. My elder brother is a medical specialist and he tells me that in the human body there are a number of "little greeblies"[2] that have no other purpose than to help the body heal. In all our experience, we have never found similar greeblies in a "self-healing" project. However, you can always hope!

Dark Side 3: Covertly Degrade Quality

This is a very well known Dark Side option. Faced with another 12 weeks of work, you tell the team to drop documentation, the online help screens, and the testing of the system. We discussed this option in Chapter 9, and when the full system is delivered the business people will be so happy with the functionality, they won't need documentation, right? The bugs are just features, after all.

Dark Side 4: Covertly Degrade Functionality

This variation is often called *descoping*. You drop nonessential functionality (assessed by you, of course) without letting anyone outside the team know. By doing this you can make up the additional 12 weeks of work. Again, by the time you deliver, many of the critical stakeholders may have moved and everyone will be happy to get the basic functionality.

Dark Side 5: Work Harder—Long-Term

This is a really terrible option. This option involves you and the team trying to work an additional 12 weeks in six elapsed weeks (in addition to the six weeks of work already scheduled). This sounds unbelievable, as we discussed in our article *Project Pathology* (our Web site, www.Thomsett.com.au, awaits you), but this option results in a suspension of belief known as *cognitive dissonance,* where the team cannot accept the reality of the situation. This option is often called the "Death March" option (we mentioned Ed Yourdon's [1997] book earlier). With luck, your exhausted team members will turn on each other and, as they tear themselves apart, you can go to your management and complain about your team's behavior and how that'll mean the project will be late!

Dark Side 6: Hire Consultants or Contractors and Blame Them

This is a powerful option. You ask for help to meet the additional work and then as the consultants and contractors arrive, you welcome them with open arms. After a respectable period, you start rumors by making comments such as, "Well, the

---

2. My medical terminology is state-of-the-art.

project was a little in trouble but, since the consultants have arrived we have seemed to find another 12 weeks of work. You know how consultants are always creating work for themselves." Then, the blame can really be shifted.

Dark Side 7: Blame Your "Users"

We discussed this behavior in Part 1. It has been a time-honored practice for IT and other specialists to blame their clients: "Those @@##!!% users. They just didn't know what they wanted. Now look! We have another 12 weeks to go. If only they could have been more specific. Blah, blah...." It is clearly a very powerful option, which is probably why it is so commonly used.

Dark Side 8: Blame Everyone—A Witch Hunt

This is another powerful option. You send a memo or e-mail to all stakeholders, your project sponsor, your management, and anyone else you can think of. In your mail you gently and politically correctly imply that everyone has not given your project the priority it deserves (which, given the number of projects typically under-way, will make sense). Then, everyone gets angry and defensive and the manage-ment calls in a consultant to review all projects. You and all your colleagues then invoke Dark Side Option 6.

Dark Side 9: Leave the Project

This is dramatic but effective. There is a time-honored joke about this option. When you leave a failing project, you write two letters, seal them and leave them for your replacement with instructions that, when they find the problems, they should open Letter 1. Letter 1 says, "Blame everything on me, the previous project manager." If that fails, the instruction says open Letter 2. Letter 2 says, "Sit down and write two letters."

Dark Side 10: Add Lots of People—The Horde Model

If you can get this option going, you're in the clear. You get management and your sponsor to hire a number of contractors and consultants from different companies. In addition, you get other people from your organization involved. Then, you can implement all of the preceding options at the same time! There are so many people, so much confusion, and so much fighting, politics, and defensive behavior that you could even leave the project and they won't know for some time: "Hey! Where's the project manager? Oh, we haven't seen him for some time. He's always at meetings. You know how it is in busy projects." Wrong! You've left.

Dark Side 11: Stop the Project

You report that the project cannot be delivered because of the frequent changes (including the 12 weeks that your team missed) and that the best action is to stop the project. Management agrees and moves you on to another project because you're one of their best project managers.

The Good Side

There are also a number of Good Side options. These will all solve the problem. They also have the advantage of being ethical (remember Chapter 22) and effective. All of these options are based on your being open with your sponsor, stakeholders, and management; that is, you tell them about the mistake and the need for an additional 12 weeks of work.

Good Side 1: Shift the Deadline

Your sponsor and your critical stakeholders evaluate the added value (ROI) impact of slipping the deadline and adding the missed requirement. Their analysis reveals that the slip of deadlines and increase in costs will be more than offset by the benefits of the additional functionality. They agree to shift the deadline.

Shifting deadlines is generally not an indication of bad management but, more likely, an indication of good project management process.[3]

Good Side 2: Shift the Requirement

As we discussed in Chapter 11, you move to a sequential release project development strategy. Your clients and sponsor agree that the deadline cannot be compromised and that the additional 12 weeks of work for the missed requirement can be treated as Release 2. The key difference here is that the sponsor and stakeholders are making the decision, not the project manager.

Good Side 3: Partition and Add People

As we also discussed in Chapter 11, you move to a concurrent release project development strategy. Your clients and sponsor really want the new functionality before the deadline. You obtain their permission to get some extra people and these people

---

3. Obviously, this depends on whether you are using the techniques covered in this book.

are scheduled to work on the missed functionality; that is, you are now running the original project and project team with a new subproject and new subproject team.

Good Side 4: Overtly Degrade Quality

This is a very effective option. With all major players in agreement, you move the team to a fast-track project development strategy. With the new functionality included, you and the team begin to reduce the effort in formal requirements gathering, design effort, documentation, testing, and other nonessential development processes. In other words, you undertake a controlled "quick and dirty" development process. However, because this decision has been made openly and with the full support of your sponsor and critical stakeholders, you also have approval for the necessary "cleanup" (i.e., evaluation and reengineering of the system before any new enhancements are undertaken). In other words, you renegotiate the quality agreement covered in Chapter 10.

Good Side 5: Change the Technology

This option tends to be more useful in larger and longer projects. By shifting to more advanced development technologies (tools such as Visual Basic, Delphi, and componentware), and with skilled people and good tools, the 12 weeks could be made up before the deadline.

Good Side 6: Change the People

This is a very powerful strategy. Recognizing the loss of time that is always consumed by new members joining a team (remember Brooks's Law), with careful planning the "skilling up" of your team could be a viable option. By selective recruitment of consultants and contractors, you can reduce the amount of time required to add the new requirement. As already discussed in a number of earlier chapters, the skills and experience of team members is one of the most significant productivity factors in the project environment.

Good Side 7: Work Harder—Short-Term

Unlike the Dark Side version of this option, short bursts of hard work can be very effective in picking up the productivity of your team. By working until around 9.00 p.m. each day and by working six or seven days a week, a team of six people can increase the amount of effort by up to 30% in a given period. However, our experience is that the difference between short-term and long-term hard work is directly related to the number of times the team members have had to work hard on previous projects: The more times the team members have had to work hard in previous projects the shorter the time period is before it becomes unacceptable.

Good Side 8: Leave the Project

This could be a very effective but humiliating option, as you have acknowledged that you are the problem. It may be that, for this particular project, you may not have the skills or, alternatively, you may have burned out. In this case, by replacing yourself with a new project manager who has more skills or who can bring a fresh perspective to the project, you could be doing yourself, the team, your sponsor, and the stakeholders a favor. Surprisingly, it could also be a good career move, as you are putting other people's expectations above your own. This could be seen as a very clear commitment on your behalf toward client service.

Good Side 9: Mix and Match

In many cases, by using a combination of some or all of the Good Side options, you maximize your team's capability of delivering the project including the additional 12 weeks' worth of requirements on time. Generally, the mix and match option is the most powerful.

Good Side 10: Stop the Project

If none of the Good Side options are available to you, the most professional option is to recommend that the project is stopped. Clearly, this is a dramatic option. However, you have to make the point that, if no other option is available, your sponsor and critical stakeholders will not get the original requirements and the additional requirements on time. If deadline extension is not an option, any additional effort or cost expended on the project will be a sunk cost.

Come to the Dark Side, Luke

If none of the Good Side options are accepted by your sponsor and stakeholders, you may be tempted to take a quick visit to the Dark Side. However, we have to warn you that quick visits to the Dark Side are a fantasy. Once you have crossed over, you most likely won't come back. Before you do, reread Chapter 22.

The Secret of Great Project Managers 25

eXtreme project management is about managing creative individuals and focusing their creativeness toward adding value for clients. It is about being passionate. It is about doing good work and having fun.

However, there is a fine line between working with creative people, having fun, and being passionate about your project management skills and becoming too passionate about the project: **The secret of great project management is to never own the project.**

Once you cross the line between being passionate about your role as a project manager and becoming passionate about your project, you start to lose your objectivity, your focus, and your career. You start getting protective and defensive. You look downward instead of outward. You work harder instead of communicating harder. Most important, you stop asking for help from your stakeholders, team, and sponsor.

We have seen many wonderful, energetic, and passionate people make this fundamental mistake.

Always remember that you don't own the project. It belongs to your organization, your sponsor, and your stakeholders. They will be the winners when your project delivers the benefits. What you own is the facilitation, integration, and communication that great project managers use to manage projects for their clients. You own the project management process, they own the project.

All the tools and techniques in this book have been developed to fully empower your stakeholders in realizing their dreams: **You are the conduit through which the dreams of your sponsor and stakeholders flow.**

References

J. L. Adams, *Flying Buttresses, Entropy and O-rings*. Boston, Harvard University Press, 1991.

Y. Akao (Ed.), *Quality Function Deployment*. Cambridge, MA, Productivity Press, 1990.

K. Beck & M. Fowler, *Planning Extreme Programming*. Boston, Addison-Wesley, 2001.

R. E. Berenbeim, "Defining Corporate Ethics," *Frontiers of Leadership*, M. Syrett & C. Hogg (eds.). Oxford, UK, Blackwell, 1992.

P. L. Bernstein, *Against The Gods*. New York, John Wiley & Sons, 1996.

A. Bhide & H. H. Stephenson, "Why Be Honest if Honesty Doesn't Pay," *Harvard Business Review*, September–October 1990, pp. 121–129.

B. W. Boehm, *Software Risk Management*. Washington, DC, IEEE Computer Society Press, 1989.

F. P. Brooks, *The Mythical Man-Month*. Reading, MA, Addison-Wesley, 1975.

R. Cialdini, *Influence: Science and Practice*. New York, Harper Collins, 1988.

L. Cohen, *Quality Function Deployment: How to Make QFD Work for You*. Reading, MA, Addison-Wesley, 1995.

J. D. Cougar & M.A. Colter, *Maintenance Programming: Improved Productivity Through Motivation*. Englewood Cliffs, NJ, Prentice-Hall, 1985.

P. Crosby, *Quality Is Free*. New York, New American Library, 1979.

M. A. Cusumano & R. W. Shelby, *Microsoft Secrets*. London, HarperCollins, 1996.

D. DeCarlo, "Quantum development," Cutter Consortium Executive Update, Vol. 2, No. 12.

W. E. Deming, *Out of the Crisis*. Cambridge, MA, MIT Center for Advanced Engineering, 1986.

P. Drucker,*The New Realities*. London, Mandarin Paperbacks, 1989.

M. Dwyer, "Business Lags on Ethics Codes: Study," *Australian Financial Review*, 18 March, 1993, p. 3.

S. Eppinger, "Innovation at the Speed of Information," *Harvard Business Review,* January 2001, pp. 149–158.

R. Fisher & W. Ury, *Getting to Yes*. London, Hutchinson, 1983.

R. Fisher & D. Ertel, *"Getting Ready to Negotiate: The Getting to Yes Workbook,"* New York, Penguin Books, 1995.

R. Frason, *Management of the Absurd*. New York, Simon & Schuster, 1996.

D. Freedman & G.M. Weinberg, *Handbook of Walkthroughs, Inspections and Technical Reviews*. Boston, Little Brown, 1977.

T. Friedman, *The Lexus and the Olive Tree*. London, HarperCollins, 1999.

J. K. Gailbraith, *The Anatomy of Power*. Boston, Houghton Mifflin, 1983.

C. Handy, *The Age of Unreason*. Boston, Harvard University Press, 1989.

D. Hughes, "The Tantrum of the Opera," The *Weekend Australian Review,* October 23–24, 1993, p. 1.

J. R. Hauser & D. Claussing, "The House of Quality," *Harvard Business Review,* Vol. 66, No. 3, May–June 1988.

V. E. Henderson, *What's Ethical in Business.* New York, McGraw Hill, 1992.

C. Jones, *Assessment and Control of Software Risks.* Englewood Cliffs, NJ, Prentice-Hall/Yourdon Press, 1994.

J. M. Juran, *Juran on Leadership for Quality.* New York, Free Press, 1989.

J. Kao, *Jamming: The Art and Discipline of Business Creativity.* San Francisco, HarperBusiness, 1997.

J. Keegan, "Chateau Leadership," *Frontiers of Leadership,* M. Syrett & C. Hogg (Eds.). Oxford, UK, Blackwell, 1992.

C. H. Kepner & B. B. Tregoe, *The New Rational Manager.* Princeton, NJ, Kepner-Tregoe, Inc., 1981.

B. King, *Better Designs in Half the Time: Implementing Q.F.D. in America.* Methuen, MA, GOAL/QPC, 1989.

P. W. Keen, *Shaping the Future. Business Design Through Information Technology.* Boston, Harvard Business School Press, 1991.

D. Kroberg & J. Bagnall, *The Universal Traveller: A Soft-Systems Guide to Creativity, Problem-Solving and the Process of Reaching Goals.* Los Altos, CA, William Kaufmann, 1974.

R. B. Maddux & D. Maddux, *Ethics in Business.* Los Altos, CA, Crisp, 1989.

J. A. McCall & M.T. Matsumoto, *Software Quality Metrics Enhancements.* Rome, NY, Rome Air Development Center Air Force Systems Command, 1980.

J. McCarthy, *Dynamics of Software Development.* Redmond, WA, Microsoft Press, 1995.

S. McConnell, *Rapid Development.* Redmond, WA, Microsoft Press, 1996.

P. Metzger, *Managing a Programming Project.* Englewood Cliffs, NJ, Prentice-Hall, 1979.

P. Miller, *Mission Critical Leadership.* New York, McGraw-Hill, 2001.

H. Mintzberg, *The Nature of Managerial Work.* New York, Harper & Row, 1973.

N. Munk, "The New Organization Man," *Fortune,* March 16, 1998, pp. 43–49.

C. Myer, *Fast Cycle Time: How to Align Purpose, Strategy and Structure for Speed.* New York, The Free Press, 1993.

C. Myers, T. Hall & D. Pitt (Eds.), *The Responsible Software Engineer: Selected Readings in IT Professionalism.* New York, Springer, 1997.

D. Osborne & T. Gaebler, *Reinventing Government.* New York, Plume, 1992.

G. Parikh, *System Maintenance Handbook.* Lincoln, NE, Ethnotech, 1979.

M. M. Parker, R. J. Benson with H. E. Trainor, *Information Economics: Linking Business Performance to Information Technology.* Englewood Cliffs, NJ, Prentice-Hall, 1988.

A. Patching, *Partnering and Personal Skills for Project Management Mastery.* Sydney, Alan Patching & Associates Pty Ltd, 1994.

T. Peters, *Thriving on Chaos.* London, Macmillan, 1988.

T. Peters, "A Brand Called You," *Fast Company, 10,* August 1997, p. 83.

L. Pinault, *Consulting Demons: Inside the Unscrupulous World of Global Corporate Consulting.* New York, Harper Business, 2000.

D. Pink, "A Free Agent Manifest," *Fast Company, 12,* December 1997/January 1998, p. 152.

M. E. Porter, *Competitive Advantage.* New York, Free Press, 1985.

L. H. Putnam & W. Myers, *Measures for Excellence: Reliable Software on Time, within Budget.* Englewood Cliffs, NJ, Yourdon Press/Prentice-Hall, 1992.

R. Rhodes, *The Making of the Atomic Bomb.* New York, Touchstone Books, 1995.

H. Rubin (Ed), *IT Metrics Strategies.* Arlington, MA, Cutter Information Systems, Vol. 1, No. 6, January 1996.

P. G. Sassone & A. P. Schwartz, "Cost-Justifying OA: A Straightforward Method for Quantifying the Benefits of Automated Office Systems," *Datamation,* Vol. 32, No. 4, February 1986, pp. 83–88.

P. Schwartz, *The Art of the Long View.* New York, Doubleday, 1991.

H. N. Schwarzkopf, *It Doesn't Take a Hero.* New York, Bantam Books, 1992.

R. Thomsett, *People & Project Management.* Englewood Cliffs, NJ, Yourdan Press, 1981.

R. Thomsett, *Third Wave Project Management.* Englewood Cliffs, NJ, Yourdon Press, 1992.

G. M. Weinberg, *The Psychology of Computer Programming.* New York, Von Nostrand Reinhold, 1971.

E. Yourdon, *Death March.* Upper Saddle River, NJ, Prentice-Hall PTR, 1997.

G. P. Zachary, *Showstopper.* London, Warner Books, 1994.

R. E. Zultner, "Quality Function Deployment for Software," *American Programmer,* Vol. 5, No. 2, February 1992.

Index

A

Active participation in planning of project, 32
Actual *versus* notional costs, 104–5
Added-value analysis
    actual *versus* notional costs, 104–5
    benefits realization, 107–8
    case study, 112–14
    contingent valuation, 106–7
    cost-effectiveness model, 108–9
    double-counted benefits, 110
    hedonic costing, 105–6
    IRACIS model, 103–4
    linked value chain, 102–3
    overview, 101
    Polaroid test, 103
    project prioritization, 110
    requirements, 73
    shadow pricing, 105–6
    value chain, 101–3
Adjustments, 219
Agile strategy, 147
Approval, critical information for project, 52
Assistance to project manager, 32
Assistance to projects, 251–53
Automated project management tools, 242

B

Bag of money and baseball bat rule, 288–90
Beam us up Scotty rule, 299–300
Benefits realization, 107–8, 268–72
Benefits reviews, 273
Black box project management, 29–30
Blame, 329–30
Brainstorm project tasks, 178–79
Brook's Law, 217
Budget, 73
Business case, 57–58, 255–56

Business culture, 324
Business risk, 159–60

C

Case studies
    added-value analysis, 112–14
    business case, 59–60
    development strategy, 153
    estimation of project, 209–10
    objectives, 92–93
    project reporting, 257
    project schedule, 225–26
    quality, 130–31
    risk analysis, 172–73
    ROI, 236–38
    scope, 92–93
    stakeholders, 92–93
    success sliders, 77
    task list development, 187
Change control process, 253–54
Classes of risk, 159
Client environment, 163
Client satisfaction surveys, 267
Common vision, 306–7
Communication with stakeholders, 88–89
Concurrent release strategy, 141–42
Consultants, 277, 329–30
Containment of risk, 167–70
Content, 25–27
Context, 25–27, 37
Contingent valuation, 106–7
Cost-benefit analysis
    estimation of costs and benefits occurring at
        different times, 99–100
    intangible benefits, 98
    lack of benefits realization planning, 98–99
    limited economic focus, 98

Cost-benefit analysis (*cont'd*)
    overview, 95–97
    poor costing models, 100
    problems, 97–100
    whole-of-life model, lack of, 100
Cost-effectiveness model, 108–9
Cost issues, 129
Covert degradation of functionality, 329
Covert degradation of quality, 329
Creative work, 244–45
Critical stakeholders, 86

D

Dark Age stage, 6
Deadlines
    meeting, 73
    shifting, 331
Defect ripple effect, 206–7
Defining product requirements, 123
Deliverable dependency, 214–15
Detailed process, 197–208
Development strategy
    agile strategy, 147
    case study, 153
    changing, 149
    concurrent release strategy, 141–42
    evolutionary strategy, 142–45
    fast track strategy, 142–45
    hybrid strategy, 145
    lite strategy, 147
    Microsoft's Daily Build strategy, 146–47
    mixing strategies, 147
    monolithic strategy, 136–39
    overview, 133–35
    production prototyping strategy, 142–45
    radical fast track strategy, 146
    RAD strategy, 146
    and risk assessment, 149–50
    selection, 148–49, 151
    sequential release strategy, 139–41
    time-boxing strategy, 146
    waterfall strategy, 136–39
Documentation, 196
Double-counted benefits, 110
Draft code of ethical behavior, 317
Dynamic stage of project management, 19–20

E

Educate as well as inform rule, 295–96
E-economy, 12–13
Elapsed days, adjust estimates to, 215
Emergencies
    adding people to project, 330, 331–32
    bad options, 328–31
    blame, 329–30
    consultants, blaming, 329–30
    covert degradation of functionality, 329
    covert degradation of quality, 329
    deadlines, shifting, 331
    good options, 331–33
    hope for change, 328–29
    leaving project, 330, 333
    overtly degrade quality, 332
    overview, 327
    people, changing, 332
    requirements, shifting, 331
    secrecy, 328
    stopping project, 331, 333
    technology, changing, 332
    users, blaming, 330
    work harder (long-term), 329
    work harder (short-term), 332–33
Engineered stage of project management, 19
Enhancement of existing products, systems, services, and infrastructure, 277
E-projects, 4
Errors, causes of, 189–93
Essential stakeholders, 86–87
Estimation of project
    case study, 209–10
    defect ripple effect, 206–7
    detailed process, 197–208
    documentation, 196
    errors, causes of, 189–93
    estimate, 194
    experts, 196
    forgetting tasks, 193
    function point estimate, 201–2
    guess, 194
    guesstimate, 194, 203–4
    miscalculating project risk, 192
    misestimating scope, 191
    misestimating stakeholders' effort, 191–92
    misunderstanding people, 193
    misunderstanding quality, 192
    no estimate, 197, 198–99
    overview, 194–95
    principles, 195–97
    process, 195
    quality, 206–8
    risk assessment, 195–96, 199–200
    sensitivity analysis, 197, 204–5
    single-person estimation, 195
    team-based estimates, 202–4
    work breakdown structures, 197, 200

Ethics
    development of internal code of ethics, 316–17
    draft code of ethical behavior, 317
    example situations, 311–13
    individual impact, 315–16
    organizational impact, 315–16
    values and attitudes in computer groups, 313–15
Evolutionary strategy, 142–45
Evolution of project management
    dynamic stage of project management, 19–20
    engineered stage of project management, 19
    eXtreme stage of project management, 20
    initial stage of project management, 19
    jazz as eXtreme project management, 21
    overview, 15–18
    stages of project management, 18–21
    waves of project management, 18–21
Expectations, 71, 320–21, 323–25
Experience of team members, 182
Experts, 196
EXtreme project management, 23–24
EXtreme stage of project management, 20

F
Facilitator, project manager as, 29–31
FAST technique, 34–35
Fast track strategy, 142–45
Feasibility study, 55–56
Feature chiefs, 127
Fifty-fifty method, 243
Fine-tune methodology, 179
First-cut network, 214–15
First-cut schedule, 215–17
5/10 day rule, 180–81
Forgetting tasks, 193
Formalizing stakeholder relationships, 89–91
Free agents, 10–12
Function point estimate, 201–2

G
Globalization, 12–13
Guess, 194
Guesstimate, 194, 203–4

H
Hedonic costing, 105–6
Help, asking for, 296–97
Hybrid strategy, 145

I
Individual impact, 315–16

Information technology, shift in control of, 4–10
Information vacuum, 293–94
Initial stage of project management, 19
Initiation process, 55–56
Inspections, 126
Intangible benefits, 98
In the absence of information, executives still
    make decisions rule, 293–94
IRACIS model, 103–4

J
Jargon, 324–25
Jazz as eXtreme project management, 21

L
Language, 324–25
Learning loop, 265–67
Leaving project, 330, 333
Level of help you get is inversely proportional to
    your delay in asking rule, 296–97
Life cycle of production systems, 280–82
Limited economic focus, 98
Linear progress, 242–43
Linked value chain, 102–3
Lite strategy, 147

M
Maintaining project management file, 255–56
Mature product or system, 281
Meeting of objectives and requirements, 72
Methodologies, 177
Microsoft's Daily Build strategy, 146–47
Miscalculating project risk, 192
Misestimating scope, 191
Misestimating stakeholders' effort, 191–92
Misunderstanding people, 193
Misunderstanding quality, 192
Mixing strategies, 147
Modified Kepner-Tregoe scope/objectives tool,
    82–83
Money, explanations in terms of, 298–99
Monolithic strategy, 136–39
Moral dilemma, 183–84
Multiple interviewees of client, 325

N
Nature of task, 182
Negotiation, 123, 308–9
New product or system, 276–77, 281
New project environment
    Dark Age stage, 6

New project environment (*cont'd*)
    E-economy, 12–13
    forces driving change in, 4–13
    free agents, 10–12
    globalization, 12–13
    information technology, shift in control of, 4–10
    outsourcing, 8
    Partnership stage, 9–10
    Payback stage, 7–9
    Tokenism stage, 7
Nonessential stakeholders, 87
No sponsor, no start rule, 300–301

O

Objectives
    case study, 92–93
    constraints compared, 85–86
    levels, 84
    modified Kepner-Tregoe scope/objectives tool, 82–83
    project objectives confused with system objectives, 85
    refining, 84–85
    scope compared, 79–82
    take it away test, 83
Old product or system, 281–82
One hundred-zero method, 243
One minute sponsor, 32
Organizational impact, 315–16
Outsourcing, 8
Overall project risk assessment, 167
Owning project, importance of never, 335–36

P

Partitioning guidelines
    by benefits, 148
    by data, 147
    by function, 147
    by stakeholder, 148
Partnership agreement, 89–91
Partnership stage, 9–10
Passive conduit rule, 290–92
Payback stage, 7–9
People, changing, 332
Physical working environment, 324
Polaroid test, 103
Poor costing models, 100
Portfolio investment effort, 277–78
Postimplementation reviews
    benefits realization planning, 268–72
    benefits reviews, 273
    client satisfaction surveys, 267
    described, 55

learning loop, 265–67
    overview, 259–62
    sponsor's role, 273
    success sliders, 262
    system support review, 268
    team for, 267–68
    timing of, 263–65
PQD process, 121–25
Problems, 97–100
Process for project management
    approval, critical information for project, 52
    business case, 57–58
    feasibility study, 55–56
    initiation process, 55–56
    overview, 49–50
    post implementation reviews, 55
    project charter, 57–58
    project justification, approval, and review, 50–52
    project planning, 52–54
    project reporting, 54
    project tracking, 54
    terms of reference, 57–58
Process work, 42
Production portfolio concept, 276–77
Production prototyping strategy, 142–45
Production support, 277
Production support portfolio, 278–80
Production system activities and support costs, 280
Product risk, 162–63
Project charter, 57–58
Project justification, approval, and review, 50–52
Project management
    active participation in planning of project, 32
    assistance to project manager, 32
    black box project management, 29–30
    content, 25–27
    context, 25–27
    context, failure due to, 37
    evolution of. *See* evolution of project management
    facilitator, project manager as, 29–31
    FAST technique, 34–35
    one minute sponsor, 32
    process for. *See* process for project management
    rapid planning, 34–35
    RAP sessions, 34–35
    reviews, 247–48
    scenario planning, 33–34
    sponsors as executive project managers, 31–33
    stages of, 18–21

technical management compared, 24–25
variables, monitoring of key project, 32
virtual teams, 36–37
white box project management, 30
whole-of-life project management, 27–29
Project managers
  behavior of, 292
  secret of great project managers, 335–36
Project metric database, 246
Project objectives confused with system
    objectives, 85
Project planning, 52–54
Project prioritization, 110
Project quality deployment, 115–18
Project reporting, 54
  assistance to projects, 251–53
  business case, 255–56
  case study, 257
  change control process, 253–54
  maintaining project management file, 255–56
  overview, 246–47
  project management reviews, 247–48
  project steering committee meeting structure,
    252–53
  radical reports, 250–51
  resolution of project conflicts, 251–52
  review process, 248–49
  stakeholders, reporting to, 253
  technical reviews, 247–48
Project risk
  assessment, 161–63
  described, 159–60
  management, 160–67
Project steering committee meeting structure,
    252–53
Project work
  categories, 43–45
  described, 41–42
  process work, conflict with, 42–43
  size of project, 45–46
Pull influence styles, 306
Push influence styles, 306

Q

QFD (quality function deployment), 117–18
Quality, 206–8
  assurance, 128, 242
  attributes, 119–21
  case study, 130–31
  cost issues, 129
  defining product requirements, 123
  feature chiefs, 127
  impact of, 128–29

index, 124–25
inspections, 126
negotiating quality attributes, 123
overview, 115–18
PQD process, 121–25
project quality deployment, 115–18
QFD (quality function deployment), 117–18
requirements, 74
review quality attributes with sponsor, 123–24
speed reviews, 126–27
stakeholders' ranking, 123
technical reviews, 126
walkthroughs, 126

R

Radical fast track strategy, 146
Radical reports, 250–51
RAD strategy, 146
Rapid planning, 34–35
RAP sessions, 34–35
  length of, 67
  overview, 61–62
  stakeholders, conflicts among, 63–65
  structure, 65–66
  technology, 67
Real-time planning, 185–86
Related projects, 87–88
Repeat process, 179–80
Requirements, 320, 331
Research and development, 277
Resolution of project conflicts, 251–52
Resources, 217–19
Responsibility issues, 290–92
Return on investment. *See* ROI
Review process, 248–49
Risk analysis
  business risk, 159–60
  case study, 172–73
  classes of risk, 159
  client environment, 163
  containment of risk, 167–70
  negative perception of, 170–71
  overall project risk assessment, 167
  overview, 155–59
  product risk, 162–63
  project risk, 159–60
  project risk assessment, 161–63
  project risk management, 160–67
  reduction of risk, 167–70
  risk assessment process, 165–67
  risk management committee, 170
  risk management plans, 169–70
  risk tracking and reporting, 170

Risk analysis (*cont'd*)
  subjective *versus* objective risk assessment,
    164–65
  system risk, 162–63
  target environment, 163
  team environment, 163
ROI
  analyzing, 235
  benefit curves, 231–32
  calculation periods, 231–32
  case study, 236–38
  cost-effectiveness, 236
  first-to-market benefit curve, 231
  fundamentals, 229–33
  future value, 234–35
  present value, 234–35
  project costs, analyzing, 234–35
  recurring benefit curve, 231
  and risk, 230
  sensitivity analysis and, 230–31
  strategic benefit curve, 231
  support costing, 232–34

S

Scenario planning, 33–34, 185–86,
    219–21
Schedule for project
  adjustments, 219
  Brook's Law, 217
  case study, 225–26
  deliverable dependency, 214–15
  elapsed days, adjust estimates to, 215
  first-cut network, 214–15
  first-cut schedule, 215–17
  overview, 211–13
  resources, 217–19
  scenario planning, 219–21
  skill models, 222–23
  staffing agreements, 221–24
  virtual team, 224
Scope
  case study, 92–93
  objectives compared, 79–82
Secrecy, 328
Selection, 148–49, 151
Sensitivity analysis, 197, 204–5
Sequential release strategy, 139–41
Shadow pricing, 105–6
Show them the money rule, 298–99
Single-person estimation, 195
Size of project, 45–46
Skill models, 222–23
Speed reviews, 126–27

Sponsors
  in the absence of information, executives still
    make decisions rule, 293–94
  agreement, 91
  bag of money and baseball bat rule, 288–90
  beam us up Scotty rule, 299–300
  behavior of project managers, 292
  educate as well as inform rule, 295–96
  as executive project managers, 31–33
  help, asking for, 296–97
  information vacuum, 293–94
  level of help you get is inversely proportional
    to your delay in asking rule, 296–97
  money, explanations in terms of, 298–99
  no sponsor, no start rule, 300–301
  overview, 287–88
  passive conduit rule, 290–92
  political power available to, 288–90
  responsibility issues, 290–92
  review quality attributes with sponsor, 123–24
  risk management, 299–300
  role of, 273
  show them the money rule, 298–99
  spending, level of authorization of, 288–90
  understanding of projects, lack of, 295–96
  you generally get the sponsor you deserve
    rule, 292
Staffing agreements, 221–24
Stakeholders
  case study, 92–93
  common vision, 306–7
  communication, 88–89
  conflicts among, 63–65
  critical stakeholders, 86
  essential stakeholders, 86–87
  formalizing stakeholder relationships,
    89–91
  influencing, 305–7
  negotiation, 308–9
  nonessential stakeholders, 87
  overview, 86–87
  partitioning guidelines, 148
  partnership agreement, 89–91
  pull influence styles, 306
  push influence styles, 306
  ranking, 123
  reasons for, 304
  related projects, 87–88
  reporting to, 253
  sponsor agreement, 91
  team members compared, 91
Stopping project, 331, 333
Strategic planning, 277
Subjective progress, 243

Subjective *versus* objective risk assessment, 164–65
Success of project
    added-value requirements, 73
    budget, meeting, 73
    criteria for, 72–74
    deadlines, meeting, 73
    expectations, 71
    meeting of objectives and requirements, 72
    overview, 69–71
    quality requirements, 74
    satisfaction, degree or level of stakeholder, 72
    success sliders, 74–77
    team satisfaction, 74
Success sliders, 74–77, 262
    business culture, 324
    case study, 77
    expectations, 320–21, 323–25
    jargon, 324–25
    language, 324–25
    multiple interviewees of client, 325
    physical working environment, 324
    requirements, 320
    uses for, 321–23
Support
    consultancy, 277
    enhancement of existing products, systems, services, and infrastructure, 277
    life cycle of production systems, 280–82
    mature product or system, 281
    new product or system, 281
    new products, systems, services, and infrastructure, 276–77
    old product or system, 281–82
    overview, 276
    portfolio investment effort, 277–78
    production portfolio concept, 276–77
    production support, 277
    production support portfolio, 278–80
    production system activities and support costs, 280
    research and development, 277
    strategic planning, 277
    system efficiency review, 278–80
    termination of production systems, 277
System efficiency review, 278–80
System risk, 162–63
System support review, 268

T

Tailor methodology, 177–78
Take it away test, 83
Target environment, 163

Task list development
    brainstorm project tasks, 178–79
    case study, 187
    experience of team members, 182
    fine-tune methodology, 179
    5/10 day rule, 180–81
    methodologies, 177
    moral dilemma, 183–84
    nature of task, 182
    overview, 175–77
    real-time planning, 185–86
    repeat process, 179–80
    review with experts, 179
    risk of task, 181–82
    scenario planning, 185–86
    tailor methodology, 177–78
    trusting your team, 182
Team
    environment, 163
    members compared, 91
    satisfaction, 74
Team-based estimates, 202–4
Technical management compared, 24–25
Technical reviews, 126, 247–48
Technology, changing, 332
Termination of production systems, 277
Terms of reference, 57–58
Time-boxing strategy, 146
Tokenism stage, 7
Tracking mechanism, 245
Tracking of project, 54
    automated project management tools, 242
    creative work, 244–45
    fifty-fifty method, 243
    linear progress, 242–43
    one hundred-zero, 243
    overview, 239–40
    project metric database, 246
    quality assurance, 242
    subjective progress, 243
    time tracking compared, 241–42
    tracking mechanism, 245
    tracking summaries, 245–46
Tracking summaries, 245–46
Trusting your team, 182

U

Understanding of projects, lack of, 295–96
Users, blaming, 330

V

Value chain, 101–3

Values and attitudes in computer groups, 313–15
Variables, monitoring of key project, 32
Virtual teams, 36–37, 224

W

Walkthroughs, 126
Waterfall strategy, 136–39
Waves of project management, 18–21
White box project management, 30

Whole-of-life project management, 27–29
Work breakdown structures, 197, 200
Work harder (long-term), 329
Work harder (short-term), 332–33

Y

You generally get the sponsor you deserve rule, 292

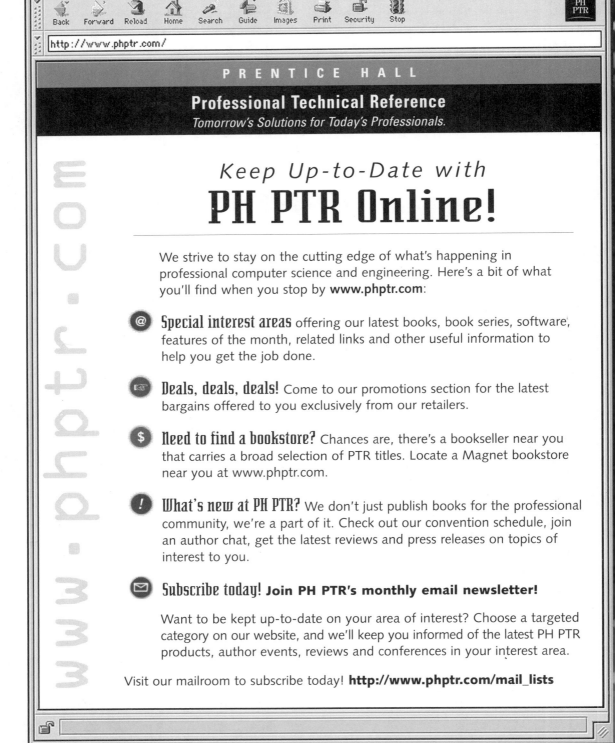